ALBERT CAMUS

THE FIRST MAN

THE FIRST MAN

by Albert Camus

*Translated from the French
by David Hapgood*

Alfred A. Knopf : New York : 1996

Copyright © 1995 by Alfred A. Knopf, Inc.

All rights reserved under International and Pan-American Copyright
Conventions. Published in the United States by Alfred A. Knopf, Inc.,
New York, and simultaneously in Canada by Alfred A. Knopf Canada, a
division of Random House of Canada Limited, Toronto. Distributed by
Random House, Inc., New York. Originally published in France as *Le
Premier Homme* by Editions Gallimard, Paris, in 1994. Copyright © 1994 by
Editions Gallimard. Louis Germain letter copyright © 1994 by
Bibliothèque Nationale.

Library of Congress Cataloguing-in-Publication Data
Camus, Albert, 1913–1960.
[Le Premier homme. English]
The first man / by Albert Camus ; translated by David Hapgood.
p.   cm.
ISBN 0-679-43937-4
1. Hapgood, David.   II. Title
PQ2605.A3734P7413   1995
843′.914—dc20   95-2668
CIP

Manufactured in the United States of America
Published September 14, 1995
Reprinted Six Times
Eighth Printing, February 1996

*This book was set in Fournier. It was composed, printed, and bound
by the Haddon Craftsmen, Scranton, Pennsylvania.
Typography and binding design by
Dorothy S. Baker.*

Editor's Note

Judith Jones, editor of the American edition of this book, has asked me for a more explanatory preface than the one I wrote for the French edition. Knopf has taken such pains with this book that I cannot refuse. But I must warn the reader that I am neither a writer, nor an academic, nor even an expert on Camus. I am just his daughter, and so I ask you to read this note with forbearance and to forgive any awkwardness in it.

Why publish this manuscript so long after my father's death? To understand this delay we must evoke the mood of 1960, the year my father died, and my mother, Francine, and his friends decided not to publish his manuscript. I shall try briefly to summarize the mood of that time by means of what is certainly an oversimplified sketch of people's opinions as they related to the question of publication.

French intellectuals were preoccupied with two topics: the Soviet Union and the war in Algeria. On the first, the prevailing opinion on the left forbade criticism of the Communist regime on the grounds that any such criticism would, by damaging the regime's credibility, delay humanity's progress toward a better world. On the second topic, the same people favored independence for Algeria under Arab rule and supported the FLN (Front de Libération Nationale).

Camus, for his part, condemned the Gulag, Stalin's trials, and totalitarianism in the Soviet Union, in the belief that ideology must serve humanity, not the contrary, and that the ends did not justify the means. He went so far as to say that the means used by totalitarian regimes destroyed any hope for a better world. As for Algeria, he advocated a federation in which the Arab and European peoples would be equally represented. Those who read this book may better understand his position.

So, in denouncing totalitarianism, and in advocating a multicultural Algeria where both communities would enjoy the same rights, Camus antagonized both the right and the left. At the time of his death he was very much isolated and subject to attacks from all sides designed to destroy the man and the artist so that his ideas would have no impact.

In these circumstances, to have published an unfinished manuscript—144 handwritten pages, often lacking periods and commas, never revised—might well have given ammunition to those who were saying Camus was through as a writer. His friends and my mother decided not to run that risk. My twin brother and I had no say in the decision, for we were only fourteen years old.

The years went by, my mother died in 1979, and I assumed the responsibility that had been hers. Between 1980 and 1985 voices began to be heard saying that perhaps Camus had not been so wrong, and little by little the old disputes died down. As for me, I first had to learn how to deal with a work of literature. I prepared Camus's *Carnet III* for publication, and then in the early 1990s my brother and I had to confront the question of *Le Premier Homme*. Two considerations persuaded us. First, we believed a manuscript of such importance would sooner or later be published unless we destroyed it. Since we had no right to destroy it, we preferred to publish it ourselves so that it would appear exactly as it was. Secondly, it seemed to us that this autobiographical account would be of exceptional value to those interested in Camus.

Finally, it is obvious that my father would never have published this manuscript as it is, first for the simple reason that he had not completed it, but also because he was a very reserved man and would no doubt have masked his own feelings far more in its final version. But it seems to me—and I say this with hesitation, for I can claim no objectivity—it seems to me that one can most clearly hear my father's voice in this text because of its very rawness. That is why I hope readers will come to it in a spirit of brotherhood.

Catherine Camus
March 1995

The text of this edition was established from the manuscript and from a first typescript by Francine Camus. Punctuation has been added as an aid to comprehension. Words that were not clear are bracketed. Words or parts of sentences that were not decipherable are shown by white space between brackets. The author's variants, written at the top of the manuscript page, appear as footnotes indicated by an asterisk; his marginal inserts are indicated by letters; the editor's or translator's notes, by numbers.

In the appendix are the author's interleaves, which have now been numbered I to V. Some of these were inserted in the manuscript (sheet I before chapter 4, II before chapter 6A), and the rest (III, IV, and V) were at the end of the manuscript.

Also in the appendix is "The First Man (Notes and Sketches)," the contents of the author's small spiral notebook with graph paper. These notes will give the reader an idea of the author's plans for the rest of the book. It seems certain that what he wrote was only the beginning of a novel that would have been longer by several hundred pages, about Algeria from the arrival of the French to the Second World War, including the war itself, and the Resistance to the German Occupation as lived by the protagonists in a love affair.

Once you have read The First Man you will understand why the appendix includes the letter Albert Camus wrote to his teacher, Louis Germain, after he received the Nobel Prize, and the last letter Louis Germain wrote to him.

PART ONE

Search for the Father

Intercessor: Widow Camus

*To you who will never be
able to read this book[a]*

Above the wagon rolling along a stony road, big thick
clouds were hurrying to the East through the dusk.
Three days ago they had inflated over the Atlantic, had
waited for a wind from the West, had set out, slowly at
first then faster and faster, had flown over the phospho-
rescent autumn waters, straight to the continent, had
unraveled[b] on the Moroccan peaks, had gathered again
in flocks on the high plateaus of Algeria, and now, at the
approaches to the Tunisian frontier, were trying to
reach the Tyrrhenian Sea to lose themselves in it. After
a journey of thousands of kilometers over what seemed
to be an immense island, shielded by the moving waters
to the North and to the South by the congealed waves of
the sands, passing scarcely any faster above this nameless country than had empires and peoples over the mil-
lennia, their momentum was wearing out and some

---

a. (add geological anonymity. Land and sea)
b. Solférino.

already were melting into occasional large raindrops that were beginning to plop on the canvas hood above the four travelers.

The wagon was creaking over a route that was fairly well marked but had scarcely any surfacing. From time to time a spark would flash under a metal wheel rim or a horse's hoof, and a stone would strike the wood of the wagon or else would sink with a muted sound into the soft soil of the ditch. Meanwhile the two small horses moved steadily ahead, occasionally flinching a bit, their chests thrust forward to pull the heavy wagon, loaded with furniture, continuously putting the road behind them as they trotted along at different paces. One of them would now and then blow the air noisily from its nostrils, and would be thrown off its pace. Then the Arab who was driving would snap the worn* reins flat on its back, and the beast would gamely pick up its rhythm.

The man who was on the front seat by the driver, a Frenchman about thirty, gazed with an impenetrable look at the two rumps moving rhythmically in front of him. He was of medium height, stocky, with a long face, a high square forehead, a strong jaw, and blue eyes. Though the season was well along, he wore a three-button duckcloth jacket, fastened at the neck in the style of that time, and a light pith helmet[a] over his close-cut hair.[b] When the rain began streaming across the

---

* split from wear and tear
a. or a kind of derby?
b. wearing heavy boots.

canvas above them, he turned toward the inside of the vehicle: "Are you all right?" he shouted.

On a second seat, wedged between the first seat and a heap of old trunks and furniture, sat a woman who, though shabbily dressed, was wrapped in a coarse woolen shawl. She smiled feebly at him. "Yes, yes," she said, with a little gesture of apology. A small four-year-old boy slept leaning against her. She had a gentle look and regular features, a warm gaze in her brown eyes, a small straight nose, and the black wavy hair of a Spanish woman. But there was something striking about that face. Not only would fatigue or something similar momentarily mask its features; no, it was more like a faraway look, a look of sweet distraction, such as you always see on some simpletons, but which would burst out only fleetingly on the beauty of this face. The kindness of that gaze, which was so noticeable, would sometimes be joined by a gleam of unreasoning fear that would as instantly vanish. With the flat of her hand, already worn with work and somewhat gnarled at the joints, she tapped her husband's back: "It's all right, it's all right," she said. And immediately she stopped smiling to watch, from under the canvas top, the road where puddles were already beginning to shine.

The man turned to the Arab, placid in his turban with its yellow cords, his body made stouter by baggy pants with a roomy seat gathered above the calf. "Do we have much farther to go?"

The Arab smiled under his big white moustache. "Eight kilometers and you're there."

The man turned to look at his wife, not smiling yet

attentive. She had kept her eyes on the road. "Give me the reins," the man said.

"As you wish," said the Arab. He handed him the reins, and the man stepped across while the old Arab slipped under him to the place just vacated. With two slaps of the flat of the reins the man took over the horses, who picked up their trot and suddenly were pulling straighter. "You know horses," the Arab said.

The husband's reply was curt and unsmiling. "Yes," he said.

The light had dimmed and all at once night settled in. The Arab took the square lantern from its catch at his left and, turning toward the back, used several crude matches to light the candle inside it. Then he replaced the lantern. Now the rain was falling gently and steadily. It shone in the weak light of the lamp, and, all around, it peopled the utter darkness with its soft sound. Now and then the wagon skirted spiny bushes; small trees were faintly lit for a few seconds. But the rest of the time it rolled through an empty space made still more vast by the dark of night. The smell of burned grass, or, suddenly, the strong odor of manure, was all that suggested they were passing by land under cultivation. The wife spoke behind the driver, who held his horses in a bit and leaned back. "There are no people here," the wife said again.

"Are you afraid?"

"What?"

The husband repeated the question, but this time he was shouting.

"No, no, not with you." But she seemed worried.

"You're in pain," the man said.

"A little."

He urged his horses on, and once more all that filled the night were the heavy sounds of the wheels crushing ridges in the road and the eight shod hooves striking its surface.

It was a night in the fall of 1913. Two hours earlier the voyagers had left the railroad station in Bône where they had arrived from Algiers after a journey of a night and a day on hard third-class benches. In the station they had found the wagon and the Arab waiting to take them to the farm located near a small village, about twenty kilometers into the interior of the country, where the husband was to take over the management. It had taken time to load the trunks and their few belongings, and then the bad road had delayed them still further. The Arab, as if aware of his companion's disquiet, said to him: "Have no fear. Here there are no bandits."

"They're everywhere," the man said. "But I have the necessary." And he slapped his tight pocket.

"You're right," said the Arab. "There's always madmen."

At that moment, the woman called her husband. "Henri," she said. "It hurts."

The man swore and pushed his horses a bit more.[a] "We're getting there," he said. After a moment, he looked at his wife again. "Does it still hurt?"

---

a. The little boy. [In the course of this chapter, the author variously places the boy in the wagon (p. 5) or in Algiers (p. 14)— *Trans.*]

She smiled at him with a strangely absent air, yet she did not seem to be suffering. "Yes, a lot."

He continued to gaze gravely at her.

Again she apologized. "It's nothing. Maybe it's the train."

"Look," the Arab said, "the village." Indeed they could see, to the left of the road and a little farther on, the lights of Solférino blurred by the rain. "But you take the road to the right," said the Arab.

The man hesitated, then turned to his wife. "Should we go to the house or the village?" he asked.

"Oh, to the house, that's better."

A bit farther, the vehicle turned to the right toward the unfamiliar house that awaited them. "Another kilometer," said the Arab.

"We're getting there," the man said, in the direction of his wife. She was bent over double, her face in her arms. "Lucie," the man said. She did not move. The man touched her with his hand. She was weeping silently. He shouted, stressing each syllable and acting out his words: "You are going to lie down there! I will go get the doctor!"

"Yes. Go get the doctor. I think this is it."

The Arab was watching them with surprise. "She's going to have a baby," the husband said. "Is there a doctor in the village?"

"Yes. I'll get him if you wish."

"No, you stay at the house. You keep watch. I'll go faster. Is there a small cart or a horse?"

"There's a cart." Then the Arab said to the wife,

"You will have a boy. Let him be a fine one." The wife smiled at him without seeming to understand.

"She doesn't hear," the man said. "At the house, you'll have to shout out loud and make signs." Suddenly the wagon was rolling almost without sound over the chalky subsurface of tuff. The road was narrower now. It passed alongside some tiled sheds behind which could be seen the first rows of the vineyard. They were met by a strong smell of fermenting grapes. They passed some large buildings with high-pitched roofs, and the wheels flattened the slag of a yard where there were no trees. The Arab took the reins without speaking and pulled them in. The horses stopped, and one of them snorted.[a] With his hand the Arab indicated a small whitewashed house. A creeping vine ran around a low door with a frame stained blue by copper sulfate. The man jumped to the ground and ran through the rain to the house. He opened the door. It led to a dark room which smelled of an empty hearth. The Arab, who was following him, walked straight through the dark to the fireplace, and, scraping an ember, lit a kerosene lamp that hung in the middle of the room over a round table. The man barely took time to notice that he was in a whitewashed kitchen with a sink of red ceramic tile, an old sideboard, and a sodden calendar on the wall. Stairs finished with the same red tiles led to the second floor. "Light the fire," he said, and he returned to the wagon.

---

a. Is it night?

(He took the little boy?) The woman was waiting in silence. He took her in his arms to set her on the ground and, holding her close for a moment, he lifted her head. "Can you walk?"

"Yes," she said, and she stroked his arm with her worn hand.

He led her to the house. "Wait," he said.

The Arab had already lit the fire, and with skillful and precise motions he was stoking it with shoots of vine. She was standing near the table, hands on her belly, and now her handsome face turned up to the lamplight was crossed by brief waves of pain. She seemed to notice neither the dampness nor the odor of neglect and poverty. The man was busy in the rooms upstairs. Then he appeared at the head of the stairs. "There's no fireplace in the bedroom?"

"No," said the Arab. "Not in the other room either."

"Come," said the man. The Arab joined him, then reappeared, walking backwards, carrying a mattress that the husband was holding by the other end. They placed it next to the fireplace. The man pulled the table to a corner, while the Arab went back upstairs and soon returned with a bolster and blankets. "Lie down there," the man said to his wife, and he led her to the mattress.

She hesitated. Now they could smell the odor of damp hair rising from the mattress. "I can't undress," she said, looking around fearfully as if she were only now seeing the place.

"Take off what you have underneath," the man said. And he repeated: "Take off your underwear." Then to the Arab: "Thanks. Unhitch a horse. I'll ride him to the village." The Arab went out. The wife went about her preparations, her back to her husband, who had also turned his back. Then she stretched out, and as soon she had done so, drawing the covers over her, she gave a single, long, full-throated howl, as if she wanted to rid herself at once of all the cries that pain had stored up in her. The man, standing by the mattress, let her cry; then, when she fell silent, he took off his pith helmet, put one knee to the ground, and kissed the fine forehead over her closed eyes. He put his hat on again and went out into the rain. The unhitched horse was turning its head, its front hooves planted in the slag. "I'll get a saddle," the Arab said.

"No, leave the reins on. I'll ride him like this. Take the trunks and the other things into the kitchen. Do you have a wife?"

"She died. She was old."

"Do you have a daughter?"

"No, God be thanked. But I have the wife of my son."

"Tell her to come."

"I'll do that. Go in peace."

The husband looked at the old Arab motionless in the fine rain and smiling at him under his wet moustache. He himself was still unsmiling, but he watched the Arab with his direct attentive gaze. Then he extended his hand. The other man took his hand in the Arab fashion, with the ends of his fingers, then lifted it to his lips. The husband turned, making the cinders crunch, strode to the horse, vaulted onto it bareback, and rode off at a lumbering trot.

As he left the property, the man headed toward the crossroads from which they had first seen the lights of the village. They were shining now with a more dazzling light, the rain had stopped falling and the road, to the right, that led toward the village was laid out straight through the vineyards where the trellis wires glistened here and there. About halfway, the horse slowed down to a walk. He was nearing a sort of rectangular shanty; one part was a room made of masonry, and a second, larger part was built of wooden planks. Projecting from this second part was a kind of counter with a big matting pulled down over it. On a door recessed in the masonry one could read: "Mme. Jacques's Farm Canteen." Light seeped under the door. The man stopped his horse right by the door, and knocked without dismounting. Immediately a firm resonant voice asked from inside, "What is it?"

"I'm the new manager of the Saint-Apôtre property. My wife is giving birth. I need help."

No one answered. After a moment bolts were drawn, bars were lifted, then dragged away, and the door opened partway. He could make out the black curly head of a European woman with plump cheeks and a flattish nose above full lips. "My name is Henri Cormery. Can you go to be with my wife? I'm going to get the doctor."

She gazed at him with the eye of one accustomed to weighing men and misfortune. He met her look squarely, but without adding a word of explanation. "I'll go," she said. "You hurry."

He thanked her and kicked the horse with his heels.

A few moments later he entered the village by passing between rampart-like walls made of dried mud. Stretching before him lay what seemed to be the only street, bordered with small one-story houses, all alike; he followed it to a small hard-surfaced square where, surprisingly, he found a metal-framed bandstand. The square, like the street, was deserted. Cormery was already headed toward one of the houses when the horse shied. An Arab, in a torn somber-colored burnoose, appeared from the shadows and came toward him. "The doctor's house," Cormery immediately asked. The Arab studied the horseman. "Come," he said after he had looked him over. They went back up the street. Written on a building with a raised ground floor reached by whitewashed stairs were the words: "Liberté, Égalité, Fraternité." Next to it was a small garden surrounded by roughly finished walls; at its far end was a house, to which the Arab pointed. "That's it," he said. Cormery jumped down from the horse, and, at a pace that showed no sign of fatigue, he crossed the garden, where all he noticed was, at the exact center, a dwarf palm with withered leaves and a rotted trunk. He knocked at the door. No one answered.[a] He turned around. The Arab was waiting in silence. The husband knocked again. From inside could be heard footsteps that stopped behind the door. But the door did not open. Cormery knocked again and said, "I'm looking for the doctor."

---

a. I fought against the Moroccans (with a cryptic look) Moroccans, they're no good.

At once the bolts were drawn and the door was opened. A man appeared. His face was young and chubby, but his hair was almost white. He was tall and well built, and his legs were squeezed into leggings. He was putting on a sort of hunting jacket. "Well! Where did you come from? I've never seen you before," he said, smiling. The husband explained. "Oh yes, the mayor told me. But, you know, this is a strange place to come to have a baby." The husband said he had been expecting the event later and that he must have made a mistake. "Well, that happens to everyone. Go ahead, I'll saddle Matador and follow you."

Halfway back, and through the rain that had begun to fall again, the doctor, mounted on a dappled gray horse, caught up with Cormery, who was now soaked through but still erect on his heavy farm horse. "Strange way to arrive," the doctor called out. "But you'll see, there's good in this place, not counting the mosquitoes and the bandits in the bush." He stayed alongside his companion. "About the mosquitoes, you know, you don't have to worry till spring. As for the bandits . . . " He laughed, but the husband rode on without a word. The doctor looked at him with curiosity. "Have no fear," he said, "it will all go well."

Cormery turned his straightforward gaze on the doctor, and, looking calmly at him, said with a touch of warmth: "I'm not afraid. I'm used to hard knocks."

"Is this your first?"

"No, I left a four-year-old boy in Algiers with my mother-in-law."

They came to the crossroads and took the road to the

property. Soon the cinders were flying under the horses' hooves. When the horses stopped and silence fell once more, they heard a loud cry from the house. The two men dismounted.

Awaiting them was a shadowy figure sheltered under a vine that was dripping water. Drawing closer, they recognized the old Arab wearing an improvised hood made of a sack. "Greetings, Kaddour," said the doctor. "How is it going?"

"I don't know, I especially don't go in where the women are," the old man said.

"Good rule," said the doctor. "Particularly when women are crying." But no cries were coming now from inside. The doctor opened the door and went in, Cormery behind him.

In front of them a big fire of vine branches flaming in the fireplace lighted the room more than did the kerosene lamp, with copper and bead trim, that hung from the middle of the ceiling. To their right, the sink was now all covered with towels and metal pitchers. The table in the middle of the room had been pushed over to the left, in front of a rickety sideboard made of unfinished wood. On it were an old traveling bag, a hatbox, and various bundles. Pieces of old luggage, including a big wicker trunk, filled all the corners of the room, leaving a space only in the middle, not far from the fire. In that space, on a mattress set at right angles to the fireplace, the wife lay stretched out, head laid back on a pillow without a case, her hair let down. The blankets now covered only half the mattress. The uncovered part of the mattress was hidden from sight by the owner of the canteen, who was on her knees to its left. She was wringing out, over a washbasin, a towel dripping reddish drops of water. To the right, sitting cross-legged, an unveiled Arab woman held out, as if making an offertory, a second, somewhat flaking enamel basin full of steaming hot water. The two women were on either side of a folded sheet that lay under the wife. The shadow and light of the fireplace rose and fell on the whitewashed walls, on the baggage that cluttered the room, and, still closer, glowed red on the faces of the two nurses and on the form of the wife, bundled up under the blankets.

When the two men entered, the Arab woman glanced quickly at them, gave a brief laugh, then turned to the fire, her thin brown arms still offering the washbasin. The owner of the canteen looked at them and joyfully exclaimed: "No more need for you, Doctor. It happened by itself." She got to her feet and the two men saw, near the patient, something shapeless and bloody stirring with a sort of still movement and making a continuing, barely perceptible sound like a muffled screeching.[a]

"So they say," said the doctor. "I hope you haven't touched the cord."

"No," said the woman, laughing. "We had to leave you something to do."

She got up and gave her place to the doctor, who again blocked the newborn from the sight of Cormery,

---

a. like that of certain cells under the microscope.

still at the door, his head uncovered. The doctor squatted and opened his case; then he took the basin from the hands of the Arab woman, who immediately withdrew from the circle of light and took refuge in the dark angle of the fireplace. The doctor washed his hands, his back still to the door, then poured on those hands some alcohol that smelled a bit like grape liquor; its odor at once filled the room. At that moment, the wife lifted her head and saw her husband. A marvelous smile transfigured that exhausted beautiful face. Cormery went over to the mattress. "He came," she said under her breath, and she reached out her hand to the infant.

"Yes," said the doctor. "But stay still." The wife gave him a questioning look.

Cormery, standing at the foot of the mattress, made a quieting gesture. "Lie down."

She lay back down again. The rain began to come down twice as hard on the old tile roof. The doctor went to work under the blanket. Then he straightened up and seemed to shake something in front of him. A small cry was heard. "It's a boy," the doctor said. "And a good sturdy one."

"There's one who's getting off to a good start," said the owner of the canteen. "By moving to a new home."

The Arab woman in the corner laughed and clapped her hands twice. Cormery glanced at her and she turned away, embarrassed.

"All right," said the doctor. "Now leave us for a moment."

Cormery looked at his wife. But her face was still tilted back. Her hands, lying relaxed on the coarse blanket, were all there was to remind him of the smile that a while ago had filled and transfigured that wretched room. He put on his helmet and headed toward the door.

"What are you going to name him?" the owner of the canteen called out.

"I don't know, we haven't thought about it." He looked at her. "Since you were here, we'll call him Jacques."

The woman burst out laughing and Cormery went out. The Arab, his head still covered with the sack, was waiting under the vine. He looked at Cormery, who said nothing to him. "Here," said the Arab, and held out an end of the sack.

Cormery took shelter. He could feel the shoulder of the old Arab against him, and he smelled the smoke given off by his clothes; he felt the rain falling on the sack over their two heads. "It's a boy," he said without looking at his companion.

"God be praised," answered the Arab. "You are a chief." The water that had come from thousands of kilometers away went on falling before them, on the cinders and the many puddles that pitted them, on the vineyards farther distant, and the trellis wires still gleamed under the raindrops. It would never get to the sea to the East, and now it was going to drench the whole country, the marshy land by the river and the mountains around them, the immense almost uninhabited territory whose powerful odor reached the two men huddled under the one sack, while behind them a feeble cry resumed from time to time.

Late in the night, Cormery was lying stretched out, in long drawers and undershirt, on a second mattress by his wife, watching the flames dance on the ceiling. The room was now pretty well tidied. On the other side of his wife, in a laundry basket, the infant slept in silence except for an occasional weak gurgle. His wife was also sleeping, her face turned toward him, her mouth partly open. The rain had stopped. Tomorrow he would have to start work. Near him, his wife's hand, already so worn it almost seemed made of wood, also reminded him of work. He reached out his own hand, placed it gently on hers, and, laying his head back, closed his eyes.

Saint-Brieuc

[a]Forty years later a man standing in the corridor of the Saint-Brieuc train was watching with an air of disapproval as the villages and ugly houses of the flat cramped countryside that stretches from Paris to the Channel marched past under the pale sun of an afternoon in spring. The meadows and fields of a land that for centuries had been cultivated to the last square meter passed, in turn, before him. With bare head and hair cut short, long face and delicate features, a direct gaze in his blue eyes, the man was of medium height, and despite his forty years he still looked slender in his raincoat. He stood with his hands firmly placed on the railing; leaning his weight on one hip, his torso at ease, he gave the impression of competence and vigor. Then the train slowed and finally stopped in a small shabby station. A moment later a rather elegant young woman passed by the window where the man was standing. She stopped

---

a. From the beginning, should show the alien in Jacques more.

to shift her suitcase from one hand to the other, and just then she noticed the traveler. He looked at her smiling, and she could not help smiling also. The man lowered the window, but the train was already leaving. "Too bad," he said. The young woman was still smiling at him.

The traveler went to sit down in his third-class compartment, where he had a seat by the window. A man with sparse plastered hair—not as old as his swollen, blotchy face suggested—was sitting huddled across from him; his eyes were closed and he was breathing hard, obviously disturbed by his labored digestion. He cast an occasional quick* glance at the traveler. On the same seat, by the corridor, a peasant woman in her Sunday best, crowned by a peculiar hat adorned with a bunch of wax grapes, was blowing the nose of a red-headed child whose face looked dim and faded. The traveler's smile disappeared. He took a magazine from his pocket and absently read an article that made him yawn.

A bit later the train stopped, and a small placard announcing "Saint-Brieuc" moved slowly into the frame of the window. The traveler immediately stood up, effortlessly lifted his suitcase with its expanding sides from the overhead rack, and, after nodding to his fellow travelers, who responded with seeming surprise, he left rapidly and hurried down the three steps of the car. On the platform, he looked at his left hand, dirty from the

---

* dim

soot that had accumulated on the railing he had just been holding, took out a handkerchief and carefully wiped it off. Then he headed toward the exit, where he was gradually joined by a group of somberly dressed travelers with blotchy faces. Under the shelter with its small posts he patiently waited his turn to hand over his ticket, waited again till the taciturn clerk returned it to him, crossed a waiting room with bare dirty walls, decorated only with old posters in which even the Riviera had taken on the colors of soot, and, striding at a lively pace through the slanting afternoon light, he went down the street that led from the station to the town.

At the hotel he asked for the room he had reserved, refused the help of the potato-faced chambermaid who wanted to carry his bag, and, after she had shown him to his room, gave her nonetheless a tip that surprised her and brought a friendly look to her features. Then he washed his hands again, and went back downstairs, still at a lively pace, without locking his door. He found the chambermaid in the lobby, asked her where the cemetery was, was given too much explanation, listened amiably, then set out in the direction she had indicated. Now he was walking down streets that were narrow and depressing, bordered by commonplace houses with ugly red tiles. Here and there he could see the crooked slates of an old half-timbered house. The few passersby did not even stop before the shopwindows that displayed the glass products, the masterpieces in plastic and nylon, the wretched ceramics that are found in every town in the contemporary Western world. Only the food shops showed any opulence. High forbidding walls surrounded the cemetery. Near its gate, meager displays of flowers and marble-cutters' shops. The traveler stopped in front of one of these shops to watch a bright-looking child in a corner who was doing his homework on a marble slab that had yet to be inscribed. Then he entered the cemetery and went to the caretaker's house. The caretaker was not there. The traveler waited in the barely furnished little office, then noticed a map, which he was studying when the caretaker entered. He was a tall gnarled man, with a big nose, who smelled of the sweat under his thick high-necked jacket. The traveler asked for the location of those who died in the war of 1914.

"Yes," the caretaker said. "That's called the square of French Remembrance. What name are you looking for?"

"Henri Cormery," said the traveler.

The caretaker opened a large book bound in wrapping paper and went down a list of names with his dirty finger. His finger came to a stop. "Cormery Henri," he said, "fatally wounded at the Battle of the Marne, died at Saint-Brieuc October 11, 1914."

"That's it," said the traveler.

The caretaker closed the book. "Come," he said. And he led the way to the first row of gravestones, some of them simple, others ugly and pretentious, all covered with that bead and marble bric-a-brac that would disgrace anyplace on earth. "Was he related to you?" he asked absently.

"He was my father."

"That's rough," the other man said.

"No, it isn't. I was less than a year old when he died. So, you see."

"Yes," said the caretaker, "but even so. Too many died."

Jacques Cormery did not answer. Surely, too many had died, but, as to his father, he could not muster a filial devotion he did not feel. For all these years he had been living in France, he had promised himself to do what his mother, who stayed in Algeria, what she[1] for such a long time had been asking him to do: visit the grave of his father that she herself had never seen. He thought this visit made no sense, first of all for himself, who had never known his father, who knew next to nothing of what he had been, and who loathed conventional gestures and behavior; and then for his mother, who never spoke of the dead man and could picture nothing of what he was going to see. But since his old mentor had retired to Saint-Brieuc and so he would have an opportunity to see him again, Cormery had made up his mind to go visit this dead stranger, and had even insisted on doing it before joining his old friend so that afterwards he would feel completely free.

"It's here," said the caretaker. They had arrived at a square-shaped area enclosed by small markers of gray stone connected with a heavy chain that had been painted black. The gravestones—and they were many—were all alike: plain inscribed rectangles set at equal intervals row on row. Each grave was decorated

---

1. *sic*

with a small bouquet of fresh flowers. "For forty years the French Remembrance has been responsible for the upkeep. Look, here he is." He indicated a stone in the first row. Jacques Cormery stopped at some distance from the grave. "I'll leave you," the caretaker said.

Cormery approached the stone and gazed vacantly at it. Yes, that was indeed his name. He looked up. Small white and gray clouds were passing slowly across the sky, which was paler now, and from it fell a light that was alternately bright and overcast. Around him, in the vast field of the dead, silence reigned. Nothing but a muffled murmur from the town came over the high walls. Occasionally a black silhouette would pass among the distant graves. Jacques Cormery, gazing up at the slow navigation of the clouds across the sky, was trying to discern, beyond the odor of damp flowers, the salty smell just then coming from the distant motionless sea when the clink of a bucket against the marble of a tombstone drew him from his reverie. At that moment he read on the tomb the date of his father's birth, which he now discovered he had not known. Then he read the two dates, "1885–1914," and automatically did the arithmetic: twenty-nine years. Suddenly he was struck by an idea that shook his very being. He was forty years old. The man buried under that slab, who had been his father, was younger than he.[a]

And the wave of tenderness and pity that at once filled his heart was not the stirring of the soul that leads

---

a. Transition.

the son to the memory of the vanished father, but the overwhelming compassion that a grown man feels for an unjustly murdered child—something here was not in the natural order and, in truth, there was no order but only madness and chaos when the son was older than the father. The course of time itself was shattering around him while he remained motionless among those tombs he now no longer saw, and the years no longer kept to their places in the great river that flows to its end. They were no more than waves and surf and eddies where Jacques Cormery was now struggling in the grip of anguish and pity.[a] He looked at the other inscriptions in that section and realized from the dates that this soil was strewn with children who had been the fathers of graying men who thought they were living in this present time. For he too believed he was living, he alone had created himself, he knew his own strength, his vigor, he could cope and he had himself well in hand. But, in the strange dizziness of that moment, the statue every man eventually erects and that hardens in the fire of the years, into which he then creeps and there awaits its final crumbling—that statue was rapidly cracking, it was already collapsing. All that was left was this anguished heart, eager to live, rebelling against the deadly order of the world that had been with him for forty years, and still struggling against the wall that separated him from the secret of all life, wanting to go farther, to go beyond, and to discover, discover before dying, dis-

---

a. enlarge on war of 1914.

cover at last in order to be, just once to be, for a single second, but forever.

He looked back on his life, a life that had been foolish, courageous, cowardly, willful, and always straining toward that goal which he knew nothing about, and actually that life had all gone by without his having tried to imagine who this man was who had given him that life and then immediately had gone off to die in a strange land on the other side of the seas. At twenty-nine, had he himself not been frail, been ailing, tense, stubborn, sensual, dreamy, cynical, and brave? Yes, he had been all that and much else besides; he had been alive, in short had been a man, and yet he had never thought of the man who slept there as a living being, but as a stranger who passed by on the land where he himself was born, of whom his mother said that he looked like him and that he died on the field of battle. Yet the secret he had eagerly sought to learn through books and people now seemed to him to be intimately linked with this dead man, this younger father, with what he had been and what he had become, and it seemed that he himself had gone far afield in search of what was close to him in time and in blood. To tell the truth, he had gotten no help. In a family where they spoke little, where no one read or wrote, with an unhappy and listless mother, who would have informed him about this young and pitiable father? No one had known him but his mother and she had forgotten him. Of that he was sure. And he had died unknown on this earth where he had fleetingly passed, like a stranger. No doubt it was up to him to ask, to inform himself. But for someone like him, who has nothing and wants the world entire, all his energy is not enough to create himself and to conquer or to understand that world. After all, it was not too late; he could still search, he could learn who this man had been who now seemed closer to him than any other being on this earth. He could . . .

Now the afternoon was coming to its end. The rustle of a skirt, a black shadow, brought him back to the landscape of tombs and sky that surrounded him. He had to leave; there was nothing more for him to do here. But he could not turn away from this name, those dates. Under that slab were left only ashes and dust. But, for him, his father was again alive, a strange silent life, and it seemed to him that again he was going to forsake him, to leave his father to haunt yet another night the endless solitude he had been hurled into and then deserted. The empty sky resounded with a sudden loud explosion: an invisible airplane had crossed the sound barrier. Turning his back on the grave, Jacques Cormery abandoned his father.

3 : *Saint-Brieuc and Malan (J.G.)*[a]

That evening at dinner, J.C. watched his old friend attack his second slice of leg of lamb with a sort of disturbing voracity; the wind that had come up was growling softly around the small low-ceilinged house in a district near the road to the beaches. On his arrival J.C. had noticed some small pieces of dry algae in the gutter bordering the sidewalk, which, with their odor of salt, were all that suggested the nearness of the sea.

Victor Malan, who spent his entire career in customs administration, had retired to this small town; he had not chosen it, but he justified the choice after the fact by saying that nothing came along to distract him from solitary meditation, neither an excess of beauty nor an excess of ugliness, nor of solitude itself. The administration of things and the management of men had taught him a great deal, but first of all, apparently, that we know very little. Yet he was immensely cul-

---

a. Chapter to be written and deleted.

tivated and J.C. admired him unreservedly, for Malan, in a day when outstanding men are so banal, was the one person who had his own way of thinking, to the extent that that is possible. At any rate, under his deceptively accommodating exterior, he was free and uncompromisingly original in his opinions.

"That's it, my son," Malan was saying. "Since you're going to see your mother, try to find out something about your father. And come back—at top speed—and tell me what happened next. I so seldom find anything to laugh about."

"Yes, it's ridiculous. But now that my curiosity is aroused I might as well try to pick up some more information. It's a bit pathological that I've never concerned myself with it."

"Not at all, it's wisdom in this case. I was married for thirty years to Marthe, whom you knew. A perfect woman and I still miss her. I always thought she liked her house."[1]

"No doubt you're right," Malan was saying, looking away, and Cormery waited for the objection that was bound to follow his approval.

"Nonetheless," Malan resumed, "I myself, and I am surely mistaken, I would restrain myself from trying to learn more than life has taught me. But I am a bad example in this respect, am I not? When all is said and done, it's surely a fault in me that I would make no such

---

1. This and the two preceding paragraphs are crossed out.

attempt. Whereas you"—and his eyes lit up mischievously—"you are a man of action."

Malan had a Chinese look, with his moon face, a somewhat flattened nose, scarcely any eyebrows, a bowl-cut hairdo, and a big moustache that failed to cover his thick, sensual lips. His soft, rounded body, the fleshy hand with pudgy fingers suggested a mandarin who disapproved of traveling by foot. When he half closed his eyes while eating heartily, you could not help seeing him in a silk robe holding chopsticks between his fingers. But the expression changed all that. The feverish dark-brown eyes, restless or suddenly intent, as if the mind was focused on a very specific point, were the eyes of an Occidental of great sensitivity and culture.

The elderly maid brought a cheese tray, which Malan ogled out of the corner of his eye. "I knew a man," he said, "who after he had lived with his wife for thirty years . . ." Cormery paid close attention: whenever Malan began with "I knew a man who . . ." or "a friend . . ." or "an Englishman who was traveling with me . . ." you could be sure he was talking about himself . . . "who didn't like pastries and his wife never ate them either. Well, after twenty years of living together, he caught his wife in the pastry shop, and by keeping an eye on her he found out that she went there several times a week to stuff herself with coffee éclairs. Yes, he thought she didn't like sweets while in fact she loved coffee éclairs."

"So," said Cormery, "we never know anyone."

"If you will. But it might perhaps be more accurate, it

seems to me, in any case I think I would prefer to say, but blame it on my inability to state anything positively— yes, suffice it to say that if twenty years of living together are not enough to know a person, then an inquiry that is bound to be superficial forty years after a man's death, runs the risk of bringing you only limited information, yes, one can say information with limited meaning about this man. Although, in another sense . . ."

He lifted a knife and, with a fatalistic air, brought it down on the goat cheese. "Excuse me. Won't you have some cheese? No? Still so abstemious! It's a hard job pleasing you!" Again there was a mischievous gleam in his half-closed eyes.

Cormery had known his old friend for twenty years now (add here why and how), and he accepted his irony with good humor. "It's not a matter of pleasing me. Eating too much makes me heavy, and I sink."

"Yes, and then you no longer soar over the rest of us."

Cormery gazed at the handsome rustic furniture that filled the low-ceilinged dining room with its white-washed beams. "My friend," he said, "you've always thought I was arrogant. I am, but not always or with everyone. With you, for example, I'm incapable of arrogance."

Malan looked away, which in him was a sign of emotion. "I know that," he said. "But why is it?"

"Because I love you," Cormery said quietly.

Malan pulled the bowl of chilled fruit toward him. He said nothing.

"Because," Cormery went on, "when I was very

young, very foolish, and very much alone—you remember, in Algiers?—you paid attention to me and,
without seeming to, you opened for me the door to
everything I love in the world."

"Oh, you were gifted."

"Of course. But even the most gifted person needs
someone to initiate him. The one that life puts in your
path one day, that person must be loved and respected
forever, even if he's not responsible. That is my faith!"

"Yes, yes," Malan said blandly.

"I know you find that hard to believe. Mind you, do
not think that my affection for you is blind. You have
great, very great faults, at least in my eyes."

Malan licked his thick lips. Suddenly he seemed interested. "What faults?"

"For example you are, let us say, thrifty. Not out of
avarice, it's true, but out of fear, fear of going without,
and so forth. All the same, it's a serious fault, one that
I generally dislike. But, above all, you cannot help
suspecting others of ulterior motives. You are instinc-
tively unable to believe that anyone has disinterested
opinions."

"Look here," said Malan as he finished his wine, "I
shouldn't have coffee, and yet . . ."

But Cormery kept his self-possession.[a] "For example,
I'm sure you couldn't bring yourself to believe me if I

---

a. I often lend money that I know I'll never get back, to people I
don't care about. It's just that I don't know how to say no, and that
exasperates me.

told you that if you were just to ask, I would immediately give you everything I have."

Malan hesitated, and now he was looking at his friend. "Oh, I know. You're generous."

"No, I am not generous. I'm stingy with my time and my energy, with anything that tires me, and that disgusts me. But what I said is true. You—you don't believe me, and that is a fault in you, that is where you are really helpless, even though you are a superior man. Because you're wrong. One word from you, right now, and everything I have is yours. You have no need of it and it's only an example. But I didn't choose it arbitrarily. Truly, everything I have is yours."

"Thank you, really," Malan said, his eyes half closed. "I am very touched."

"All right, I'm embarrassing you. You don't like people to speak too openly. I just wanted to tell you that with all your faults I love you. I love or revere very few people. As for the rest, I'm ashamed of my indifference to them. But for those I love, nothing and no one, neither I nor certainly they themselves, can ever make me stop loving them. It took me a long time to learn that; now I know it. That being said, let's go on with our conversation: you don't approve of my trying to find out about my father."

"No—that is to say, I do approve. I was just afraid you'd be disappointed. A friend of mine who was very attracted to a young woman and wanted to marry her made the mistake of asking others about her."

"A bourgeois," Cormery said.

"Yes," Malan said, "I was the one." They both burst

out laughing. "I was young. I collected such contradictory opinions about her that my own view of her became confused. I wasn't sure whether or not I loved her. In short, I married another woman."

"I can't find myself a second father."

"No, and luckily so. One is enough, if I can go by my own experience."

"All right," said Cormery. "Anyhow, I have to go see my mother in a few weeks. That gives me an opportunity. I spoke to you about it particularly because I was disturbed a while back by that difference in age in my favor. Yes, in my favor."

"Yes, I understand."

Cormery looked at Malan.

"Tell yourself he never grew old," Malan said. "He was spared that suffering, and it is long."

"Along with a certain number of pleasures."

"Yes, you love life. You have to, since that's all you believe in." Malan seated himself heavily in a cretonne-covered easy chair, and suddenly a look of inexpressible melancholy came over his face.

"You're right," said Cormery. "I've loved life, I'm hungry for it. At the same time, life seems horrible to me, it seems inaccessible. That is why I am a believer, out of skepticism. Yes, I want to believe, I want to live, forever." Cormery fell silent.

"At sixty-five, every year is a stay of execution," Malan said. "I would like to die in peace, and dying frightens me. I have accomplished nothing."

"There are people who vindicate the world, who help others live just by their presence."

"Yes, and they die," Malan said.

They were silent, and the wind blew a little harder around the house.

"You're right, Jacques," said Malan. "Go find out. You no longer need a father. You brought yourself up alone. Now you could love him as you know how to love. But . . ." he said, and he hesitated. "Come back to see me. I don't have much time left. And forgive me . . ."

"Forgive you?" said Cormery. "I owe everything to you."

"No, you don't owe me very much. Just forgive me for sometimes not knowing how to respond to your affection."

Malan gazed at the antique lamp hanging over the table, and his voice was hollow when he said what a few minutes later Cormery, alone in the wind in the deserted neighborhood, would keep on hearing over and over:

"There is a terrible emptiness in me, an indifference that hurts . . ."[a]

---

a. Jacques / I tried to find out for myself, from the start, when I was a child, what was right and what was wrong—because no one around me could tell me. And now that everything is leaving me I realize I need someone to show me the way and to blame me and praise me, by right not of power but of authority, I need my father.

I thought I knew it, and that I had myself in hand, I don't [know?] any longer.

4 : *The Child's Games*

A gentle short swell was making the ship roll in the July heat. Jacques Cormery, lying half naked in his cabin, watched the fragmented reflection of the sunlight on the sea dancing on the copper rim of the porthole. He jumped to his feet to turn off the fan that was drying the perspiration in his pores before it even began to trickle down his chest; it was better to sweat. Then he relaxed on his bunk, narrow and hard as he liked a bed to be. Now the dull sound of the engines rose from the depths of the ship in muffled vibrations, like an enormous army forever on the march. He liked the sound these big steamers made, night and day, and the sensation of walking on a volcano, while all around the immense sea offered its open reaches to his view. But it was too hot on the deck; after lunch, passengers besotted with food had collapsed in the deck chairs on the covered deck or had fled down the passageways belowdecks at siesta time. Jacques did not like to take a siesta. *"A benidor,"* he thought bitterly: that was the bizarre expression his grandmother used when he was a child in Algiers and she was making him join her for the siesta. The three rooms of the small apartment in an Algiers neighborhood were enveloped in the striped shade of the carefully closed shutters.[a] Outside, the heat was baking the dry dusty streets, and, in the half-light of the rooms, one or two big energetic flies were buzzing around like airplanes as they searched tirelessly for a way out. It was too hot to read *Pardaillan* or *L'Intrépide*.[b] On rare occasions when his grandmother wasn't home or was chatting with the neighbor, the child would poke his nose through the shutters in the living room that faced the street. The street was deserted. The red and yellow canvas shades had been pulled down in front of the shoe and notions stores across the street, a curtain of multicolored beads masked the entrance to the tobacco shop, and Jean's café was empty except for the cat lying on the sill between the sawdust-covered floor and the dusty sidewalk, and sleeping as if it were dead.

The child then turned back to the sparse whitewashed room, furnished with a square table in the middle, and, against the walls, a sideboard, a small desk that was scarred and spotted with ink, and, on the floor, a small mattress covered with a blanket where, after nightfall, his half-mute uncle slept; and five chairs.[c] In a

---

a. Around his tenth year.

b. Those big books printed on newsprint, with crudely colored covers on which the price was printed in bigger type than the title or the name of the author.

c. extreme cleanliness.

A wardrobe, a wooden dressing table with a marble top. A bed-corner, on a mantelpiece of which only the shelf was made of marble, stood a small flowered vase with slender neck, of the kind one finds at a fair. The child, caught between the two deserts of sunlight and shade, started circling the table at a hurried pace, repeating like a litany: "I'm bored! I'm bored!" He was bored, yet in that boredom was a game, a delight, a kind of excitement, for rage would seize him as he heard his grandmother calling *a benidor* when at last she came home. But his protests were in vain. The grandmother had raised nine children in the bush, and she had her own ideas on upbringing. With a single shove she pushed him into the bedroom. It was one of two rooms that looked out onto the yard. The other had two beds, his mother's and the one he shared with his brother. His grandmother was entitled to a room of her own. But she would take the child in her big high wooden bed, often for the night and always for the siesta. He would take off his sandals and lift himself onto the bed. He had to take his place at the back, against the wall, ever since the day he slipped to the floor while his grandmother was sleeping, to resume circling around the table and reciting his litany. Once in his place, he would watch his grandmother take off her dress and drop her coarse linen shift, fastened at the top by a drawstring with a ribbon that she would undo. Then she in turn got up on the bed, and the child smelled beside him the odor of el-

---

side rug with knotted stitches, worn and dirty, frayed at the edges. And in a corner, a big trunk covered with an old tasseled Arab rug.

derly flesh while he stared at the big blue veins and old-age spots that marred his grandmother's feet. "Go on," she would say. "*A benidor*." She went to sleep very quickly, while the child, his eyes open, followed the comings and goings of the tireless flies.

Yes, he had hated that for years; and even later, as a grown man, and until he had been gravely ill, he could not bring himself to stretch out after lunch during the hot season. If he happened nonetheless to fall asleep, he would awaken nauseous and ill at ease. Only recently, since he had been suffering from insomnia, could he sleep for half an hour during the day and awaken fresh and alert. *A benidor* . . .

The wind must have dropped, flattened by the sun. The ship had stopped its gentle rolling and now seemed to be proceeding in a straight line, the engines at full speed, the propeller boring directly through the depths of the water, and the sound of the pistons so steady that it could no longer be distinguished from the soft cease-less murmur of the sunlight on the sea. Jacques was half asleep, and he was filled with a kind of happy anxiety at the prospect of returning to Algiers and the small poor home in the old neighborhood. So it was every time he left Paris for Africa, his heart swelling with a secret ex-ultation, with the satisfaction of one who has made good his escape and is laughing at the thought of the look on the guards' faces. Just as, each time he returned to Paris, whether by road or by train, his heart would sink when he arrived, without quite knowing how, at those first houses of the outskirts, lacking any frontier of trees or water and which, like an ill-fated cancer, reached out its ganglions of poverty and ugliness to absorb this foreign body and take him to the center of the city, where a splendid stage set would sometimes make him forget the forest of concrete and steel that imprisoned him day and night and invaded even his insomnia. But he had escaped, he could breathe, on the giant back of the sea he was breathing in waves, rocked by the great sun, at last he could sleep and he could come back to the childhood from which he had never recovered, to the secret of the light, of the warm poverty that had enabled him to survive and to overcome everything. That fragmented reflection on the copper of the porthole, now almost motionless, came from the same sun that pressed with all its weight on the shutters of the dark room where the grandmother was sleeping and plunged a very slender sword into the darkness through the one opening that a sprung knot had left in the butt-strap of the shutters. The flies were missing, it was not they who were peopling and nourishing his reverie; there are no flies at sea, and besides they were dead, those flies the child had loved because they were noisy, the only living beings in that world chloroformed by the heat, and all the men and animals were lying inert on their flanks—except himself, it's true; he was turning over on the bed in the narrow space left to him between the wall and his grandmother, and he wanted also to live, and it seemed to him that the time for sleep was being subtracted from his time for living and playing. His playmates were waiting for him, that was certain, in rue Prévost-Paradol, with its small gardens that in the evening smelled of damp from their watering and of the honeysuckle that grew everywhere, whether or not it was watered. As soon as his grandmother awakened, he would dash out, down to the rue de Lyon, still deserted under its ficus trees, run as far as the fountain at the corner of Prévost-Paradol, quickly turn the cast-iron crank at the top of the fountain, putting his head under the faucet to receive the gushing stream that would fill his nostrils and his ears, run down the open neck of his shirt to his belly and down his legs under his shorts to his sandals. Then, happily feeling the water foam between his feet and the leather of the soles, he would run breathlessly to join Pierre[a] and the others who were sitting at the hall entrance of the only two-story house on the street, sharpening the cigar-shaped piece of wood they would soon be using to play *canette vinga*[1] with the blue wooden racquet.

As soon as they were all there, they went off, scraping the racquet along the rusty garden fences in front of the houses, which made enough noise to awaken the neighborhood and make the cats jump out of their sleep under the dusty wisteria. They ran, crossing the street, trying to catch each other, already covered with sweat, but always in the same direction, toward the "green field" not far from their school, four or five blocks away. But there was an obligatory stop at what was

---

a. His friend Pierre was also the son of a war widow, who worked in the post office.

1. See the author's explanation below.

known as the waterspout, an enormous round fountain on two levels in a rather large square, where the water never ran, but the basin, long since clogged up, would on occasion be filled to the brim by the country's torrential rains. Then the water, covered with old moss, melon rinds, orange peels, and all sorts of refuse, would stagnate until the sun sucked it up or the municipal authorities roused themselves and decided to pump it out, and a filthy dry cracking sludge remained for a long time at the bottom of the basin, waiting till the sun, pursuing its efforts, reduced it to dust and the wind or the brooms of the street sweepers blew it onto the shiny leaves of the ficus that surrounded the square. In summer, at any rate, the basin was dry, and its broad edge of shiny dark stone, made slippery by thousands of hands and trouser bottoms, was available to Jacques, Pierre, and the others to play at jousting, swiveling in their seats until the inevitable fall hurled them into the shallow basin that smelled of urine and sun.

Then, still running, through the heat and the dust that covered their feet and their sandals with a single gray layer, they dashed on to the green field. It was a vacant lot behind a cooperage, where among rusted hoops and old rotting barrel bottoms bunches of anemic grass sprouted between patches of chalky tuff. There amidst loud cries they would draw a circle in the tuff. One of them would take up a position in the circle, racquet in hand, and the others would take turns hurling the wooden cigar into the circle. If the cigar landed in the circle, the thrower took the racquet, and then he defended the circle. The more skillful among them[a] would hit the cigar on the fly and drive it far away. In that case they had the right to go where it had landed, make the cigar jump in the air by hitting its end with the edge of the racquet, then drive it still farther, and so on until either they missed their swing or the others caught it on the fly, and they hurried back again to defend the circle from the cigar hurled quickly and expertly by the opponent. This poor man's tennis, which had a few more complex rules, would take up the whole afternoon. Pierre was the best player. He was thinner than Jacques, and smaller, almost frail; his hair was as much blond as brown hanging down to his eyebrows beneath which his blue eyes were direct and vulnerable, a bit hurt, astonished; though clumsy in his manner, in action he was sure and accurate. As for Jacques, he would make impossible parries and miss routine backhands. Because of the former, and the successes that caused his comrades to admire him, he thought he was the best player and often bragged about it. In fact, Pierre beat him all the time and never said a word. But after the game he would straighten up to his full height and smile to himself while he listened to the others.[b]

When either the weather or their mood did not lend itself to running around the streets and vacant lots, they would first gather in the hall of Jacques's house. From

---

a. put the skillful defender in the singular.

b. The green field was where the *donnades* took place. [Fights between boys that followed a strict ritual. See pp. 153–54—*Trans.*]

there they went out the back door and down into a small yard enclosed on three sides by the walls of houses. On the fourth side a big orange tree stretched its branches over a garden wall; when it was in flower, its scent rose alongside the wretched houses, drifting through the hall or down a small stone stairs to the yard. Along one side and half of another a small L-shaped building housed the Spanish barber whose shop was on the street, and an Arab household[a] where on some evenings the wife would be roasting coffee in the yard. On the third side, the tenants kept hens up in high dilapidated coops made of wood and wire screening. Finally, on the fourth side, the black maws of the building's cellars gaped on either side of the stairs: caverns without exit or lighting, cut into the earth itself, without any partitions, sweating with humidity, reached by four steps covered with green mold, where the tenants piled at random their surplus possessions, that is, almost nothing: old sacks were rotting there, scraps of chests, rusty old washbasins with holes in them, things you find lying around vacant lots that even the poorest have no use for. It was there, in one of those cellars, that the children would gather. Jean and Joseph, the two sons of the Spanish barber, were in the habit of playing there. Since it was at the door to their hovel, the cellar was their own territory. Joseph, plump and mischievous, was always laughing and would give away everything he had. The short and thin

---

a. Omar is the son of this couple—the father is a city street sweeper.

Jean was forever picking up even the smallest nail or screw that he found, and he was particularly stingy with his marbles and with the apricot pits that were necessary for one of their favorite games.[a] You could not imagine more opposite types than these inseparable brothers. With Pierre, Jacques, and Max, the last of the accomplices, they would plunge into the humid stinking cellar. They would take torn sacks that were rotting on the ground and, after ridding them of the gray cockroaches with jointed shells that they called guinea pigs, they would stretch them over rusty iron uprights. And under this vile tent, in their own place at last (when none of them had ever had a room or even a bed he could call his own), they would light a little fire that, confined in that damp air, would die out in smoke and drive them out of their den until they covered it over with some damp earth they had scraped up from the yard itself. Then they would share, not without an argument from little Jean, the big mint-flavored caramels, the dried and salted peanuts and chick-peas, the salted lupine seeds called "tramousses," and the barley sugar that came in loud colors, sold by the Arabs who displayed their wares in front of the nearby movie theatre on a fly-besieged stand made by mounting a plain wooden box on rollers. On days when it rained heavily, the excess water would

---

a. You put one pit on top of a tripod of three other pits. Someone tries to knock this structure down by throwing another pit at it from a given distance. If he succeeds, he picks up the four pits. If he misses, his pit belongs to the owner of the pile.

run off the saturated yard and flood the cellars, and the children, standing on old boxes, would play Robinson Crusoe far from the open sky and the sea breezes, triumphant in their kingdom of poverty.[a]

But the best* days were those in summer when, under one pretext or another, the boys managed by a clever lie to escape the siesta. Then, since they never had money for the trolley, they would walk the long way to the experimental garden, through a succession of the neighborhood's yellow-and-gray streets, crossing the district of the stables, the big coachhouses belonging to businesses or individuals who supplied the regions of the interior with their horse-drawn trucks, then passing alongside big sliding doors behind which they heard the horses stamping, the sudden snorts that would make the animals' lips smack, the sound of the metal chains used as halters hitting against the wood of the manger, while the boys breathed with delight the odors of manure, of straw, and of sweat that came from these forbidden places that Jacques would still be dreaming about while he went to sleep. They lingered in front of an open stable where the horses were being groomed, heavyset big-hoofed animals that came from France; they were beaten down by the heat and the flies, and their eyes were those of exiles. Then, chased away by the teamsters, the children ran on to the huge garden where the rarest of species were raised. There, on the broad walk

---

a. Galoufa.
* biggest.

that led past a great vista of pools and flowers to the sea, they were under the suspicious eyes of the guards, and they affected the manner of casual, worldly strollers. But at the first transverse path, they would head toward the eastern part of the garden, through rows of enormous mangroves so dense that in their shade it seemed almost night, then past the big rubber trees[a] where you could not tell the drooping branches from their multiple roots, which grew from the first branches to reach the ground; and still farther, to the real objective of their expedition, the big palms that bore at their tops tightly packed bunches of round orange fruits that they called "cocoses." Once there, they first had to reconnoiter in all directions to make sure no guards were nearby. Then began the search for ammunition—that is, stones. When they had all returned with their pockets full, they took turns firing stones at the bunches of fruit swaying gently in the sky above all the other trees. Each stone that struck home knocked down a few fruits, which belonged to the winning marksman. The others had to wait till he had picked up his loot before they fired in their turn. Jacques, who had a good arm, equaled Pierre at this game. But they both shared their booty with those who were less successful. The worst among them at this game was Max, who wore glasses and had poor eyesight. He was squat and solidly built, and the boys had respected him ever since the day they saw him fight. The others, and especially Jacques, who could not con-

---

a. give the name of the trees.

trol his violent temper, were in the habit during their
frequent street fights of hurling themselves at the adversary in an attempt to inflict as much pain as quickly as
possible, even at the risk of being hit hard in return. But
when Max, whose name sounded German, was called a
dirty Hun by the butcher's fat son, nicknamed "Gigot,"
he calmly removed his glasses, which he entrusted to
Joseph, took up the boxer's stance they had seen pictured in the newspapers, and invited the other boy to re-
peat his insult. Then, not seeming to raise a sweat, he
dodged each attack by Gigot, hit him several times
without being even touched in return, and finally, the
supreme glory, he gave Gigot a black eye. Since that
day, Max's popularity in the little group had been as-
sured. Now, with their hands and pockets sticky with
fruit, they hurried out of the garden toward the sea, and
once they were outside the boundary, they ate the
cocoses stacked on their dirty handkerchiefs, chewing
delightedly on fibrous berries that were nauseatingly
sweet and rich, yet as light and savory as victory. Then
they scurried off to the beach.

To get there they had to cross what was called the
sheep's trail, because in fact flocks of sheep often traveled it to or from the Maison-Carrée market, east of Algiers. Actually it was a lateral road that divided the sea
from the city spread out on its hills like the arc of an am-
phitheatre. Between the road and the sea lay factories,
brickyards, and a gasworks separated by stretches of
sand covered with patches of clay or lime dust where
scraps of iron and wood were turning white. You
crossed this barren land to reach the Sablettes beach. Its

sand was somewhat dirty, and the water in the first
waves was not always clear. To the right, the public
baths offered cabins, and its hall, a big wooden box on
pilings, was available for dancing on holidays. Every
day, during the season, a french-fries peddler would
start up his stove. Seldom did the little group have even
the price of a single paper cornet of fried potatoes. If by
chance one of them had the required coin,[a] he would
buy his twist, march solemnly to the beach, followed respectfully by the retinue of his comrades, and, in the
shade of an old derelict barge by the sea, he would set
his feet in the sand and drop to a sitting position while
holding his twist vertical in one hand and covered with
the other, to make sure he did not lose a single one of
the crusty fries. The custom was that he would then
give his comrades one fry apiece, and they would reverently savor the single tidbit, hot and smelling of strong
oil, that he permitted them. They would watch while
the favored boy gravely relished the remaining fries one
by one. There were always crumbs left at the bottom of
the paper twist, which they would implore the glutted
owner to share. Most of the time, unless it was Jean, he
would unfold the oily paper, spread out the potato
crumbs, and authorize them to take a single crumb each.
All it took then was an eenie, meenie, minie, moe to decide who would go first and thus get the biggest crumb.
When their feast was over, both pleasure and frustration
immediately forgotten, they would race under the harsh

---

a. 2 SOUS

sun toward the western end of the beach, until they came to a half-destroyed masonry structure that must have been the foundation for a now vanished bungalow, behind which they could undress. In a few seconds they were naked, a moment later in the water, swimming with clumsy vigor, shouting,[a] drooling and spitting, daring each other to dive or vying as to who could stay underwater the longest. The sea was gentle and warm, the sun fell lightly on their soaked heads, and the glory of the light filled their young bodies with a joy that made them cry out incessantly. They reigned over life and over the sea, and, like nobles certain that their riches were limitless, they heedlessly consumed the most gorgeous of this world's offerings.

They forgot the time as they ran back and forth between beach and sea, drying the salt water that made them sticky while they were on the sand, then in the water washing off the sand that clothed them in gray. They ran on and on, and the swifts with their quick cries were beginning to fly lower over the factories and the beach. The sky, emptied of the hot haze of the day, became clearer, then turned greenish, the light slackened, and on the other side of the bay, till now enveloped in a sort of fog, the sweep of houses and the city became more distinct. It was still day, but already lamps were being lit in preparation for Africa's brief twilight. Pierre was usually the first to sound the alarm: "It's

---

a. If you drown, your mother'll kill you. Aren't you ashamed to let everything hang out like that. Where's your mother.

late," and right away came the stampede, the quick fare-well. Jacques with Joseph and Jean ran toward their homes without worrying about the others. They galloped till they were out of breath: Joseph's mother was quick with her hand. And as for Jacques's grand-mother . . . They ran on through the rapidly falling night, panicked when the first gaslamp went on, the trolleys with their lights on receding before them; they ran faster, dismayed to see that night had already fallen, and parted on the doorstep without even a goodbye. On such evenings Jacques would stop on the dark stinking stairs, lean against the wall, and wait for his throbbing heart to quiet down. But he could not wait, and the knowledge made him gasp still more. In three strides he was on the landing; he passed by the door to the toilet for the floor, and he opened his door. There was a light in the dining room at the end of the hall, and, chilled, he heard the rattle of spoons against dishes. He entered. At the table his half-mute uncle[a] went on noisily sucking up his soup; his mother, still young, her brown hair abundant, gazed at him with her lovely gentle look. "You know perfectly well—" she began.

But his grandmother, of whom he only saw the back, interrupted her daughter; she was erect in her black dress, her mouth firmly set, her eyes direct and stern. "Where were you?" she asked.

"Pierre was showing me the arithmetic homework."

The grandmother stood and came over to him. She

---

a. the brother.

sniffed his hair, then ran her hands over his ankles still covered with sand. "You were at the beach."

"Then you're liar," the uncle managed to articulate.

The grandmother passed behind him to get the crude whip, known as a bull's pizzle, that was hanging behind the door, and she gave him three or four lashes on his legs and buttocks that burned till he howled. A little while later, sitting with tears filling his mouth and throat before the plate of soup that the uncle, moved to pity, had served him, he strained every nerve to keep those tears from overflowing. And his mother, after a glance at the grandmother, would turn to him that face he so loved: "Eat your soup," she would say. "It's all over. It's all over." That was when he let go and wept.

Jacques Cormery awakened. The sun was no longer reflected in the copper of the porthole, but had dropped to the horizon and was lighting up the wainscoting across the cabin. He dressed and went out on the deck. He would find Algiers at the end of the night.

5 : The Father. His Death
The War. The Bombing

He held her in his arms, right at the door, still out of breath from racing up the stairs four at a time, in a single surefooted dash not missing a step, as if his body still remembered the exact height of each stair. When he had gotten out of the taxi, the street was already lively and still sparkling in spots from the morning's[a] sprinkling, which the burgeoning heat was beginning to disperse in mist; he saw her there where she had been long ago, on the apartment's single narrow balcony between the two rooms, over the barber's roof—but this barber was no longer the father of Jean and Joseph; he died of tuberculosis; it goes with the trade, his wife would say, always having to breathe hair—the corrugated-iron roof still carried the same load of ficus berries, bits of crumpled paper, and old cigarette butts. She was there, her hair still abundant but turned white years ago, still erect despite her seventy-two years; she looked ten years

---

a. Sunday.

younger because she was so slender and her strength was still evident—they were all like that in the family, a clan of lean people with a nonchalant manner whose energy was inexhaustible; old age did not seem to have any hold on them. At fifty his half-mute Uncle Émile[1] looked like a young man. The grandmother had died without bowing her head. And as for his mother, toward whom he was now running, it seemed that nothing could erode her gentle endurance, since decades of exhausting labor had spared the young woman in her that Cormery as a child had admired with all his heart.

When he arrived on the doorstep, his mother opened the door and threw herself in his arms. And there, as she did every time they were reunited, she kissed him two or three times, holding him against her with all her strength; and in his arms he felt her ribs, the hard jutting bones of her shoulders, trembling a bit, while he breathed the soft smell of her skin that made him remember the spot, under her larynx, between the two jugular tendons, that he no longer dared to kiss, but that as a child he had loved to nuzzle and fondle on those infrequent occasions when she took him on her knees and he pretended to sleep, his nose in the little hollow that to him had the scent of a tenderness all too rare in his young life. She embraced him, and then, having let go of him, she looked at him and took him again in her

---

1. Later called Ernest.

arms to kiss him once more, as if she had measured in herself all the love she had or could express and found that one measure was still missing. "My son," she said, "you were far away."[a] And immediately she turned away, went back into the apartment, and seated herself in the dining room that faced the street; she no longer seemed to be thinking of him nor for that matter of anything, and she even looked at him from time to time with an odd expression, as if—or so at least it seemed to him—he were now in the way, were disturbing the narrow, empty, closed universe which she circled in her solitude. What was more, once he was seated by her, she seemed on this day to be seized with some sort of anxiety, and occasionally she would glance furtively out at the street with her lovely melancholy expression, her eyes feverish until she turned to Jacques and they became peaceful.

The street was getting noisier, and the heavy red trolleys were rattling by more often. Cormery watched his mother, in her small gray blouse set off by a white collar, sitting in profile on the same uncomfortable chair [ ][1] by the window where she had always sat, her back a bit rounded by age, but still not seeking the support of the chair, her hands clasped around a small handkerchief that now and then she would roll into a ball with her stiffened fingers, then leave in the hollow of her dress between her motionless hands, her head turned a

----

a. transition.

1. Two illegible marks.

little toward the window. She was just as she had been thirty years ago, and behind the wrinkles he once more discovered the same miraculously young face, the arch of her brows as smooth and polished as if they had been cast with the forehead, her small straight nose, the mouth still clearly delineated despite the tension at the corners of her lips from her dentures. The neck itself, which is so soon laid waste, had kept its form although the tendons were knotty and the chin a bit slack.

"You went to the hairdresser," Jacques said.

She smiled with her look of a little girl caught in some misdeed. "Yes, you know, you were coming." She had always been coquettish in her almost invisible way. And, as plainly as she might be dressed, Jacques did not remember ever seeing her wear anything ugly. Even now, the grays and blacks in which she dressed were well chosen. That was the way of the clan, who were always wretched, or just poor, or occasionally, in the case of certain cousins, somewhat well off. But all of them, especially the men, insisted like all Mediterraneans on white shirts and pressed pants, finding it natural that this work of upkeep—constant, given their meager wardrobes—should be added to the labor of the women, whether mothers or spouses. As for his mother,[a] she had always reckoned that it was not enough to wash other people's laundry and do their housework, and as far back as he could remember, Jacques had

---

a. the bony polished brow where the dark and feverish eye was shining.

seen her ironing the single pair of pants that he and his brother each had, until he left to go off into the world of women who neither iron nor do laundry.

"It's the Italian," his mother said. "The hairdresser. He does good work."

"Yes," said Jacques. He was going to say: "You're very beautiful," and he stopped himself. He had always thought that of his mother and had never dared to tell her so. It was not that he feared being rebuffed nor that he doubted such a compliment would please her. But it would have meant breaching the invisible barrier behind which for all his life he had seen her take shelter—gentle, polite, complaisant, even passive, and yet never conquered by anyone or anything, isolated by her semideafness, her difficulty in expressing herself, beautiful surely but virtually inaccessible, and never more so than when she was full of smiles and when his own heart most went out to her—yes, all his life she had had the same manner, fearful and submissive, yet also distant, the same look she had thirty years ago when she watched without intervening while her mother beat Jacques with a whip, she who had never touched or even really scolded her children; there was no doubt that those blows wounded her too, but she could not intervene because she was exhausted, because she could not find the words, and because of the respect she owed her mother; she had not interfered, she had endured through the long days and the years, had endured those blows for her children, just as for herself she endured the hard days of working in the service of others, washing floors on her knees, living without a man and without solace in the midst of the greasy leavings and dirty linen of other people's lives, the long days of labor adding up one by one to a life that, by dint of being deprived of hope, had become also a life without any sort of resentment, unaware, persevering, a life resigned to all kinds of suffering, her own as well as that of others. He had never heard her complain, other than to say she was tired or that her back hurt after a big washday. He had never heard her speak ill of anyone, other than to say a sister or aunt had not been nice to her, or was "stuck up." But on the other hand, he had seldom heard her laugh wholeheartedly. She laughed a little more now that she was no longer working because her children were paying for all her needs. Jacques looked around the room, which had also remained unchanged. She had not wanted to leave this apartment where she had her own routines, this neighborhood where everything was easy for her, to go to a more comfortable place where everything would have become difficult for her. Yes, it was the same room. They had replaced the furniture; it was decent now, less wretched. But the pieces themselves were still bare, still pushed back against the wall.

"You're always poking around," his mother said.

Yes, he could not keep himself from opening the buffet, which still contained only the bare necessities, despite all his entreaties; its nakedness fascinated him. He also opened the drawers of the sideboard that housed the two or three medications with which this household made do, mixed in with two or three old newspapers, bits of string, a little cardboard box filled with odd buttons, an old identification photo. Here even the unnecessary was shabby, because they never had anything superfluous. And Jacques was well aware that had his mother been put in a standard household where objects were as plentiful as they were in his present home, she would only have made use of what was strictly necessary. He knew that in the next room, his mother's, furnished with a small wardrobe, a narrow bed, a wooden dressing table, and a straw-bottomed chair, its one window hung with a crocheted curtain, he would find no articles at all, except, now and then, the small rolled-up handkerchief that she would leave on the bare wooden top of the dressing table.

That was just what had struck him when he first saw other households, those of his classmates at the *lycée* or later those of a more well-to-do world: the number of vases, bowls, statuettes, paintings that crowded those rooms. In his home, his family said "the vase that's on the mantelpiece"; the pot, the soup dishes, and the few articles you might find had no names. At his uncle's, on the other hand, one was made to admire the glazed earthenware from the Vosges and you ate off the Quimper dinner service. Jacques had grown up in the midst of a poverty naked as death, among things named with common nouns; it was at his uncle's that he discovered those proper nouns. And still today, in this room with freshly washed tiles, on this plain shiny furniture, there was nothing except an Arab ashtray made of chased copper, there because he was coming, and a post office calendar on the wall. There was nothing to see here, and little to say, and that was why he knew nothing about his mother except what he learned from his own experience. Nor about his father.

"Papa?"

She looked at him, and now she was paying attention.[a]

"Yes."

"His name was Henri, and what else?"

"I don't know."

"Didn't he have any other name?"

"I think he did, but I don't remember." Suddenly distracted, she gazed at the street where the sun was now beating down with all its force.

"He looked like me?"

"Yes, he was your spitting image. He had blue eyes. And his forehead was like yours."

"What year was he born?"

"I don't know. I was four years older."

"And you, what year were you born?"

"I don't know. Look in the family book."

Jacques went into the bedroom and opened the wardrobe. Among the towels, on the top shelf, were the family record book, a pension book, and some old documents in Spanish. He came back with the papers.

"He was born in 1885 and you in 1882. You were three years older."

"Ah! I thought it was four. It was a long time ago."

---

a. The father—interrogation—war of 14—Attack.

"You told me he lost his father and mother when he was very young, and his brothers put him in an orphanage."

"Yes. His sister too."

"His parents had a farm?"

"Yes. They were Alsatians."

"At Ouled-Fayet."

"Yes. And we were at Chéragas. It's right nearby."

"How old was he when he lost his parents?"

"I don't know. Oh, he was young. His sister left him. That wasn't right. He didn't want to see them anymore."

"How old was his sister?"

"I don't know."

"And his brothers? Was he the youngest?"

"No. He was the second one."

"But then his brothers were too young to look after him."

"Yes, that's it."

"Then it wasn't their fault."

"No, he held it against them. After the orphanage, when he was sixteen, he went to his sister's farm. They made him work too much. It was too much."

"He came to Chéragas."

"Yes, to our place."

"That's where you met him?"

"Yes." Again she turned her head away, toward the street, and he felt himself unable to continue along that line. But she herself went in another direction. "You have to understand, he didn't know how to read. They didn't learn anything in the orphanage."

"But you showed me postcards he sent you from the war."

"Yes, he learned from M. Classiault."

"At Ricome."

"Yes. M. Classiault was the boss. He taught him to read and write."

"How old was he?"

"Twenty, I think. I don't know. All that was long ago. But when we were married, he had learned about wines and he could work anywhere. He had a good head on his shoulders." She looked at him. "Like you."

"And then?"

"And then? Your brother came. Your father was working for Ricome, and Ricome sent him to his farm at Saint-Lapôtre."

"Saint-Apôtre?"

"Yes. And then there was the war. He died. They sent me the shell splinter."

The shell fragment that had split his father's skull was in a little biscuit can behind those same towels in that same wardrobe, with the dry and terse cards written from the front that he could recite by heart. "My dear Lucie. I'm well. We're changing quarters tomorrow. Take good care of the children. I kiss you. Your husband."

Yes, in the depths of the night when he was born during their move, an emigrant, child of emigrants, Europe was already tuning its cannons that would go off in unison several months later, chasing the Cormerys from Saint-Apôtre, he to his army corps in Algiers, she to her mother's little apartment in that wretched neighbor-

hood, carrying in her arms the baby swollen with mosquito bites from the Seybouse. "Don't trouble yourself,
Mother. We'll leave when Henri comes back."

And the grandmother, erect, white hair pulled back,
her eyes bright and hard: "Daughter, you'll have to go
to work."

"He was in the Zouaves."

"Yes. He was in the war in Morocco."

It was true. He had forgotten. In 1905 his father was
twenty years old. He had been on active duty, as they
say, against the Moroccans.[a] Jacques recalled what M.
Levesque, the principal of his school, had told him when
he ran into him on the streets of Algiers several years
earlier. M. Levesque had been called up at the same time
as his father. But they spent only a month in the same
unit. According to him, he did not know Cormery well,
for the latter had little to say. Hardened to fatigue,
closemouthed, but easygoing and fair-minded. On just
one occasion, Cormery had seemed beside himself. It
was at night, after a scorching day, someplace out in the
Atlas Mountains where the detail had made camp at the
top of a hill protected by a rocky pass. Cormery and Levesque were supposed to relieve the sentinel at the bottom of the pass. No one answered their call. And, at the
foot of a hedge of prickly pears, they found their comrade with his head back, bizarrely facing toward the
moon. And at first they did not recognize his head because of its strange shape. But it was very simple. His

---

a. 14

throat had been cut and that ghastly swelling in his mouth was his entire sexual organ. That was when they saw the body, with the legs spread wide, the Zouave's pantaloons slashed, and, in the middle of the gap, that swampy puddle, which they could see by the now indirect light of the moon.[a] A hundred meters farther on, this time behind a large rock, the second sentinel was displayed in the same position. The alarm was sounded, the number of sentries doubled. At dawn, when they had gone back up to the camp, Cormery said their enemies were not men. Levesque, who was thinking about it, answered that for them that was how men should act, that we were in their country, that they fought by any and all means.

Cormery's face was dead set. "Maybe. But they're wrong. A man doesn't do that."

Levesque said that according to the other side, there were certain circumstances in which a man was supposed to do anything and [destroy everything].

But Cormery had shouted as if crazed with anger: "No, a man doesn't let himself do that kind of thing! That's what makes a man, or otherwise . . ." Then he calmed down. "As for me," he said in a low voice, "I'm poor, I came from an orphanage, they put me in this uniform, they dragged me into the war, but I wouldn't let myself do that."

"There are Frenchmen who do do it," [said] Levesque.

---

a. Croak with it or without it, you're still dead, the sergeant said.

"Then they too, they aren't men." And suddenly he cried out: "A filthy race! What a race! All of them, all of them . . ." And, white as a sheet, he went into his tent.

When he thought about it, Jacques realized that the most he had learned about his father was from this old teacher, of whom he had now lost track. But it was no more, except in the details, than what he had been able to surmise from his mother's silences. A hard man and a bitter one, who had worked all his life, had killed on command, had submitted to everything that could not be avoided, but had preserved some part of himself where he allowed no one to trespass. A poor man, after all. For poverty is not a choice one makes, but a poor person can protect himself. And Jacques tried, with the little he knew from his mother, to picture the same man nine years later, married, father of two, who had achieved a somewhat better position in life and then was summoned back to Algiers to be mobilized,[a] the long journey by night with the patient wife and the unbearable children, the parting at the station and then, three days later, at the little apartment in Belcourt, his sudden appearance in the Zouave regiment's handsome red-and-blue uniform with its baggy pantaloons, sweating under the thick wool in the July* heat, a straw hat in his hand because he had neither tarboosh nor helmet, after he had sneaked out of the depot under the arches of the docks and run to kiss his wife and children

---

a. 1814 newspapers in Algiers. [*Sic—Ed.*]

* August.

before shipping out that night for the France he had never seen,[a] on the sea that had never before carried him; and he embraced them, strongly and quickly, and he left at the same pace, and the woman on the little balcony waved to him and he responded on the run, turning to wave the straw hat, before once more racing down the street that was gray with dust and heat, and then he disappeared in front of the movie theatre, farther on, into the radiant light of the morning from which he would never return. Jacques would have to imagine the rest. Not through what could be told to him by his mother, who had no idea what history and geography might be, who knew only that she lived on land near the sea, that France was on the other side of that sea which she too had never traveled, France in any case being an obscure place lost in a dim night which one reached through a port named Marseilles, which she pictured like the port of Algiers, where there was a shining city they said was very beautiful and that was called Paris, where there was also a region named Alsace that her husband's family came from—it was a long time ago, they were fleeing enemies called Germans to settle in Algeria, and now that same region had to be taken back from those same enemies who were always evil and cruel, especially with the French, and for no reason at all. The French were always obliged to defend themselves against these quarrelsome, implacable men. It was there, along with Spain, which she could

---

a. He had never seen France. He saw it and was killed.

not locate but in any case it was not far away, from where her own family, natives of Mahon, had emigrated as long ago as her husband's family to come to Algeria, because they were dying of hunger in Mahon, and she did not even know that it was on an island, not knowing anyway what an island was, for she had never seen one. About other countries, she might sometimes be struck by the names without always being able to pronounce them correctly. And in any case she had never heard of Austria-Hungary nor of Serbia, Russia—like England—was a difficult name, she did not know what an archduke was, and she could never have articulated the four syllables of Sarajevo. The war was there, like an evil cloud thick with dark menace, but you could not keep it from invading the sky, no more than you could stop the locusts or the devastating storms that would swoop down on the high plains of Algeria. The Germans were forcing France into war once again, and we were going to suffer—there were no causes for it, she did not know the history of France, nor what history was. She knew a little of her own history, barely knew the history of those she loved, and those she loved had to suffer as she did. Into the night of the world she could not imagine, and the history she did not know, a still darker night had just come; mysterious orders had arrived, brought out into the bush by a sweating, weary constable, and they had to leave the farm where they were just getting ready to harvest the grapes—the parish priest was at the station in Bône for the draftees' departure: "We must pray," he said to her, and she had answered, "Yes, Monsieur Curé," but actually she had not heard him, for he had not spoken loudly enough, and besides the idea of praying would never have entered her mind, she never wanted to bother anyone—and now her husband was gone away in his handsome multicolored outfit; he would come back soon, that was what everyone was saying, the Germans would be punished, but in the meantime she had to find work. Luckily, a neighbor had told the grandmother that they needed women in the cartridge factory at the armory and that they would give preference to the wives of men in service, especially if they had family responsibilities, and she would have the good fortune to work ten hours a day arranging little cardboard tubes according to their thickness and color; she would be able to bring money home to the grandmother, the children would have enough to eat until the Germans were punished and Henri came home. Of course, she did not know there was a Russian front, nor what a front was, nor that the war could spread to the Balkans, to the Middle East, to the planet; everything was going on in France, where the Germans had entered without giving warning and were attacking children. Actually everything over there was happening with the troops from Africa, among them H. Cormery, transported as quickly as possible, led as they were to a mysterious region people were talking about, the Marne, and there was no time to find them helmets; the sun was not strong enough to erase colors as it did in Algeria, so that waves of Arab and French Algerians, dressed in smart shining colors, straw hats on their heads, red-and-blue targets you could see for hundreds of meters, went over the top in droves into the fire, were destroyed in droves, and began to fertilize a narrow stretch of land where for four years men who came from all over the world, crouching in muddy lairs, would struggle for each meter under a sky bristling with flares, with shells screaming while great artillery barrages proclaimed their futile assaults.[a] But for the moment there were no dugouts, only the African troops who melted away under fire like multicolored wax dolls, and each day hundreds of new orphans, Arab and French, awakened in every corner of Algeria, sons and daughters without fathers who would now have to learn to live without guidance and without heritage. A few weeks passed and then on a Sunday morning, on the small indoor landing of the only upper floor, between the stairs and the two unlit toilets—black holes dug Turkish-style through the masonry, constantly being cleaned with cresyl and always stinking—Lucie Cormery and her mother were sitting on two low chairs picking over lentils by the light of the window at the top of the stairs, and the baby in a small laundry basket was sucking a carrot covered with his drool, when a grave and well-dressed gentleman appeared on the stairs with a sort of envelope. The two surprised women put down the dishes they were sort-

---

a. to develop

ing lentils into, from a pot set between them, and were wiping off their hands when the gentleman, who had stopped on the next to last step, bade them not to disturb themselves, and asked for Mme. Cormery. "There she is," the grandmother said, "I'm her mother," and the gentleman said he was the district mayor, that he was bearing painful news, that her husband had died on the field of honor, and that France mourned him and at the same time was proud of him. Lucie Cormery had not heard him, but got to her feet and very respectfully offered him her hand; the grandmother stiffened, hand over her mouth, and was saying "My God" in Spanish again and again. The gentleman held Lucie's hand in his, then squeezed it between both his hands, and murmured his words of condolence; then he handed her his envelope, turned, and descended the stairs at a heavy gait.

"What did he say?" Lucie asked.

"Henri is dead. He was killed."

Lucie had stared at the envelope without opening it, neither she nor her mother could read; she turned it over, without a word, without a tear, unable to imagine this death, so far away in the depths of a mysterious night. And then she put the envelope in the pocket of her apron, passed by the baby without looking at him, went into the bedroom she shared with her two children, closed the door and the shutters of the window that looked out on the yard, and stretched out on her bed, where she remained for many hours silent and without tears, squeezing the envelope in her pocket and staring into the dark at the misfortune she did not understand.[a]

"*Maman,*" said Jacques.

She was still gazing at the street, in her same manner, and she did not hear him. He touched her thin wrinkled arm, and she turned smiling to him.

"Papa's cards, you know, the ones from the hospital."

"Yes."

"You received them after the mayor came?"

"Yes."

A shell fragment had split open his skull and he had been transported in one of those ambulance trains dripping blood, scattered with straw and bandages, that shuttled between the slaughterhouse and the evacuation hospitals at Saint-Brieuc. There he was able to scrawl two cards, by guesswork since he could no longer see: "I'm wounded. It's nothing. Your husband." Then after a few days he died. The nurse wrote: "It was better this way. He would have been left blind or insane. He was very brave." And then she received the shell fragment.

A patrol of three armed parachutists was passing by in single file on the street, looking in all directions. One of them was black; he was tall and supple and he

---

a. she thinks shells explode by their own volition.

looked like a splendid animal in the spotted skin of his camouflage.

"It's for the bandits," she said. "And I'm glad you went to his grave. As for me, I'm too old and besides it's far. Is it beautiful?"

"What, the grave?"

"Yes."

"It's beautiful. There are flowers."

"Yes. The French are good people."

She said it and she believed it, but without giving any further thought to her husband, forgotten now, along with the misfortune of long ago. And nothing was left, neither in her nor in this house, of that man who was consumed in a cosmic fire and of whom there remained only a memory as imperceptible as the ashes of a butterfly wing incinerated in a forest fire.

"The stew is going to burn, wait a minute."

[a]She had gotten up to go to the kitchen and he had taken her place, gazing down in his turn at the street, unchanged after so many years, with the same stores, their colors faded and flaked by the sun. Only the tobacconist across the street had put up long strips of multicolored plastic in place of the curtain of little hollow reeds that made a special sound—which today Jacques could still hear—when he used to go through it to penetrate into the exquisite odor of newsprint and tobacco and to buy *L'Intrépide* where he would thrill to tales of

---

a. changes in the apartment

honor and courage. Now the street was experiencing the liveliness of a Sunday morning. Workingmen in freshly washed and ironed white shirts were chatting on their way to the three or four cafés, which smelled of cool shade and anise. Some Arabs were passing by, poor also but decently dressed, their wives still veiled but wearing Louis XV shoes. Now and then entire Arab families went by in their Sunday best. One of these families had three children in tow, one of them dressed up as a parachutist. And just then the patrol of parachutists came back along the street, relaxed and seemingly indifferent. The explosion resounded at the very moment Lucie Cormery came back to the room.

It sounded very close, enormous, as if it would never stop reverberating. It seemed that they had long since stopped hearing it, but the bulb in the dining-room light was still shaking behind its glass shell. His mother had recoiled to the back of the room, pale, her dark eyes full of a fear she could not control, and she was unsteady on her feet.

"It's here. It's here," she was saying.

"No," Jacques said, and he ran to the window. People were fleeing in the street, he did not know where to; an Arab family had gone into the notions store across the street, hurrying their children inside, and the shop-keeper let them in, closed the door and removed the door handle, then stood behind the window watching the street. At that moment the parachute patrol came back, running at top speed in the opposite direction. Cars pulled up hastily on the sidewalk and stopped. The street had emptied in a few seconds. But by leaning forward, Jacques could see a big crowd in motion farther away, between the Musset movie theatre and the trolley stop. "I'm going to go see," he said.

At the corner of the rue Prévost-Paradol,[a] [1]a group of men were shouting.

"That filthy race," a short worker in an undershirt said, looking in the direction of an Arab standing as if glued in a gateway near the café.

"I didn't do anything," the Arab said.

"You're all in it together, all you fucking sons of bitches," and he started toward him. The other men held him back. Jacques said to the Arab: "Come with me," and he took him into the café, which was now run by Jean, his childhood friend, the son of the barber. Jean was there, still the same, but wrinkled, short and thin, his face sly and alert.

"He didn't do anything," said Jacques. "Take him into your home."

Jean looked the Arab over while he wiped off the counter. "Come," he said, and they disappeared out the back.

Jacques went outside, and the worker scowled at him.

"He hasn't done anything," Jacques said.

"We should kill them all."

---

a. —He saw it before coming to see his mother?

—Rework the *Kessous* bombing in the third part, and in that case only mention it here.

—Farther along.

1. This entire section up to "you could not tell which" is circled with a question mark.

"That's what you say when you're angry. Think it over."

The worker shrugged. "Go over there and see what you say after you've seen the mess."

Ambulance sirens were rising, rapid, urgent. Jacques ran to the trolley stop. The bomb had exploded by the line pole close to the stop. A lot of people, all in their Sunday dress, had been waiting for the trolley. The little café nearby was full of cries of anger or suffering, you could not tell which.

He went back to his mother. She was standing erect now and very pale. "Sit down," and he led her to the chair close to the table. He sat by her and took her hands.

"Twice this week," she said. "I'm afraid to go out."

"It's nothing," Jacques said. "It'll stop."

"Yes," she said. She looked at him with an odd air of indecision, as if she were divided between her faith in her son's intelligence and her conviction that *life in its entirety* was a misfortune you could not struggle against but could only endure.

"You see," she said, "I'm old. I can't run anymore."

Now the blood was returning to her cheeks. In the distance could be heard the sirens of the ambulances, urgent, rapid. But she did not hear them. She breathed deeply, calmed herself a little more, and smiled at her son with her beautiful brave smile. Like all her people, she had grown up with danger, and danger might wring her heart but she would endure it as she did everything else. It was he who could not bear that pinched look of a dying person he had suddenly seen on her face.

"Come with me to France," he said to her, but she shook her head with resolute sorrow: "Oh no, it's cold over there. I'm too old now. I want to stay home."

6 : The Family

"Ah!" his mother said to him, "I'm glad when you're here.[a] But come in the evening, I'll be less bored. It's the evenings especially, in winter it gets dark early. If only I knew how to read. I can't knit either in this light, my eyes hurt. So when Étienne's not here, I lie down and wait till it's time to eat. It's a long time, two hours like that. If I had the little girls with me, I'd talk with them. But they come and they go away. I'm too old. Maybe I smell bad. So it's like that, and all alone . . ."

She spoke all at once, in short simple sentences that followed each other as if she were emptying herself of thoughts that till then had been silent. And then, her thoughts run dry, she was again silent, her lips tight, her look gentle and dejected, gazing through the closed dining-room shutters at the suffocating light coming up from the street, still at her same place on the same un-

---

a. She never used a subjunctive.

comfortable chair and her son going around the table in the middle of the room as he used to do.[a]

She watched him as once more he circled the table.[b]

"Solférino, it's pretty?"

"Yes, it's spotless. But it must have changed since the last time you saw it."

"Yes, things change."

"The doctor sends you his greetings. You remember him?"

"No. It was long ago."

"No one remembers Papa."

"We didn't stay long. And besides, he didn't say much."

"*Maman?*" She looked at him, unsmiling, with a mild and vacant expression. "I thought you and Papa never lived together in Algiers."

"No, no."

"Did you understand me?" She had not understood; he could guess as much from her slightly frightened manner, as if she were apologizing, and he articulated the words as he repeated the question: "You never lived together in Algiers?"

"No," she said.

"But how about the time Papa went to see them cut off Pirette's head?"

He hit his neck with the side of his hand to make himself understood. But she answered immediately: "Yes, he got up at three o'clock to go to Barberousse."

---

a. Relations with brother Henri: the fights.
b. what they ate: stew of innards, codfish stew, chick-peas, etc.

"So you were in Algiers?"

"Yes."

"But when was it?"

"I don't know. He was working for Ricome."

"Before you went to Solférino?"

"Yes."

She said yes, maybe it was no; she had to reach back in time through a clouded memory, nothing was certain. To begin with, poor people's memory is less nourished than that of the rich; it has fewer landmarks in space because they seldom leave the place where they live, and fewer reference points in time throughout lives that are gray and featureless. Of course there is the memory of the heart that they say is the surest kind, but the heart wears out with sorrow and labor, it forgets sooner under the weight of fatigue. Remembrance of things past is just for the rich. For the poor it only marks the faint traces on the path to death. And besides, in order to bear up well one must not remember too much, but rather stick close to the passing day, hour by hour, as his mother did, somewhat by necessity no doubt, since that childhood illness (by the way, according to his grandmother, it was typhoid. But typhoid does not have such aftereffects. Typhus perhaps. Or else? Here again, all was darkness) since that childhood illness had left her deaf and speaking with difficulty, then prevented her from learning what is taught to even the most wretched, so her mute resignation was forced on her, but it was also the only way she had found to face up to her life, and what else could she have done, who in her place could have found another way? He wanted her to be fascinated by describing for him a man who had died forty years earlier and whose life she had shared (and had she really shared it?) for five years. She could not do that; he did not even know if she had passionately loved that man, and in any case he could not ask it of her, for in her presence he too was in his own way mute and crippled; at heart he did not even want to know what there had been between them, and so he had to give up on learning anything from her. Even the one circumstance that had made such an impression on him as a child, had pursued him throughout his life and even into his dreams, his father getting up at three o'clock to attend the execution of a notorious criminal—even that he had learned from his grandmother. Pirette was an agricultural laborer on a farm in the Sahel, quite close to Algiers. He had killed his employers and the three children in the house with a hammer. "To rob them?" Jacques asked as a child. "Yes," said Uncle Étienne. "No," said his grandmother, but without any further explanation. They found the disfigured corpses, the house splattered with blood right up to the ceiling, and, under one of the beds, the youngest child still breathing; he died also, but he had found the strength to write on the whitewashed wall with his blood-soaked finger: "It's Pirette." They searched for the murderer and found him, dazed, out in the countryside. Horrified public opinion demanded the death penalty; it was readily granted, and the execution took place before Barberousse prison in the presence of a considerable number of spectators. Jacques's father had gotten up in the night and gone to attend the exemplary punishment

of a crime that, according to the grandmother, had out-
raged him. But they never knew what had happened.
Apparently the execution had taken place without incident. But Jacques's father was livid when he came
home; he went to bed, then got up several times to
vomit, and went back to bed. He never wanted to talk
about what he had seen. And on the night he heard the
story, Jacques himself, when he was lying huddled on
the side of the bed to avoid touching his brother, with
whom he slept, choked back his nausea and his horror
as he relived the details he had heard and those he imag-
ined. And throughout his life those images had followed
him even into his sleep when now and then, but regularly, a recurrent nightmare would haunt him, taking
many forms, but always having the one theme: they
were coming to take him, Jacques, to be executed. And
for a long time when he awakened he would shake off
his fear and anguish and return to that soothing reality
where there was absolutely no chance that he would be
executed. Then, by the time he had come of age, world
events around him were such that his execution was no
longer so unlikely a possibility, and reality no longer as-
suaged his dreams, but on the contrary was fed during a
very [precise] number of years by the same dread that so
distressed his father and that he had left to his son as his
only clear and certain legacy. But it was a mysterious
bond that connected him to the dead stranger of Saint-
Brieuc (who, after all, had not thought he would die a
violent death either), a bond beyond the reach of his
mother, who had known that story, had seen his vomiting, and had forgotten that morning, just as she had not

realized later on that times had changed. For her the times were always the same: disaster could emerge at any moment without calling out a warning.

His grandmother,[a] on the other hand, had a more accurate picture of things. "You'll end up on the gallows," she would often tell Jacques. Why not? It was no longer unusual. She did not know that but, being the person she was, nothing would have surprised her. Erect in her long black robe of a prophetess, uninformed and stubborn, she at least had never known resignation. And she more than anyone else had dominated Jacques's childhood. Raised by her parents from Mahon on a small farm in the Sahel, she was very young when she married a slender and delicate man, also of Mahon origin, whose brothers had already settled in Algeria by 1848, after the tragic death of the paternal grandfather, a sometime poet who composed his verses mounted on a donkey and riding around the island between stone walls that bordered vegetable gardens. It was during the course of one of these outings that a scorned husband shot poetry in the back, in the belief that he was punishing a lover but misled by the silhouette and the broad-brimmed black hat, thus killing a model of familial virtue, who, however, left nothing to his children. The eventual result of this tragic misunderstanding in which a poet found his death was the settling on the Algerian shore of a nest of illiterates who multiplied, far from any school, harnessed to a life of exhausting labor under a

---

a. Transition.

ferocious sun. But the husband of Jacques's grandmother, judging by his photos, had kept something of
his poet grandfather's inspiration, and his thin face with
its clear-cut features under a lofty brow, and his
dreamer's expression, did not suggest that he could hold
his own against his young, beautiful, and vigorous
spouse. She gave him nine children, of whom two died
in infancy, another was saved only at the price of being
handicapped, and the last was born deaf and partly
mute. She raised her brood on that somber little farm
while doing her share of their hard common labor; she
sat at the end of the table with a long stick at hand that
spared her any superfluous speech, the guilty one being
immediately hit over the head. She held sway,
demanding respect for herself and her husband, whom
the children had to address in the polite form of speech,
according to Spanish practice. Her husband would not
long enjoy this respect: he died prematurely, worn out
by sun and labor, and perhaps by his marriage, without
Jacques ever being able to discover what disease he died
of. Left alone, the grandmother disposed of the little
farm and went to live in Algiers with her younger children, the others having been sent out to work as soon as
they were old enough to be apprenticed.

When Jacques had grown up enough to observe her,
she was impaired by neither poverty nor adversity.
Only three children were still with her. Catherine,[1] who

---

1. On page 8 Jacques Cormery's mother is given the name
Lucie. From here on, she is named Catherine.

did housework for others; the youngest, the handicapped one, who had become an energetic cooper; and
Joseph, who had not married and who worked for the
railroad. All three earned paltry wages that, combined,
had to support a family of five. His grandmother
managed the household's money, and that is why the
first thing that struck Jacques about her was her penny-
pinching—not that she was a miser except in the sense
that we are miserly with the air we breathe that keeps us
alive.

It was she who bought the children's clothes.
Jacques's mother came home late in the day, and was
satisfied to watch and listen to what was said, overwhelmed by the energy of the grandmother, to whom
she relinquished everything. Thus it was that Jacques,
throughout his life as a child, had to wear raincoats that
were too long, for his grandmother bought them to last
and counted on nature for the child's size to catch up
with that of the clothing. But Jacques grew slowly, not
really deciding to sprout till he was fifteen, and his raincoat would wear out before he grew into it. Another
would be bought on the same thrifty principle, and
Jacques, whose classmates mocked his dress, had no re-
course but to puff out his raincoat at the waist in order
to make what was ridiculous look original. Anyway,
these brief episodes of shame were quickly forgotten in
the classroom, where Jacques regained the upper hand,
and on the playground, where soccer was his kingdom.
But that kingdom was prohibited, because the playground was made of cement and soles would be worn
out so quickly that his grandmother had forbidden

Jacques to play soccer during recess. She herself bought her grandsons thick solid boots that she hoped would prove immortal. In order to stretch out their longevity, she would also have the soles studded with enormous cone-shaped nails, which were doubly useful: you had to wear out the studs before wearing out the sole, and they enabled her to detect infractions of the ban on playing soccer. Running on the cement yard did in fact quickly wear down the studs and give them a shine that betrayed the guilty one. Every day when he got home, Jacques had to report to the kitchen, where Cassandra presided over the black pots, and, with knee bent and sole facing up, in the posture of a horse being shod, he would have to show her his soles. Of course he could not resist the call of his friends and the lure of his favorite sport, and he would apply himself not to attempting an impossible virtue but to disguising the resulting sin. So on leaving school, and later the *lycée,* he would spend a good deal of time rubbing his soles in damp earth. Sometimes this ruse was successful. But the time would come when the wear on the studs was glaringly obvious, or sometimes the sole itself would be damaged, or—the worst of catastrophes—the upper sole would be detached from the lower by an awkward kick against the ground or the grille that protected the trees, and Jacques would come home with a string tied around his shoe to hold it together. Those were nights for the leather whip. The only consolation his mother offered the weeping Jacques was: "You know they're expensive. Why can't you be more careful?" But she herself never laid a hand on her children. The next day, they put Jacques in espadrilles and took his shoes to the shoemaker. Two or three days later he would get them back dotted with new studs, and once more he would have to learn to keep his balance on his slippery unstable soles.

The grandmother was capable of going still further, and even after so many years Jacques could not recall this story without a shiver of shame and disgust.* He and his brother were given no pocket money, except occasionally when they would agree to go visit a shopkeeper uncle or an aunt who had married well. It was easy in the case of the uncle because they liked him. But the aunt had a way of rubbing in her comparative wealth, and, rather than feel humiliated, the two children preferred to go without money and the pleasures it would procure them. In any event, and although the pleasures of the sea, the sun, and the neighborhood games were free, fries, caramels, Arab pastries, and in Jacques's case certain soccer matches required a little money, at least a few centimes. One evening Jacques was coming home after doing errands, holding at arm's length the dish of potatoes and cheese that he had taken to the neighborhood baker to be baked (they had neither gas nor range in their home, and they cooked on an alcohol stove. So there was no oven, and when they had something to bake they would take it all prepared to the baker, who for a few centimes would put the dish in the oven and keep an eye on it), the dish before him steam-

---

* where shame and disgust mingle

ing through the dishtowel that protected it from the dust of the street and made it possible for him to hold it around the edges. The string bag filled with provisions bought in very small quantities (a half-pound of sugar, a quarter-pound of butter, twenty-five centimes' worth of grated cheese, etc.) did not weigh heavily in the crook of his right arm and Jacques sniffed the good smell of potatoes and cheese as he made his way nimbly through the working-class crowd that at this hour was milling around on the sidewalks of the neighborhood. At that moment a two-franc piece slipped through a hole in his pocket and fell clinking on the sidewalk. Jacques picked it up, counted his change, which was all there, and put it in his other pocket. "I could have lost it," he thought suddenly. And the next day's match, which till then he had banished from his thoughts, now returned to his mind.

No one had actually taught the child what was right and what was wrong. Some things were forbidden and any infraction was severely punished. Others were not. Only his teachers would sometimes talk about morality, when the curriculum left them the time, but there again the prohibitions were more explicit than the reasons for them. All that Jacques had been able to see and experience concerning morality was daily life in a working-class family where it was evident no one had ever thought there was any way other than the hardest kind of labor to acquire the money necessary to their survival. But that was a lesson in courage, not morals. Nonetheless, Jacques knew it was wrong to hide those two francs. And he didn't want to do it. And he would not do it; maybe he could do what he'd done before, squeeze between two boards to get in the old stadium at the parade grounds and see the match free. That was why he himself did not understand why he did not immediately give back the change, and why, a little later, he came from the toilet and declared that a two-franc piece had fallen in the hole when he dropped his pants. Even "toilet" was too exalted a term for the small space that had been improvised in the masonry of the landing of the one upper floor. A Turkish-style hole had been drilled in a mid-size pedestal jammed between the door and the back wall. The place was without air, without electric light, without faucet, and they had to pour jerry cans of water in the hole after each use. But nothing could keep the stink from overflowing into the stairs. Jacques's explanation was plausible.[a] It saved him from being sent back out on the street to look for the lost coin, and it cut short any further action. Yet Jacques felt a pang as he announced his bad news. His grandmother was in the kitchen chopping garlic and parsley on an old board that was green and pitted with use. She stopped and looked at Jacques, who was waiting for her to explode. But she remained silent and studied him with her icy-clear eyes. "You're sure?" she said at last.

"Yes, I felt it drop."

She was still studying him. "Very well," she said. "We shall see."

---

a. No. It was because he had already claimed to have lost the coin in the street that he had to find another explanation.

And Jacques, horrified, saw her roll up her right sleeve, baring her knotty white arm, and go out on the landing. He dashed into the dining room, on the verge of throwing up. When she summoned him, he found her at the washbasin. Her arm was covered with gray soap, which she was rinsing off in a gush of water. "There was nothing there," she said. "You're a liar."

He stammered: "But it could have been washed down."

She hesitated. "Maybe. But if you're lying, it'll be your tough luck."

Yes, it was his tough luck, for in that instant he understood it was not avarice that caused his grandmother to grope around in the excrement, but the terrible need that made two francs a significant amount in this home. He understood it, and now he clearly saw, with a spasm of shame, that he had stolen those two francs from his family's labor. Even today, watching his mother at the window, Jacques could not explain how he could have failed to return those two francs and yet have enjoyed going to the match the next day.

His grandmother was also linked with other shameful memories for which there was less legitimate cause. She had wanted Henri, his older brother, to have violin lessons. Jacques had dodged this by claiming he could not continue to do so well in school with this extra work. So his brother had learned to scrape a few horrible sounds from a frigid violin, he could play popular songs with a few false notes. For fun, Jacques, whose voice was quite true, had learned the same songs, without any idea of the calamitous consequences of this innocent pastime.

Sure enough, on Sunday, when his grandmother's married daughters,[a] two of whom were war widows, would call on her, or her sister, who still lived on a farm in the Sahel and spoke the Mahon dialect more readily than Spanish, would come to visit, after she had served big bowls of black coffee on the oilcloth-covered table, his grandmother summoned her grandchildren to give an impromptu concert. The dismayed boys brought the metal music stand and the two-page scores of well-known tunes. They had to perform. Jacques followed the zigzags of Henri's violin as best he could, singing "Ramona," "I had a wonderful dream, Ramona, we'd gone away just you and I," or "Dance, O my Djalmé, this night it's you I want to love," or else, staying in the Orient, "Nights of China, nights of caresses, night of love, night of ecstasy, of tenderness . . ." On other occasions the grandmother would make a special request for more true-to-life songs. So Jacques would sing: "Is it really you my man, you whom I so loved, you who vowed, God knows you did, never to make me cry." As it happened, this was the only song Jacques could sing with real feeling, for at the end its heroine repeats its touching refrain in the middle of a crowd watching the execution of her wayward lover. But the grandmother's favorite song was one she no doubt loved for its melancholy and tenderness, which one would seek in vain in her own nature. It was Toselli's "Serenade," which Henri and Jacques brought out with quite a bit of brio,

---

a. Her nieces.

although the Algerian accent was not really suited to the enchanted hour evoked by the song. On a sunny afternoon, four or five women dressed in black, all of whom except the grandmother had put aside the black mantillas that Spanish women wear, were seated in a row around the poorly furnished room with its rough-cast white walls, and were nodding gently in approval of the outpouring of the music and the lyrics—until the grandmother, who had never been able to tell a *do* from a *si*, and for that matter did not even know the names of the notes of the scale, would break the spell with a curt "You made a mistake," which took the wind out of the performers' sails. We were *there*, the grandmother would say when the thorny passage had been gotten through in a way satisfying to her taste; once again the women would rock in time to the music, and at the end they applauded the two virtuosi, who hastily packed up their equipment and went out to join their comrades in the street. Only Catherine Cormery had remained silent in a corner. And Jacques still remembered that Sunday afternoon when, as he was about to leave with his music, his mother had said, in reply to one of the aunts who complimented her about him, "Yes, that was good. He's intelligent," as if there were any connection between the two statements. But when he had looked back, he understood the connection. Her face was quivering, her gentle eyes feverish, and she gazed at him with an expression that made him recoil, hesitate, then flee. "She loves me, then she loves me," he said to himself in the staircase, and at the same time he realized how desperately he loved her, that he had craved her love with all his heart, and that until that moment he had always doubted whether she loved him.

Performances at the movies held other pleasures in store for the child . . . The ritual took place on Sunday afternoon and sometimes on Thursday. The neighborhood movie house was just down the street from their building and bore the name of a Romantic poet, as did the street alongside it. Before going in, you had to pass an obstacle course of Arab peddlers' stands bearing helter-skelter displays of peanuts, dried salted chick-peas, lupine seeds, barley sugar coated in loud colors, and sticky sourballs. Others sold gaudy pastries, among them a pyramid of creamy swirls sprinkled with pink sugar, and still others displayed Arab fritters dripping with oil and honey. A swarm of flies and children, both attracted by the same sweets, buzzed and shouted as they chased each other around the stands amidst the curses of the peddlers, who feared for the stability of their goods and who brushed both flies and children away with a single gesture. Some of the peddlers had found shelter under the marquee that extended over one side, others had put their gummy riches out under the strong sunlight and the dust raised by the children's games. Jacques would escort his grandmother, who had sleeked back her white hair for the occasion and fastened her eternal black dress with a silver brooch. She would sedately part the howling kids who blocked the entrance and present herself at the one ticket window to buy "reserved" seats. Actually the only choice was between these "reserved" seats, uncomfortable folding chairs that opened noisily, and the benches toward which the children surged at the last moment, bickering over their places, when a side door was opened for them. At each end of the benches was stationed an usher, armed with a leather whip, who was responsible for keeping order, and it was not unusual to see him expel an overly boisterous child or adult. In those days the theatre showed silent films, the newsreel first, then a short comedy, the main feature, and finally a serial shown at the rate of one episode per week. The grand-mother particularly liked these serials, where each episode ended in suspense. For example, the muscular hero carrying the wounded blond girl in his arms would start out on a vine bridge over a canyon torrent. And the last frame of the weekly episode would show a tattooed hand severing the vines of the bridge with a crude knife. The hero would continue proudly on his way despite the warnings shouted by the spectators in the benches.[a] The question then was not whether the couple would escape—no doubt on that score being permitted—but only how they would extricate themselves, which explains why so many spectators, both Arab and French, would come back the next week to see the lovers stopped in their mortal plunge by a providential tree. The show was accompanied throughout on the piano by an old maiden lady, who met the jeers of the benches with the calm stillness of her thin back shaped like a bottle of mineral water capped with a lace collar. At the time, Jacques thought it a mark of distinction that this

a. Riveccio.

impressive lady wore her fingerless gloves during the most torrid hot spells. Nor was her job as easy as one might have thought. Providing musical commentary to the news, in particular, required her to change melodies according to the nature of the events being shown on the screen. She would go without transition from a lively quadrille accompanying the spring fashion shows to Chopin's Funeral March for a flood in China or the funeral of a personage important on the national or international scene. Whatever the piece, it was always imperturbably performed, as if ten little mechanical instruments were executing precise maneuvers on the old yellowed keyboard that had been ordained once and for all by clockwork. In that hall with bare walls, its floor littered with peanut shells, the smell of cresyl mingled with a strong odor of humanity. It was the pianist, in any case, who silenced the deafening racket by launching with full pedal into the prelude that was supposed to set the mood for the matinée show. A great throbbing sound announced that the projector was starting, and that was when Jacques's ordeal began.

Since they were silent, the films would project a certain amount of written text intended to clarify the plot. As his grandmother was illiterate, it was Jacques's job to read these texts to her. Despite her age, his grandmother was not at all hard of hearing. But first of all he had to make himself heard over the sound of the piano and that of the audience, whose vocal responses were plentiful. Furthermore, though the texts were extremely simple, his grandmother was not very familiar with some words and others were completely unknown to her. Jacques, for his part, did not want to disturb their neighbors and was especially anxious not to tell the entire hall that his grandmother did not know how to read (sometimes she herself would be embarrassed enough to say, raising her voice, at the beginning of the show: "You'll have to read to me, I forgot my glasses"), so he would not read the text as loudly as he might have. The result was that the grandmother only half understood, and would insist that he read it again and louder. Jacques would try to raise his voice, the shushes would plunge him into a vile shame, he stammered, the grandmother scolded him, and soon another text appeared, all the more mysterious to the poor old woman because she had not understood the preceding one. Confusion would only compound until Jacques found enough presence of mind to sum up in a few words a crucial moment in, for example, *The Mark of Zorro*, with Douglas Fairbanks, Sr. "The villain wants to take the girl away from him," Jacques would firmly articulate, taking advantage of a pause in the sound of the piano or the audience. It all became clear, the film went on, and the child could breathe easier. Usually that was the extent of his worries. But some films on the order of *Les Deux Orphelines* were really too complicated, and, caught between his grandmother's demands and the ever-angrier reprimands of their neighbors, Jacques would end by remaining completely silent. He still remembered one of these performances when the grandmother, beside herself, had finally walked out, while he followed her in tears, distressed at the thought that he had spoiled one of the poor woman's rare pleasures and that it had been paid for out of their meager funds.[a]

As for his mother, she never came to these performances. She could not read either, and she was half deaf besides. Beyond that, her vocabulary was even more limited than her mother's. Even today, her life was without distractions. In forty years she had been to the movies two or three times, had understood nothing, and it was only in order not to displease those who invited her that she would say the dresses were pretty or that the one with the moustache looked like a very bad man. Nor could she listen to the radio. And as to the newspapers, sometimes she would leaf through those that were illustrated, would get her sons or granddaughters to explain the pictures, would decide that the Queen of England seemed sad, and close the pages to gaze once more out the same window and watch the activity on the same street that she had been contemplating through half her lifetime.[b]

----

a. add symptoms of poverty—unemployment—holiday camp summer in Miliana—blowing the bugle—expelled—Doesn't dare tell her. Speak up: well we'll drink coffee tonight. From time to time it changes. He looks at her. He's often read stories of poverty where the woman is valiant. She didn't smile. She left to go in the kitchen, valiant—Not resigned.

b. Bring on Uncle Ernest *old, before*—his portrait in the room where Jacques and his mother were. Or have him come *after*.

Étienne

In a sense, she was less involved in life than her brother Ernest,[1] who lived with them; he was stone deaf, and he expressed himself as much by onomatopoeic sounds and gestures as with the hundred-odd words at his disposal. But Ernest, who could not be put out to work when he was young, had haphazardly attended school and learned to make out the letters of the alphabet. He did go to the movies sometimes, and he would come home with an account of the film that astounded those who had already seen it, as the wealth of his imagination would make up for what he had missed. Moreover, he was shrewd and crafty, and a sort of native intelligence enabled him to make his way in a world and among people who nonetheless remained obdurately silent to him. Thanks to that same intelligence, he would bury himself every day in the newspaper, where he could

---

1. Sometimes named Ernest, sometimes Étienne, it is always the same person: Jacques's uncle.

make out the headlines and so have at least a nodding acquaintance with world affairs. "Hitler," he would say, for example, to Jacques when he had come of age, "no good, eh."

"No, that wasn't good."

"The Huns, always the same," the uncle added.

"No, it wasn't that."

"Yes, there're some good ones," his uncle acknowledged. "But Hitler that's no good," and right after, his love of a joke gaining the upper hand: "Levy" (that was the mercer across the street) "he's scared." And he guffawed. Jacques would try to explain. His uncle would become serious again: "Yes. Why he wants to hurt the Jews? They're like other people."

He always loved Jacques, in his fashion. He admired his success in school. He would rub the child's skull with his hard hand on which tools and manual labor had left a hornlike callus. "Got a good head, this one. Hard"—and he tapped his own head with his big fist—"but good." Sometimes he added: "Like his father."

One day Jacques took the opportunity to ask if his father had been intelligent.

"Your father, hard head. Did what he wanted, always. Your mother always yes yes."

Jacques was unable to get any more out of him.

In any case, Ernest would often take the child with him. His energy and vitality, finding no outlet in speech or in the complex relations of social life, would explode in his physical life and its sensations. Even on awakening, when someone shook him out of the hermetic sleep of the deaf, he would rear up wild-eyed, bellowing "huhn huhn!" like a prehistoric beast that wakens each day to a strange and hostile world. But once he was awake, his body and its functioning made him secure on his feet. Despite the hard labor of his job as a cooper, he liked to go swimming and hunting. When Jacques was still a child,[a] his uncle would take him to Sablettes beach, make him get up on his back, and immediately set out to sea with a rudimentary but powerful stroke, making inarticulate sounds that translated first his surprise at the coldness of the water, then his pleasure at being there or his anger at an errant wave. "You not scared," he would say from time to time to Jacques. Yes, he was afraid but did not say so; he was spellbound by the solitude where they were, between the sky and the sea, one as vast as the other; when he glanced back, the beach seemed like an invisible line, and an acid fear would grip his stomach and, with the beginnings of panic, he pictured the immense dark depths below where he would sink like a stone if ever his uncle should let him loose. Then the child would clutch the swimmer's neck a little tighter. "You scared," his uncle said right away.

"No, but go back."

Docile, the uncle turned, took a few breaths, and set off again as confidently as if he were on terra firma. On the beach, and hardly out of breath, he rubbed Jacques vigorously, with great gusts of laughter, turned aside to urinate with a loud splash, still laughing, then would

---

a. 9 years

congratulate himself on the fine functioning of his blad-
der, slapping his belly with the "Good, good" that accompanied all his enjoyable sensations, among which he
made no distinction, whether they were of excretion or
of nutrition, stressing in each case and with the same
innocence the pleasure they gave him, and always
wanting his family to share his pleasure, which at the
dining-room table would provoke a protest from the
grandmother, who accepted that these things were discussed, and even spoke of them herself, but, as she
would say, "Not while we're eating," though she put up
with his watermelon act; the fruit had a great reputation
as a diuretic; Ernest adored it and he would begin his
consumption of it by laughing, by mischievous winks at
the grandmother, by an assortment of sounds of inhal-
ing, regurgitating, and slurping, and after the first few
mouthfuls that he would bite right down to the skin, he
would perform a whole pantomime in which with his
hand he would repeatedly demonstrate the journey the
handsome rose and white fruit was supposed to make
from his mouth to his penis, while he made faces and
rolled his eyes to illustrate how spectacularly he was en-
joying himself, all this accompanied by: "Good, good.
Washes you out. Good, good"—until it was so irresist-
ible that everyone would burst out laughing. This
Adam-like innocence caused him to attach exaggerated
importance to a series of fleeting ailments he would
complain of, frowning, his gaze turned inward as if he
were scrutinizing the mysterious night of his organs. He
claimed to be suffering from a "stitch," its location
varying widely, or a "lump" that wandered all over the

place. Later, when Jacques was attending the *lycée*, his uncle would question him, in the belief that there was one science that applied equally to everyone, showing him the small of his back: "Right there, it pulls," he would say. "That's bad?" No, it was nothing. And Ernest would go out relieved, descending the stairs with his small hurried steps to join his comrades in the neighborhood cafés, with their wood furnishings and zinc bar, smelling of anisette and sawdust, where Jacques sometimes had to go fetch him at dinnertime. It was not the least of the child's surprises to find this deaf-mute at the bar surrounded by his comrades and talking his head off while they all laughed, laughter in which there was no mockery, for his friends adored Ernest for his good nature and his generosity.[a b c d]

---

a. the money he'd set aside and gave to Jacques.

b. Of medium height, a bit bowlegged, his shoulders somewhat stooped under a thick shell of muscle, he gave the impression despite his slender build of an extraordinarily virile strength. And yet his face was and for a long time would remain that of an adolescent, delicate regular features, a bit [ ] [a word crossed out—*Ed.*] with his sister's beautiful chestnut eyes, a very straight nose, bare eyebrows, regular chin, and beautiful thick hair—no, a little wavy. His physical beauty in itself was why despite his handicap he had had several adventures with women, which could not lead to marriage and were necessarily brief, but at times had the appearance of what is usually called love, like that affair he'd had with a married shopkeeper in the neighborhood, and sometimes he would take Jacques to the Saturday night concert in Bresson Square that looked out on the sea, and the military orchestra on the bandstand played *The Bells of Corneville* or tunes from *Lakmé*, while in the

Jacques would be well aware of that when his uncle took him hunting with his comrades, all of whom were coopers or workers at the port or on the railroad. They got up at dawn. Jacques was responsible for awakening his uncle, whom no alarm could rouse from his sleep. Jacques himself responded to the ringing, his brother turned over in bed grumbling, and his mother, in the other bed, stirred softly without awakening. He got up groping his way, struck a match, and lit the small kerosene lamp on the night table that stood between the two beds. (Ah! the furnishings in that room: two iron beds—one single, where the mother slept, the other double, where the two children slept—a night table between the two beds, and, across from the night table, a wardrobe with a mirror. At the foot of the mother's bed was a window that faced the yard. Below that window was a cane trunk covered with a crocheted blanket. While he was still small, Jacques had to kneel on the trunk to close the shutters of the window. And no chair.) Then he would go to the dining room, shake his uncle, who bellowed, looked up in terror at the lamp over his eyes, and finally came to his senses. They

---

midst of the crowd that was moving around the [ ], Ernest in his Sunday best would make sure his path crossed that of the café owner's wife dressed in raw silk, and they would exchange smiles of friendship, the husband occasionally saying a few amicable words to Ernest, whom he surely never saw as a potential rival.

c. the la mouna laundry [words circled by the author—*Ed.*]

d. the beach pieces of bleached wood, corks, sea-worn fragments of glass . . . reeds from cork trees.

dressed. And Jacques heated leftover coffee on the little alcohol burner while his uncle packed sacks with provisions: a cheese, *sobrasada* sausages, tomatoes with salt and pepper, and a half loaf of bread cut in two where a big omelet made by the grandmother had been inserted. Then the uncle for the last time checked the double-barreled shotgun and the cartridges, over which a great ceremony had taken place the night before. After dinner they had cleared the table and carefully cleaned its oil-cloth cover. The uncle had seated himself at one side of the table and gravely set before him, by the light of the big kerosene lamp lifted down from its hanging position, the pieces of the disassembled gun that he had painstakingly greased. Sitting at the other side, Jacques waited his turn. So did the dog Brillant. For there was a dog, a mongrel setter, boundlessly good-natured, who couldn't hurt a fly, the proof of that being that if he happened to catch one on the wing, he would spit it out with a disgusted look accompanied by a great display of outstretched tongue and smacking of his chops. Ernest and his dog were inseparable, and there was a perfect understanding between them. You could not help thinking of them as a couple (and only one who neither knew nor loved dogs would see that as ridiculous). And the dog owed the man obedience and love, while the man agreed to have only this single responsibility. They lived together and never left each other, sleeping together (the man on the dining room couch, the dog on a skimpy bedside rug that was threadbare), went to work together (the dog would lie on a bed of wood shavings,

made just for him, under a workbench in the shop),
went out to cafés together, the dog waiting patiently between his master's legs until his performance had come
to an end. They spoke in onomatopoeia and relished
each other's smells. One must never tell Ernest that his
seldom-washed dog gave off a strong odor, especially
after it had rained. "Him," he would say, "no smell,"
and he would lovingly sniff the inside of the dog's big
quivering ears. Hunting was a spree for both of them,
their night on the town. Ernest had only to bring out the
knapsack for the dog to race madly around the little dining room, setting the chairs to dancing by bumping
them with his rear, and thumping his tail against the
sideboard. Ernest would laugh. "He understands, he
understands," and he would calm the animal, who
would then place his muzzle on the table and watch their
minute preparations, yawning discreetly from time to
time but never leaving the delightful spectacle until it
was over.[a][b]

When the shotgun was once more assembled, his
uncle handed it to him. Jacques received it reverently,
and he shined its barrels with an old linen rag. Meanwhile the uncle was preparing his cartridges. He had
before him some brightly colored cardboard tubes with
copper bases in a sack from which he also removed
gourd-shaped metal flasks containing the powder and

---

a. the hunt? could be cut.
b. the book should be heavy with things and flesh.

shot and brown felt wadding. He carefully filled the tubes with powder and wadding. The tubes would be fitted into a small machine he also took from the sack. A little crank worked a cap that crimped the tops of the tubes down to the level of the wadding. When the cartridges were ready, Ernest handed them one by one to Jacques, who devoutly placed them in the cartridge belt he had in front of him. In the morning one knew they were leaving when Ernest put the heavy cartridge belt around his belly, which had already been augmented by two layers of sweaters. Jacques buckled the belt behind his back. And Brillant, who since waking had been coming and going in silence, trained to control his delight so as not to awaken anyone, but who was breathing his feverishness on every object within his reach, would now rear up against his master, paws on his chest, and try by stretching his back and neck to give that beloved face a good strong licking.

They hurried toward the Agha station under a sky that was already growing light, the fresh smell of the ficus trees floating in the air, with the dog racing at full speed ahead of them on a zigzagging course that sometimes ended with him sliding on sidewalks still wet from the night's humidity, then coming back just as fast, visibly terrified that he had lost them, Étienne carrying the shotgun muzzle-down in its heavy canvas case, as well as a sack and a game bag, Jacques with his hands in the pockets of his shorts and a big knapsack on his back. Their friends were at the station with their dogs, who did not leave their masters except to make quick inspections under their fellows' tails. There were Daniel and

Pierre,[a] brothers who worked in the shop with Ernest, Daniel always laughing and full of optimism, Pierre more contained, more methodical, full of opinions and words of wisdom about people and things. Also there was Georges, who was employed at the gasworks but who would earn some extra pay by boxing an occasional match. And often two or three others besides, all good fellows, at least for this occasion, happy to have escaped for a day from the workshop, from small overcrowded apartments, sometimes from their wives also, uninhibited and in a mood of amused tolerance that is peculiar to men when they have gotten together among themselves for some brief violent pleasure. They climbed cheerfully into one of those cars where every compartment opens to the platform, they handed each other the knapsacks, they made the dogs get in, and they settled down, happy now to feel themselves sitting side to side sharing the same warmth. On these Sundays Jacques learned that the company of men was good and could nourish the soul. The train started out, then picked up speed with short puffs and an occasional brief sleepy whistle. They were crossing one end of the Sahel, and on reaching the first fields these loud sturdy men fell oddly silent and watched the day dawn over carefully cultivated fields where morning mists trailed like scarves on the hedges of big dry reeds that separated the fields. Now and then clumps of trees would slip past the window with the whitewashed farmhouse they pro-

---

a. careful, change the names.

tected, where everyone was sleeping. A bird that was flushed out of the ditch alongside the embankment came suddenly up to their level, then flew in the same direction as the train, as if trying to race it, until it abruptly set off at a right angle to the course of the train, and now it seemed as if it had been pulled away from the window and hurled to the rear of the train by the wind of their passage. The green horizon turned pink, then all at once red, and the sun appeared and rose visibly in the sky. It sucked the mists off all the expanse of fields, kept on rising, and suddenly it was hot in the compartment; the men took off one sweater after another, made the fidgety dogs lie down, traded some jokes, and already Ernest was telling stories in his manner about food, about sickness, and also [about] fights in which he always had the upper hand. Sometimes one of the comrades would ask Jacques about his school; then they talked of other things or called him to witness one of Ernest's charades. "He's tops, your uncle!"

The countryside was changing, becoming more rocky, the orange trees gave way to oaks, and the little train chugged harder and harder and gave off great blasts of steam. Suddenly it was colder, for the mountain had come between the sun and the travelers, and then they realized it was still only seven o'clock. At last the train gave a final whistle, reduced its speed, slowly rounded a tight curve, and arrived at a small station that was alone in the valley, deserted and silent, for it only served some distant mines; it was planted with big eucalyptuses whose sickle-shaped leaves shivered in the morning breeze. They left the train with the usual hubbub, the dogs tumbling out of the compartment, missing the two steep steps down, the men again lining up to pass each other the sacks and guns. But at the exit of the station, where the first slopes began immediately, the silence of wild nature bit by bit drowned out their exclamations and shouts; the little troop finished climbing the hill in silence, while the dogs circled in endless figure eights. Jacques would not let his vigorous companions leave him behind. Daniel, his favorite, had taken his knapsack, over his objections, but he still had to take two steps for one of theirs to keep up, and the sharp morning air was scorching his lungs. After an hour they at last came to the edge of a vast and gently undulating plateau wooded with dwarf oaks and junipers, over which a fresh and softly sunlit sky stretched its immense space. This was their hunting terrain. The dogs came back, as if they already knew, and gathered around the men. They agreed to meet for lunch at two o'clock in the afternoon at a pine thicket, where a small spring was conveniently located at the edge of the plateau and where they could see over the valley and far out on the plain. They synchronized their watches. The hunters grouped themselves in pairs, whistled to their dogs, and set out in different directions. Ernest and Daniel were paired. Jacques was given the game bag, and he put it carefully over his shoulder. Ernest, from a distance, announced to the others that he would bring back more rabbits and partridges than anyone else. They laughed, waved, and disappeared.

Now for Jacques began a time of ecstasy that he would always cherish nostalgically with wonder in his heart: the two men two meters apart but staying abreast, the dog in front, himself always kept at the rear, his uncle, whose eye was suddenly wild and cunning, always checking to make sure he kept his distance, and the interminable walking in silence, through bushes from which a bird they passed up would sometimes fly with a piercing cry, going down small ravines full of scents where they would follow the bottom ground, going back up toward the sky, radiant and warmer and warmer, the rising heat rapidly drying soil that was still damp when they set out. Gunshots across the ravine, the sharp clacking of a covey of dust-colored partridges flushed out by the dog, the double report repeated almost immediately, the dog's dash ahead, his return with eyes madly flashing and holding in his blood-covered jaws a bundle of feathers that Ernest and Daniel took from him, and that Jacques received a moment later with mingled excitement and horror; the search for more victims, and when they saw them fall, Ernest's yelping that you sometimes could not distinguish from Brillant's; and again the progress forward, Jacques sagging now under the sun despite his little straw hat, while the plateau around them was beginning to vibrate heavily like an anvil under the hammer of the sun, and occasionally a gunshot or two, but never more, for only one of the hunters had seen the hare or rabbit scurry off, it was doomed if it was in Ernest's line of fire, he was always as agile as a monkey and now he was running almost as fast as his dog, baying like him, to pick up the dead creature by its hind legs and display it from far away to Daniel and Jacques, who arrived jubilant and out of breath. Jacques opened wide the game bag to receive the new trophy before setting off again, staggering under the sun his master, and so, for hours without end on a land without boundaries, his head lost in the unremitting light and the immense space of the sky, Jacques felt himself to be the richest of children. As the hunters returned toward the place where they were to meet for lunch, they kept an eye out for any opportunity, but their hearts were no longer in it. They were dragging their feet, they were mopping their brows, they were hungry. They arrived two by two, showing their prizes to each other from a distance, deriding the empty game bags, declaring that the same ones were always empty, all recounting their catches at the same time, each having some special detail to add. But the great braggart was Ernest, who finally got the floor and mimed, with an accuracy that Jacques and Daniel were well placed to judge, the way the partridges took off, and the scurrying rabbit zigzagged twice then rolled on his back like a rugby player making a try from behind the goal. Meanwhile the methodical Pierre poured anisette in the metal goblets he had collected from each person and went to fill them with fresh water at the spring trickling by the edge of the pines. They improvised a makeshift table with dishtowels, and each one brought out his provisions. But Ernest, who was talented as a cook (summertime fishing expeditions always began with a bouillabaisse that he would put together on the spot and that he spiced so generously it would have burned the tongue off a tortoise), whittled some sticks until they were sharp, speared pieces of the *sobrasada* he had brought, and grilled them over a little wood fire till they burst and a red liquid dripped on the embers where it sizzled and caught fire. He put the scorching hot and fragrant sausages between two pieces of bread and handed them to the others, who greeted them with exclamations and devoured them, washed down with rosé wine they had cooled in the spring. Then there was laughter, and stories about their jobs, and jokes, but Jacques, who was dirty and worn out, his mouth and hands sticky, was barely listening because he was falling asleep. But, in fact, all of them were sleepy, and for some time they drowsed, gazing vacantly at the distant plain under its haze of heat, or else, like Ernest, they went sound asleep, each with a handkerchief covering his face. However, at four o'clock they had to start down to catch the train, which would come at half past five. Now they were in their compartment, crammed together in fatigue, the worn-out dogs under the seats or between the men's legs, bloodthirsty dreams running through their heavy sleep. The day was beginning to fade at the edges of the plain; then it was the brief African twilight, and the night, always disturbing on those wide-open spaces, would fall without transition. Later on, in the station, they were in a hurry to get home to eat and go to bed early for the next day's work, so they parted quickly in the dark, almost without words but with great friendly backslapping. Jacques heard them moving away, he listened to their warm rough voices, he loved them. Then he fell in step with Ernest, whose pace was still spirited, while his own feet were dragging.

Near their home, Ernest turned to him in the dark street: "You happy?" Jacques did not answer. Ernest laughed and whistled to his dog. But, a few steps farther, the child slipped his small hand in the hard calloused hand of his uncle, who squeezed it very hard. And so they went home in silence.

[a] [b]Ernest was, however, subject to an anger as immediate and wholehearted as his pleasures. The impossibility of reasoning or even talking with him made his rages seem like a natural phenomenon. You see a storm gathering, you wait for it to break. Nothing else to do. Like many deaf people, Ernest had a very well-developed sense of smell (except when it concerned his dog). This privileged condition brought him great delights, as when he inhaled the odor of split-pea soup or those dishes he loved above all others, squid in its ink, sausage omelet, or the stew of innards made with beef heart and lung, the bourguignon of the poor, which was the grandmother's great success, and often appeared on their table because it was cheap; or on Sundays when he would sprinkle himself with cheap eau de cologne or the lotion known as [Pompero] (that Jacques's mother also used), its mild and lemony bergamot-based scent always lingered in the dining room and in Ernest's hair, and he would sniff deeply at the bottle with an air of rap-

---

a. Tolstoy or Gorki (I) *The Father* From that background came Dostoevsky (II) *The Son* which returning to its origins gives the writer of the period (III) *The Mother*

b. M. Germain—the *lycée*—religion—death of the grandmother—End with Ernest's hand?

ture . . . But his sensitivity in this regard also caused him trouble. He would not tolerate certain odors that could not be detected by the normal nose. For example, he had gotten in the habit of sniffing his plate before beginning his meal, and he would turn red with anger when he discovered what he claimed was the smell of egg. The grandmother would then take the suspect plate, sniff it, declare that she smelled nothing there, and hand it to her daughter for her opinion. Catherine Cormery would pass her delicate nose over the porcelain, and, without even sniffing, say softly that no, it didn't smell. They sniffed the other plates in order better to form a definitive judgment, except those of the children, who ate from iron dishes. (The reasons for that matter were a mystery, lack of china perhaps, or, as the grandmother once stated, to save breakage, though neither he nor his brother was clumsy with his hands. But family traditions are often no more soundly based, and ethnologists certainly make me laugh when they seek the reasons for so many mysterious rituals. The real mystery, in many cases, is that there is no reason at all.) Then the grandmother would pronounce the verdict: it did not smell. In truth she never would have decided otherwise, especially if it was she who did the dishes the night before. She would not have given an inch on her honor as a housekeeper. But that was when Ernest's real anger exploded, and all the more so because he could not find the words to express his conviction.[a] One had to let the

---

a. microtragedies

tempest run its course, whether he sulked instead of eating, or picked with a disgusted air at his plate, though the grandmother had changed it, or even left the table and stormed out declaring that he was going to a restaurant; in fact he had never set foot in that kind of place, nor had anyone in their home, although when any dissatisfaction was expressed at the table, the grandmother would never fail to pronounce the fateful line: "Go to a restaurant." From that time on the restaurant appeared to all to be one of those sinful and falsely alluring places where everything seems easy provided you can afford it, but where the very first guilty delights it dispenses will one day or another be dearly paid for by your stomach. In any event the grandmother never responded to her youngest child's anger. On the one hand because she knew it was useless, on the other because she had always had an odd weakness for him, which Jacques, once he had done some reading, attributed to the fact that Ernest was handicapped (though we have so many examples of parents who, despite our preconceptions, will turn away from the handicapped child), and which he better understood one day much later when, catching a tenderness he had never seen in his grandmother's usually hard eyes, he turned to see his uncle putting on the jacket of his Sunday outfit. The dark cloth made him look even more slender, his features were delicate and youthful, he was freshly shaved and his hair carefully combed, and for once he was wearing a fresh collar and a tie—he had the look of a Greek shepherd in holiday dress—and Jacques saw his uncle as he really was, which was very handsome. And then he understood that his grandmother's love for her son was physical, that, like everyone, she was in love with the grace and strength of Ernest, and her weakness for him that had seemed unusual was after all very common; it softens us all more or less, and delightfully so besides, and helps make the world bearable—it is our weakness for beauty.

Jacques also remembered another of Uncle Ernest's rages, this one more serious since it almost ended in a fistfight with Uncle Josephin, the one who worked for the railroad. Josephin did not sleep at his mother's home (and indeed where would he have slept?). He had a room in the neighborhood (where he had never actually invited any of the family and which Jacques, for example, had never seen) and took his meals with his mother, to whom he paid a small amount for his board. Josephin was as different from his brother as he could be. Ten years older, with a short moustache and a crew cut, he was also more stolid, more reserved, and especially more calculating. Ernest often accused him of avarice. Actually he expressed it more simply: "He Mzabite." To him the Mzabites were the neighborhood grocers; they did in fact come from Mzab, and for many years they would live behind their shops, which smelled of oil and cinnamon, living without wives on next to nothing in order to support their families in the five towns of Mzab, out in the desert, where this tribe of heretics, puritans of Islam, persecuted unto death by the orthodox, had landed centuries ago, in a place they had chosen because they were quite sure no one would fight them for it, there being nothing there but stone—

it was as far from the half-civilized world of the coast as a lifeless cratered planet might be from the earth; there they did in fact settle and build five towns around stingy waterholes, and conceived this strange ascetic life of sending their able-bodied men to the coast to engage in business in order to support this creation of the spirit and the spirit alone, until those men could be replaced by others and return to their earth-and-mud-fortified towns to enjoy the kingdom they had at last won for their faith. Thus the sparse lives and the avarice of these Mzabites could only be judged in the light of their profound aims. But the working-class people of the neighborhood, who knew nothing of Islam and its heresies, saw only the surface. And for Ernest, or anyone else, to call his brother a Mzabite was the same as comparing him to Harpagon.[1] Josephin was in fact pretty close with his money, in contrast to Ernest, who, according to the grandmother, was "openhanded." (It is true that when she was in a fury with him, she would accuse him of letting money run through the fingers of that same hand.) But beyond their different natures was the fact that Josephin earned a little bit more than Ernest and it is always easier to be extravagant when you have nothing. Few indeed are those who continue to be openhanded after they have acquired the means for it. Such as these are princes among men, before whom one must bow down. Certainly Josephin was not rolling in money, but in addition to his salary, which he managed

---

1. Protagonist of Molière's *The Miser—Trans.*

with care (he practiced the so-called envelope system, but, too cheap to buy real envelopes, he would make them out of newspapers or grocery bags), he made extra money with some small well-calculated deals. Working for the railroad, he was entitled to travel free once every two weeks. So every other Sunday he would take the train into what was called the "interior"—that is, the bush—and he would go around the Arab farms buying eggs, scrawny chickens or rabbits at low cost. He would bring back this merchandise and sell it to his neighbors at a fair profit. His life was well ordered in every aspect. He was not known to have a woman. In any case, between his week of work and his Sundays devoted to trade, he lacked the time needed to pursue sensual pleasures. But he had always proclaimed that at forty he would marry a well-placed woman. Until then he would stay in his room, amassing money and continuing to live part time at his mother's. Strange as it seemed, given his lack of charm, he nonetheless carried out his plan as he had said, and married a piano teacher who was far from ugly and who, with her furniture, brought him at least a few years of bourgeois bliss. It is true that Josephin ended up keeping the furniture and not the wife. But that was another story, and all Josephin had not foreseen was that after his quarrel with Ernest he would not be able to take his meals with his mother but would have to resort to the costly delights of the restaurant. Jacques no longer remembered the origin of the drama. Obscure feuds sometimes would divide his family, and in truth no one could sort out their causes, especially because all of them were so lacking in memory that no one could recall the reasons for the feud but would confine themselves to keeping alive consequences they had accepted and digested once and for all. About that day, all he could remember was Ernest standing at the table in the middle of the meal shouting insults, incomprehensible other than "Mzabite," at his brother, who remained seated and went on eating. Then Ernest struck his brother, who got up and fell back before coming at him. But the grandmother was already hanging on to Ernest, and Jacques's mother, white with emotion, was pulling at Josephin from behind. "Let him be, let him be," she was saying, and the two children, their faces pale and their mouths open, watched motionless and listened to the flood of enraged curses that were all flowing in one direction until Josephin said sullenly, "He's a dumb animal. You can't do anything to him," and circled the table while the grandmother held on to Ernest, who wanted to run after his brother.

Ernest was still struggling after the door had slammed. "Let me go, let me go," he said to his mother. "I'll hurt you."

But she had seized him by the hair and was shaking him: "You, you, you'd hit your mother?"

And Ernest dropped into his chair sobbing, "No, no, not you. You like the good Lord for me!"

Jacques's mother went to bed without finishing her meal, and the next day she had a headache. From that day on, Josephin never returned home, except once in a while when he was sure Ernest was not there, to visit his mother.

[a]There was another rage Jacques did not like to recall because he himself did not want to know its cause. For quite a while a certain M. Antoine, with whom Ernest was vaguely acquainted—a fishmonger in the market, of Maltese origin, quite handsome in bearing, slender and tall, who always wore a strange dark derby and at the same time a checkered bandanna that he rolled and knotted around his neck inside his shirt—would come by their home regularly before dinner. Thinking about it later, Jacques saw what had not struck him at the time, that his mother was dressing a bit more smartly; she was wearing brightly colored aprons, and you could even see a hint of rouge on her cheeks. This was also the time when women were beginning to cut their hair, which until then they had worn long. Jacques liked to watch his mother or his grandmother perform the ceremony of combing and fixing her hair. With a napkin around the shoulders and a mouth full of hairpins, they would comb their waist-length hair for a long time, then put it up, pull a headband very tight around the bun at the nape of the neck, riddle it with hairpins that they would withdraw one at a time from the mouth, their lips parted and teeth clenched, and would stick one by one in the thick mass of the bun. The new style seemed both ridiculous and shameful to the grandmother, who, underestimating the true power of fashion, declared without bothering

---

a. The household of Ernest, Catherine after the death of the grandmother.

about logic that only women who "walked the streets" would let themselves so be made ridiculous. His mother had taken that for granted, and yet a year later, at about the time Antoine was calling, she came home one evening with her hair cut, looking fresh and rejuvenated; she said, outwardly cheerful but behind it one could sense her anxiety, that she had wanted to give them a surprise.

It was a surprise indeed to the grandmother, who, eyeing her from head to foot and contemplating this irremediable disaster, merely said to her, in front of her son, that now she looked like a whore. Then she went back to her kitchen. Catherine Cormery stopped smiling, and all the sorrow and weariness of the world appeared on her face. Then she saw her son's intent expression, and tried to smile again, but her lips trembled and she dashed weeping to her bedroom, to the bed that was her only refuge for rest, for solitude, and for sorrow. Jacques, bewildered, went to her. She had buried her face in the pillow; her neck, exposed by her short curls, and her thin back were shaking with sobs.

"*Maman, maman,*" Jacques said, touching her timidly with his hand. "You're very beautiful like this."

But she had not heard him, and with her hand she asked him to leave her. He retreated to the doorway and, leaning against the jamb, he too began to weep with helplessness and love.*

For the next several days the grandmother did not

---

* tears of helpless love

speak a word to her daughter. At the same time, Antoine was received more coolly when he called. Ernest, especially, kept a distant manner. Though he was a swell and a smooth talker, Antoine could certainly sense something. What was going on? Several times Jacques saw signs of tears in his mother's beautiful eyes. Ernest would usually remain silent and would scuffle with Brillant. One summer evening, Jacques noticed that his uncle seemed to be watching something from the balcony.

"Is Daniel coming?" the child asked.

His uncle grunted. And suddenly Jacques saw Antoine arrive after not having come for several days. Ernest rushed out, and a few seconds later muffled sounds came up the stairs. Jacques dashed out and saw the two men fighting silently in the dark. Ernest, heedless of the blows he was taking, was striking and striking with fists hard as iron, and a moment later Antoine rolled down the stairs, got up with his mouth bloody, and took out a handkerchief to wipe off the blood, all the while keeping his eyes on Ernest, who went off like a madman. When he went back inside, Jacques found his mother sitting in the dining room, not moving, her face still. He also sat down without speaking.[a] And then Ernest came back, grumbling curses, and darted a furious look at his sister. Dinner took place as usual, except that his mother did not eat; she simply said "I'm not hungry" when her mother insisted. Once the meal was over, she went to

---

a. bring on much earlier—fight not Lucien.

her room. During the night, Jacques woke up and heard her turn over in her bed. Starting the following day, she went back to her black or gray dresses, nothing but the clothing of the poor. Jacques found her just as beautiful, even more beautiful for being more distant and absent in spirit, now that she was settled forever in poverty, in solitude, and in old age soon to come.[a]

For a long time Jacques held a grudge against his uncle, without knowing just what he was blaming him for. But, at the same time, he knew he could not hold him to blame, and that if the poverty, the infirmities, the elemental need in which all his family lived did not excuse everything, in any case they made it impossible to pass judgment on those who were its victims.

They hurt each other without wanting to, just because each represented to the others the cruel and demanding necessity of their lives. And, in any event, he could not doubt his uncle's animal-like devotion first of all to the grandmother and then to Jacques's mother and her children. He had felt that devotion to himself the day of the accident at the cooperage.[b] Jacques went to the cooperage every Thursday. If he had any homework, he would dash it off rapidly, and then run very fast to the workshop, going as gaily as he would on

---

a. for old age would come—at the time Jacques thought his mother was old and she was barely the age he was now, but youth is above all a collection of possibilities, and for him to whom life had been generous . . . [passage crossed out—*Ed.*]

b. put cooperage before rages and maybe even at beginning profile Ernest.

other days when he went to meet his playmates of the
streets. The barrel works was near the parade grounds.
It was a yard cluttered with rubbish, old hoops, slag,
and extinguished fires. At one side had been erected a
sort of roof of bricks supported at regular intervals by
pillars made of rubble. The five or six artisans worked
under that roof. Each one was supposed to have his
own area: a workbench against the wall and in front of
it a space where the barrels and wine casks could be assembled, and, separating it from the next area, a sort of
bench with a rather large slot cut in it into which the
barrelhead was slid and then shaped by hand with a
tool that resembled a chopping knife,* but with the
sharp side facing the man who held it by its two han-
dles. Actually this layout was not evident at first glance.
Certainly that was how it had been originally designed,
but little by little the benches were moved around,
hoops piled up between the workbenches, cases of rivets lay here and there, and it took lengthy observation
or, which amounted to the same thing, a long stay to
see that everything each artisan did took place in his
separate area. Before he reached the shop carrying his
uncle's snack, Jacques could recognize the sound of
hammering on the hoop-drivers that drove the metal
hoops down around the barrel after the staves had been
put in place, and the worker pounded one end of the
driver while deftly moving its other end all around the

---

* look up the name of the tool

hoop—or else Jacques would guess from a louder, less frequent sound that someone was riveting a hoop fastened in the shop's vise. When he arrived in the midst of the hammering racket, he was greeted joyfully and the dance of the hammers would resume. Ernest, dressed in old patched blue pants, espadrilles covered with sawdust, a sleeveless gray flannel shirt, and a faded old tarboosh that protected his handsome hair from dust and shavings, would embrace him and suggest that he help out. Sometimes Jacques would hold the hoop in place on the anvil where it was wedged while his uncle would drive the rivets in with mighty blows. The hoop vibrated in Jacques's hands, and with each blow of the hammer would dig into his palms—or else while Ernest seated himself astride one end of the bench, Jacques sat the same way at the other end, holding the bottom of the barrel while Ernest shaped it. But what he liked best was bringing the staves out to the middle of the yard for Ernest to assemble roughly, keeping them in place with a hoop. In this barrel, open at both ends, Ernest would place a pile of shavings that it was Jacques's responsibility to set on fire. The fire caused the iron to expand more than the wood, and Ernest would take advantage of that to drive the hoop down with great blows of his hammer and driver, while the smoke brought tears to their eyes. When the hoop had been driven in place, Jacques would bring big wooden buckets he had filled with water at the pump at the end of the yard, then move aside while Ernest threw the water hard against the barrel, thus chilling the hoop, which shrank so it bit deeper into the wood, softened by the water, all amidst a great blowing of steam.[a]

At the break they left things as they were to have their snack, and the workers would gather, in winter around a fire of wood and shavings, in summer in the shade of the roof. There was Abder, the Arab laborer who wore Arab pantaloons, the seat hanging in folds and the legs ending in mid-calf, a tarboosh, and an old jacket over a tattered sweater, and who in an odd accent called Jacques "my colleague" because when he helped his uncle he was doing the same work as the Arab. The boss, M. [ ],[1] was actually an old barrelmaker who with his helpers filled orders for a bigger, nameless cooperage. An Italian worker who was always sad and always had a cold. And especially the joyful Daniel, who always took Jacques aside to joke and play with him. Jacques would make his escape, wander around the shop—his black apron covered with sawdust, bare feet in worn-out sandals if it was hot, covered with earth and shavings—savoring the smell of sawdust, the fresher smell of the shavings, then come back to the fire to smack his lips over its delicious smoke, or else cautiously to try out the tool used to edge the barrel bottoms on a piece of wood he wedged in the vise, and he would delight in his manual skill, for which the workers would praise him.

It was during one of these breaks that he foolishly

---

a. finish the barrel
1. An illegible name.

stood up on the bench with wet soles. Suddenly he slid forward while the bench tipped over backwards, and he fell with all his weight on the bench, his right hand squeezed under it. Immediately he felt a dull pain in his hand, but he stood up laughing for the workers who had come running over. But even before he had stopped laughing Ernest rushed to him, picked him up in his arms, and dashed out of the shop, running as fast he could and stammering: "To doctor, to doctor." Then Jacques saw the middle finger of his right hand had been completely squashed at the end into a shapeless dirty pulp that was dripping blood. His heart skipped a beat and he fainted. Five minutes later they were at the Arab doctor's who lived across the street from their home. "It's nothing, Doctor, nothing, eh?" said Ernest, white as a sheet.

"Go wait next door," the doctor said. "He's going to be brave." He had to be; his strangely patched-up finger bore witness to that even today. But once the staples were inserted and it was bandaged, the doctor gave him a sweet drink and awarded him a badge for courage. Even so, Ernest wanted to carry him across the street and, in the stairs of their building, he embraced the child, sobbing and hugging him close till it hurt.

"Maman," Jacques said, "someone's knocking at the door."

"It's Ernest," his mother said. "Go open it for him. I lock it now because of the bandits."

When he discovered Jacques on the doorstep, Ernest gave an exclamation of surprise, something that sounded like the English "how," and he straightened up and embraced him. Despite hair that was now entirely white, his face was surprisingly youthful, his features still regular and harmonious. But he was even more bowlegged, his shoulders completely rounded, and he walked swinging wide his arms and legs.

"How are you?" Jacques said.

Not so good, he had stitches, rheumatisms, it was going badly; and Jacques? Yes, all was well, he was in good shape, she (and he pointed to Catherine) was glad to see him. Since the grandmother had died and the children had left home, brother and sister had been living together and could not do without each other. He needed someone to look after him, and from that standpoint she was his wife, preparing meals, doing his laundry, caring for him when necessary. What she needed was not money, for her sons paid for her needs, but a man's companionship, and Ernest had been watching over her in his fashion for the years they had lived together; yes, like man and wife, not in the flesh but in the blood, helping each other to survive when their handicaps made life so difficult, carrying on a mute dialogue lit up from time to time by scraps of sentences, but more connected and better informed about each other than many normal couples.

"Yes, yes," said Ernest. "Jacques, Jacques, always she's saying."

"Well, here I am," said Jacques. And here he was indeed, he was with the two of them as he used to be; he was never able to talk to them and he had never stopped loving them, them above all, and he cherished them all the more for his ability to love them when he had failed to love so many who deserved it.

"And Daniel?"

"He's all right, he's old like me. Pierrot his brother in prison."

"What for?"

"He says the union. Me, I think he's with the Arabs." And suddenly worried: "Say, the bandits, that's all right?"

"No," said Jacques, "the other Arabs yes, the bandits no."

"Right, I said to your mother the bosses too tough. It's crazy but bandits too much."

"That's it," said Jacques. "But we have to do something for Pierrot."

"Good, I'll tell Daniel."

"And Donat?" (That was the man at the gasworks who boxed.)

"He's dead. Cancer. We're all old."

Yes, Donat was dead. And Aunt Marguerite, his mother's sister, was dead; that was where his grandmother would drag him on Sunday afternoons, and he was horribly bored, except when Uncle Michel, a teamster—who was also bored by these conversations in the dark dining room, over bowls of black coffee on the oilcloth table covering—would take him to his nearby stable, and there, in the shadowy light, while the afternoon sun was still warming the streets outside, first Jacques would smell the good smell of horsehair, of straw and manure, hear the harness chains rattle against the wooden manger, the horses turning their long-lashed eyes to him, and Uncle Michel, tall and spare with a long moustache, who himself smelled of straw, would lift him onto one of the horses that would placidly plunge his nose back into the manger and crunch his oats, while his uncle gave the child some carobs, which he chewed and sucked with delight, full of friendship for this uncle who in his mind was always associated with horses, and it was with him that they went with the whole family on Easter Monday for a mouna treat to the Sidi-Ferruch forest, and Michel rented one of those horse-drawn trams that ran between the district where they lived and downtown Algiers, a big sort of latticework cage equipped with back-to-back benches, to which the horses were harnessed, the lead horse chosen by Michel from his stable, and early in the morning they loaded the tram with big laundry baskets filled with the coarse brioches called "mounas" and the light crumbly pastries called "oreillettes" that all the women of the house made at Aunt Marguerite's over the two days before the outing, flattening out the dough with a rolling pin on the oilcloth dusted with flour till it covered almost the entire cloth, then, with a small boxwood cutter, cutting out the pastries that the children would carry on plates to be dropped into big copper basins full of boiling oil, then to be carefully set in rows in the big laundry baskets, from which would come the exquisite odor of vanilla that accompanied them all the way to Sidi-Ferruch, mingling with the smell of the surf that rose from the sea to the shore road, vigorously inhaled by the four horses over which Michel[a] would crack his whip, which he handed occasionally to Jacques beside him. Jacques was fascinated by the four enormous rumps rocking before him with a great noise of bells or else opening as the tail went up and he would see the savory dung form then drop to the ground while the horseshoes sparked and the bells rang faster as the horses tossed their heads. In the forest, while the others settled the baskets and dishtowels under the trees, Jacques helped Michel rub down the horses and fasten around their necks the gray-brown canvas nose bags, in which the horses chomped their jaws, opening and closing their large brotherly eyes or chasing away a fly with an impatient hoof. The forest was full of people; they ate side by side while here and there people were dancing to the sound of an accordion or a guitar, and the sea was rumbling nearby—it was never hot enough to swim, but always enough to go barefoot in the shallowest waves—while others were taking their siesta, and the imperceptible softening of the light made the reaches of the sky still more vast, so vast that the child felt tears coming to his eyes along with a great cry of joy and gratitude for this wonderful life. But Aunt Marguerite was dead, she was so beautiful, and always stylish—too coquettish, people said—but she had not been wrong, for diabetes would soon nail her to her armchair, and she would begin to swell up in that neglected apartment

---

a. bring Michel back during the Orléansville earthquake.

until she was so enormous, so bloated she could hardly breathe, so ugly it was frightening, and around her were her daughters and her lame son who was a cobbler, all watching sick at heart to see whether her breath would fail her.[a] [b] She grew fatter still, stuffed with insulin, and at the end her breath did give out.[c]

But Aunt Jeanne was dead too, the grandmother's sister, the one who attended the Sunday afternoon concerts and who held out for a long time in her white-washed farmhouse with her three war-widowed daughters, always talking about her husband, who had died long since.[d] Uncle Joseph, who only spoke the Mahon dialect and whom Jacques admired for the white hair topping his handsome pink face and the black sombrero he wore, even at the dinner table, with an inimitably noble air, a real peasant patriarch, who nonetheless would occasionally lift himself slightly during the meal to let loose an incongruous sound, for which he would courteously excuse himself in response to his wife's resigned reproaches. And his grandmother's neighbors, the Massons, they were all dead, the old woman first and then the older sister, the tall Alexandra and [ ][1] the

---

a. Book six in the second part.

b. And Francis was dead too (see latest notes)

c. Denise leaves home at eighteen to be a prostitute—Comes back rich at twenty-one, sells her jewels, does over her father's whole stable—killed by an epidemic

d. the daughters?

1. Illegible name.

brother with the ears that stuck out, who was a contor-
tionist and sang at the matinées at the Alcazar movie
house. All of them, yes, even the youngest daughter,
Marthe, whom his brother Henri had courted and more
than courted.

No one ever talked about them. Neither his mother
nor his uncle ever spoke of the departed relatives. Nor
of the father whose traces he was seeking, nor of the
others. They went on living in poverty, though they
were no longer in need, but they were set in their ways,
and they looked on life with a resigned suspicion; they
loved it as animals do, but they knew from experience
that it would regularly give birth to disaster without
even showing any sign that it was carrying it.[a] And
then, the way these two were with him, silent and drawn
in on themselves, empty of memories and only holding
on to a few blurred images; they lived now in proximity
to death—that is always in the present. Never would he
learn from them who his father had been, and even
though by their presence alone they reopened springs
within him reaching back to his poor and happy childhood, he could not be sure whether these very rich
memories gushing out of him were really faithful to the
child he had been. It was far more certain, on the contrary, that he was left with two or three favorite pictures
that joined him to them, made him one with them, that
blotted out what he had tried to be for so many years

a. but are they after all aliens? (no, he was the a.)

and reduced him to the blind anonymous being that for so many years had survived through his family and that made him truly distinctive.

The picture, for example, of those hot evenings when after dinner the whole family would take chairs down to the sidewalk in front of the door to the building, where the air coming down from the dust-covered ficus trees was hot and dusty, while the people of the neighborhood came and went in front of them, and Jacques,[a] with his head on his mother's thin shoulder, leaning back a little in his chair, would gaze up through the branches at the stars of the summer sky; or that other picture of the Christmas night when, coming home from Aunt Marguerite's after midnight without Ernest, they saw a man lying in front of the restaurant near their door, with another man dancing around him. The two men had been drinking and had wanted to drink some more. The owner, a frail young blond man, had told them to leave. They had kicked his pregnant wife. And the owner fired a shot. The bullet lodged in the man's right temple. Now on the sidewalk that head was resting on the wound. Drunk on alcohol and fright, the other man had started dancing around him, and while the restaurant closed up, everyone fled before the police arrived. And in that out-of-the-way corner of the neighborhood where they stood squeezed together, the two women holding the children tight against them, a rare beam of light gleaming on the street slick with re-

---

a. humble and proud sovereign of the beauty of the night.

cent rainfall, the long wet tracks of cars, the occasional
arrival of the noisy brightly lit trolleys full of joyous
travelers indifferent to this scene from another world—
all this engraved on Jacques's terrified heart an image
that until now had survived all others: the sweet and
persistent image of the neighborhood where he reigned
all day long, innocent and eager, but which the ending
of the days would turn suddenly mysterious and disturbing, when the streets would begin to be peopled
with shadows—or rather, a single anonymous shadow
would sometimes emerge, accompanied by soft footsteps and the indistinct sound of voices, and be bathed
in the blood-red splendor of a pharmacy's globe light,
and the child would be suddenly filled with dread and
would run to his wretched home to be back among his
own.

6A : School[1]

[a]This man had never known his father, but he often spoke to Jacques of him in a rather mythological way, and in any case at a critical time he knew how to take the father's role. That is why Jacques had never forgotten him, as if, having never really felt the lack of a father he had never known, he had nonetheless subconsciously recognized, first as a child, then during the rest of his life, the one paternal act—both well thought out and crucial—that had affected his life as a child. For M. Bernard, his teacher for the year of the *certificat d'études*,[2] had at a given moment used all his weight as a man to change the destiny of this child in his charge, and he had in fact changed it.

Right now M. Bernard was facing Jacques in his small

---

1. See appendix, sheet II, pp. 286–87, that the author inserted between pages 68 and 69 of the manuscript.

a. Transition from 6?

2. The last year of elementary school, and at the time the last year of compulsory public education—*Trans*.

apartment in the winding streets of the Rovigo, almost at the foot of the Casbah, a district that overlooked the city and the sea, occupied by small shopkeepers of all races and all religions, where the homes smelled at once of spices and of poverty. He was there, grown old, his hair more sparse, old-age splotches under the now glassy tissue of his cheeks and hands, moving more slowly than in the old days, and visibly glad when he could sit back down in his rattan armchair, by the window that faced the street of shops, where a canary was chirping; age had also softened him and he let his feelings show, which he had not done before, but he was still erect, his voice strong and firm, as it had been back when, standing before his class, he would say: "In line two by two. By two! I didn't say by five!" And the scrambling would stop; the pupils, who both feared and adored M. Bernard, would line up along the wall outside the classroom, in the second-floor corridor, until, when the rows were at last still and straight, and the children quiet, a "Come in now, you bunch of *tramousses*" would liberate them and give them the signal to move but at a more subdued pace, which M. Bernard, robust, elegantly dressed, his strong face with its regular features crowned by hair that was thinning but still smooth, smelling of cologne, would watch over with good-natured strictness.

The school was located in a relatively new part of that old neighborhood, among two- and three-story houses built not long after the war of 1870 and more recent warehouses that eventually connected the main street of the neighborhood, where Jacques's home was, to the inner harbor and the coaling docks. So Jacques went on foot twice a day to that building he had begun attending at the age of four, when he went to nursery school, about which he remembered nothing except a dark stone lavatory that took up one whole end of the covered playground where he landed one day headfirst, got up all bloody with a cut eyebrow, amidst the panic of teachers, and it was then he became acquainted with medical staples and, in fact, his had hardly been removed when they had to put one on his other eyebrow, his brother having conceived the idea of dressing him up at home in an old bowler that blinded him and an old coat that hobbled his feet, with the result that he wound up with his head hitting a loose tile and was covered with blood once again. But now he was going to nursery school with Pierre, who was a year or almost so older, who lived in a nearby street with his mother, also a war widow and now working in the post office, and two of his uncles who worked on the railroad. Their families were vaguely friends, or—the way people are in these neighborhoods—they valued one another but hardly ever exchanged visits, and they were firmly resolved to help each other out but almost never had the occasion to do so. Only the children had really become friends, from that first day when Jacques was still wearing a dress and was entrusted to Pierre, who was aware that he was wearing pants and had responsibilities as the older boy, the two children went together to nursery school. They then went through every grade together up to the year of the *certificat d'études*, which Jacques entered at the age of nine. For five years they made the same journey four times a day, one blond, the other brown-haired, one placid, the other hot-blooded, destined from the beginning to be friends, good students both and also tireless at play. Jacques shone more in some subjects, but his conduct, his flightiness, and his desire to show off were forever leading him into all sorts of foolish behavior, and this gave the advantage back to the more sober and discreet Pierre. So they alternated at the head of the class, but, in contrast to their families, they did not think to take pride in this. Their pleasures were different. Each morning, Jacques would wait for Pierre outside his house. They would leave before the passage of the scavengers—or more precisely a cart drawn by a broken-kneed horse driven by an old Arab. The sidewalk was still moist from the humidity of the night, the air coming from the sea tasted of salt. Pierre's street, which led to the market, was dotted with garbage cans that famished Arabs or Moors, or sometimes an old Spanish tramp, had pried open at dawn to see if there was still something to be retrieved from what poor and thrifty families had so disdained they would throw it away. The lids of these cans were usually off, and by this hour of the morning the neighborhood's thin vigorous cats had taken the place of the ragged people. The idea was for the two children to creep up to the garbage can so noiselessly that they could suddenly slap the lid down on the cat inside. This exploit was not easy, for cats born and raised in a poor district were as vigilant and agile as animals used to fighting for their right to live. But sometimes, hypnotized by an appetizing find that was hard to extract from the pile of garbage, a cat would let itself be caught unawares. The lid would slam

noisily down, the cat would give a terrified howl, con-
vulsively arch its back and claws, and manage to raise
the roof of its zinc prison, then scramble out, its hair
standing on end with fear, and tear off as if there were a
pack of hounds at its heels—to bursts of laughter from
its tormentors, who were hardly aware of their cruelty.[a]

To tell the truth, these tormentors were also incon-
sistent, for they directed their hatred at the dogcatcher,
nicknamed "Galoufa"[1] (which in Spanish . . .) by the
neighborhood children. This municipal employee oper-
ated at about this same time of day, but if necessary he
would also come around in the afternoon. He was an
Arab in European dress who was usually stationed at
the rear of a strange cart drawn by two horses and
driven by an impassive old Arab. The body of this cart
consisted of a kind of cube made of wood, with a double
row of cages with strong bars installed along each side.
It included a total of sixteen cages that could each hold a
dog, that would then find itself squeezed between the
bars and the back of the cage. Since the dogcatcher was
perched on a little running board at the back of the cart,
his nose was even with the roof of the cages and thus he
would survey his hunting grounds. The cart rolled
slowly through wet streets that were beginning to be
peopled by children on their way to school, housewives
in flannelette housecoats decorated with garish flowers

---

a. Exoticism pea soup.

1. The name originated with the first person to take this position
and who was in fact named Galoufa.

going for their bread or milk, and Arab peddlers returning to the market, their little folded stands over one
shoulder, holding in the other hand enormous hampers
of braided straw that contained their merchandise. And
suddenly, at a word from the dogcatcher, the old Arab
would pull back on the reins and the cart would stop.
The dogcatcher had spotted one of his wretched victims
digging feverishly in a garbage can, glancing back fran-
tically at regular intervals, or else trotting rapidly along
a wall with the hurried and anxious look of an under-
nourished dog. Galoufa then seized from the top of the
cart a leather rod with a chain that ran through a ring
down the handle. He moved toward the animal at the
supple, rapid, and silent pace of a trapper, and when he
had caught up with the beast, if it was not wearing the
collar that proves membership in a good family, he
would run at it, in a sudden burst of astonishing speed,
and put his weapon around the dog's neck, so that it
served as an iron and leather lasso. Suddenly strangled,
the animal struggled wildly while making inarticulate
groans. But the man quickly dragged [it] to the cart,
opened one of the cage doors, lifted the dog, strangling
it more and more, and shoved it into the cage, making
sure to put the handle of his lasso through the bars.
Once the dog was captured, he loosened the iron chain
and freed the neck of the now imprisoned animal. At
least that is how things happened when the dog was not
under the protection of the neighborhood children. For
they were all in league against Galoufa. They knew the
captured dogs were taken to the municipal pound, kept
for three days, after which, if no one claimed them, the

animals were put to death. And if they had not known it, the pitiful spectacle of that death cart returning after a fruitful journey, loaded with wretched animals of all colors and sizes, terrified behind their bars and leaving behind the vehicle a trail of cries and mortal howls, would have been enough to rouse the children's indignation. So, as soon as the prison van appeared in the area, the children would alert each other. They would scatter throughout the streets of the neighborhood, they too hunting down the dogs, but in order to chase them off to other parts of the city, far from the terrible lasso. If despite these precautions the dogcatcher found a stray dog in their presence, as happened several times to Pierre and Jacques, their tactics were always the same. Before the dogcatcher could get close enough to his quarry, Jacques and Pierre would start screaming "Galoufa! Galoufa!" in voices so piercing and so terrifying that the dog would flee as fast as he could and would soon be out of reach. Now it was the children's turn to prove their skill as sprinters, for the unfortunate Galoufa, who was paid a bounty for each dog he caught, was wild with anger, and he would chase them brandishing his leather rod. The grown-ups usually helped them escape, either by hindering Galoufa or by stopping him outright and telling him to stick to his dogs. The workingmen of the neighborhood were all hunters and as a rule liked dogs; they had no respect for this strange occupation. As Uncle Ernest would say: "He loafer!" The old Arab who drove the cart presided silent and impassive over all the fuss, or, if the arguments stretched out, would calmly start rolling a cigarette.

Whether they had captured cats or saved dogs, the children would then hasten—wearing short capes for the wind if it was winter, their leather sandals (known as "mevas") flapping if it was summer—toward school and work. While crossing the market, they would glance quickly at the displays of fruit, mountains of oranges and tangerines, of medlars, apricots, peaches, tangerines,[1] melons, and watermelons rushing past them, of which they would get to taste only the least expensive, and that in small quantities; two or three turns at jousting on the broad shiny rim of the basin at the waterspout, and they would go alongside the warehouses on Boulevard Thiers, where they would be hit in the face with the smell of oranges coming from factories that peeled them to make liqueurs with their rinds; up a small street of gardens and villas, and they would come out finally on rue Aumerat into a swarm of children who, while chattering away at each other, were waiting for the doors to open.

Then came class. With M. Bernard, this class was always interesting for the simple reason that he loved his work with a passion. Outside, the sun might blare on the tawny walls while the heat crackled in the classroom itself, though it was shaded by awnings with big yellow and white stripes. Or the rain might fall, as it does in Algeria, in endless deluges, making a wet dark well of the street, but the class was hardly distracted. Only the flies during a storm could sometimes divert the children's at-

---

1. *sic*

tention. They would be captured and grounded in the inkwells, where they suffered a hideous death, drowned in the purple ink that filled the little cone-shaped wells that were set in holes in the table. But M. Bernard's method, which consisted of strict control on behavior while at the same time making his teaching lively and entertaining, would win out over even the flies. He always knew the right moment to bring from his treasure chest the mineral collection, the herbarium, the mounted butterflies and insects, the maps or . . . to revive his pupils' flagging interest. He was the only person in the school to have obtained a magic lantern, and twice a month he would do projections on some subject in natural history or geography. In arithmetic, he instituted a contest in mental calculation that forced the students to think quickly. He would put forth a problem to the class, all sitting with their arms folded, in division, or multiplication, or sometimes a somewhat complex addition. How much is $1,267 + 691$? The first one to give the correct answer was awarded a plus that counted toward the monthly ranking. Besides, he used the textbooks with competence and accuracy . . . The texts were always those used in France. And these children, who knew only the sirocco, the dust, the short torrential cloudbursts, the sand of the beaches, and the sea in flames under the sun, would assiduously read—accenting the commas and periods—stories that to them were mythical, where children in hoods and mufflers, their feet in wooden shoes, would come home dragging bundles of sticks along snowy paths until they saw the snow-covered roof of the house where the smoking chimney told them the pea soup was cooking in the hearth. For Jacques, these stories were as exotic as they could possibly be. He dreamed about them, filled his compositions with descriptions of a world he had never seen, and was forever questioning his grandmother about a snowfall lasting one hour that had taken place in the Algiers area twenty years earlier. For him these stories were part of the powerful poetry of school, which was nourished also by the smell of varnished rulers and pen cases; the delicious taste of the strap on his satchel that he would chew on at length while laboring over his lessons; the sharp bitter smell of purple ink, especially when his turn came to fill the inkwells from a huge dark bottle with a cork through which a bent glass tube had been pushed, and Jacques would happily sniff the opening of the tube; the soft feel of the smooth glossy pages in certain books, which also gave off the good smell of print and glue; and, finally, on rainy days, the smell of wet wool that emanated from the wool coats at the back of the classroom and seemed to be a harbinger of that Garden of Eden where children in wooden shoes and woolen hoods ran through the snow to their warm homes.

Only school gave Jacques and Pierre these joys. And no doubt what they so passionately loved in school was that they were not at home, where want and ignorance made life harder and more bleak, as if closed in on itself; poverty is a fortress without drawbridges.

But it was not just that, for Jacques considered himself the most unfortunate of children when, to get rid of this tireless brat during vacations, his grandmother would send him to a holiday camp, with fifty or so other children and a handful of counselors, at Miliana in the Zaccar Mountains; there they lived in a school that had dormitories, ate and slept comfortably, played or wandered around all day long, watched over by some nice nurses, and despite all that, when evening came—when shadows rose so rapidly on the mountain slopes and from the neighboring barracks the bugle began to throw the melancholy notes of curfew into the enormous silence of this small town lost in the mountains, a hundred kilometers from any really traveled location—the child felt a limitless despair rising in him and in silence he cried for the destitute home of his entire childhood.[a]

No, school did not just provide them an escape from family life. At least in M. Bernard's class, it fed a hunger in them more basic even to the child than to the man, and that is the hunger for discovery. No doubt they were taught many things in their other classes, but it was somewhat the way geese are stuffed: food was presented to them and they were asked to please swallow it. In M. Germain's[1] class, they felt for the first time that they existed and that they were the objects of the highest regard: they were judged worthy to discover the world. And even their teacher did not devote himself just to what he was paid to teach them; he welcomed them with simplicity into his personal life, he lived that life with them, told them about his childhood and the

---

a. stretch out and exalt secular school.

1. Here the author uses the teacher's real name.

lives of children he had known, shared with them his philosophy but not his opinions, for though he was for example anti-clerical, like many of his colleagues, he never said a word against religion in class, nor against anything that could be the object of a choice or a belief, but he would condemn with all the more vigor those evils over which there could be no argument—theft, betrayal, rudeness, dirtiness.

But most of all he talked to them about the war that was still recent, which he had fought for four years, and about the suffering of the soldiers, their courage and their endurance, and the joy of the armistice. At the end of each term, before sending them home for vacation, and from time to time when the schedule allowed him to, he would read them long excerpts from Dorgelès's *Les Croix de Bois*.[a] For Jacques these readings again opened the door to the exotic, but this time an exotic world stalked by fear and misfortune, although he never made any but a theoretical connection with the father he never knew. He just listened with all his heart to a story that his teacher read with all *his* heart and that spoke to him again of snow and his cherished winter, but also of a special kind of men, dressed in heavy cloth stiff with mud, who spoke a strange language and lived in holes under a ceiling of shells and flares and bullets. Pierre and he awaited each reading with ever-increasing impatience. That war everyone was still talking about (and Jacques listened silent but with ears wide open when

---

a. see the book. [A novel of the First World War—*Trans.*]

Daniel would tell in his own way about the Battle of the Marne, where he fought and he still did not know how he had come out alive when they, the Zouaves, he said, they were put out in front and then at the charge down a ravine they charged and there was no one ahead of them and they were advancing and all of a sudden the machine gunners when they were halfway down they were dropping one on top of the other and the bed of the ravine was all full of blood and the ones crying for *maman* it was awful) that the survivors could not forget and that cast its shadow over everything in the children's world and shaped all the ideas they had for fascinating stories more extraordinary than the fairy tales read in other classes, and that would have disappointed and bored them if M. Bernard had taken it into his head to change his curriculum. But he went on with it, funny scenes alternating with terrifying descriptions, and little by little the African children made the acquaintance . . . of x y z, who became part of their world; they talked about them among themselves as if they were old friends who were right there and so much alive that Jacques at least could not for a moment imagine that though they were living in the war, there was any chance they could be victims of it. And on the day at the end of the year when, as they arrived at the end of the book,* M. Bernard read them the death of D. in a subdued voice, when he closed the book in silence, facing his own memories and emotions, then raised his eyes to his silent, overwhelmed

---

* novel

class, he saw Jacques in the first row staring at him with his face bathed in tears and shaking with sobs that seemed as if they would never end. "Come come, child," M. Bernard said in a barely audible voice, and he stood up to return the book to the case, his back to the class.

"Wait a minute, kiddo," M. Bernard said. Now he stood up with difficulty, ran his index finger over the bars of the cage, so that the canary chirped all the more: "Ah! Casimir, we're hungry, we're asking our father," and [got himself] to his little schoolboy's desk on the other side of the room, near the fireplace. He rummaged in a drawer, closed it, opened another, pulled out something. "Here," he said, "this is for you." Jacques received a book bound in grocery-store paper with no writing on its cover. Before he even opened it, he knew it was *Les Croix de Bois,* the very copy M. Bernard had read to the class.

"No, no," he said, "it's . . ." He wanted to say: "it's too beautiful." He could not find the words.

M. Bernard shook his old head. "You cried that last day, you remember? Since that day the book's belonged to you." And he turned away to hide his suddenly reddened eyes. He went back again to his desk, turned to Jacques with his hands behind his back, then, brandishing a short solid red ruler* in his face, he said, laughing, "You remember the 'sugar cane'?"

---

* The punishments.

"Oh, M. Bernard," said Jacques, "so you kept it! You know it's forbidden now."

"Pooh, it was forbidden then too. But you're a witness that I used it!"

Jacques was indeed a witness, for M. Bernard was in favor of corporal punishment. True, the everyday punishment only consisted of minus marks that he would deduct at the end of the month from the number of points accumulated by the pupil, thus bringing him down in his overall ranking. But in more serious cases M. Bernard did not bother to send the offender to the principal's office, as did many of his colleagues. He followed an unalterable ritual. "My poor Robert," he would say, calmly and still with good humor, "we shall have to resort to the 'sugar cane.' " No one in the class reacted (except to snicker behind his hand, according to the eternal rule of the human heart that the punishment of one is felt by the others as pleasure).[a] The child would stand, pale but in most cases trying to put a good face on it (some were already swallowing their tears when they left their table and headed toward the desk that M. Bernard was standing beside, in front of the blackboard). Still conforming to the ritual, and here there was a touch of sadism, Robert or Joseph had to go to the desk himself to get the "sugar cane" and present it to the sacrificer.

The "sugar cane" was a red wood ruler, short and thick, spotted with ink, marred with nicks and slashes,

---

a. or, what punishes one makes the others rejoice.

that M. Bernard had long ago confiscated from some forgotten pupil; the boy would now hand it to M. Bernard, who usually received it with a mocking air, then held his legs apart. The child had to put his head between the knees of the teacher, who by tightening his thighs would hold him firmly. And on the buttocks thus presented, M. Bernard would inflict some solid blows with the ruler, the number varying according to the offense and equally divided between the two cheeks. Reactions to this punishment differed according to the pupil. Some began sobbing even before being hit, and the unfazed teacher would observe that they were getting ahead of themselves; others would naively try to protect their bottom with their hands, which M. Bernard would slap aside with a casual blow. Still others, smarting under the blows of the ruler, would buck desperately. There were also those, among them Jacques, who took the blows without a word, shivering, and returned to their places holding back a flood of tears. On the whole, however, this punishment was accepted without bitterness: first, because almost all these children were beaten at home and so physical punishment seemed to them a natural method of upbringing; then too because the teacher was absolutely fair, they all knew in advance which infractions, always the same ones, would result in the ceremony of atonement, and those who went beyond the limit of actions that resulted only in minus points knew the chance they were taking; and finally because the sentence was imposed with hearty impartiality on the best students as well as the worst. Jacques, whom M. Bernard obviously loved very much, suffered it like the rest, and he even had to undergo it the day after M. Bernard had publicly shown his preference for him. When Jacques at the blackboard had given a good answer and M. Bernard had patted his cheek and a voice in the classroom whispered, "teacher's pet," M. Bernard had pulled him close and said with a kind of solemnity: "Yes, I am partial to Cormery as I am to all those among you who lost their fathers in the war. I fought the war with their fathers and I survived. I try at least here to take the place of my dead comrades. And now if someone wants to say I have 'pets,' let him speak up!" This speech was received in absolute silence. At the end of the day, Jacques asked who had called him "teacher's pet." To take such an insult without responding would have meant a loss of honor.

"I did," said Munoz, a big blond boy, rather flabby and insipid, who though undemonstrative had always shown his antipathy to Jacques.

"All right," said Jacques. "Then your mother's a whore."[a] That too was a ritual insult that led immediately to battle, for to insult mothers and the dead had been from time immemorial the most serious of affronts known to the shores of the Mediterranean. Even so, Munoz hesitated. But a ritual is a ritual, and others spoke for him: "Come on, it's the green field." The green field was a sort of vacant lot, not far from the school, where sickly grass grew in scabby bunches, littered with old hoops, tin cans, and rotting barrels. This

---

a. and your ancestors are whores.

was where the *donnades* took place. A *donnade* was just a
duel, with the fist taking the place of the sword, but
obeying the same ceremonial rules, at least in spirit. Its
aim was to settle a quarrel where the honor of one of the
adversaries was at stake, either because someone had insulted his parents or his ancestors, or had belittled his
nationality or his race, or had been informed on or had
accused another of informing, had stolen or been accused of it, or else for the more obscure reasons that
come up every day in a society of children. When a
pupil reckoned, or especially when others reckoned for
him (and he was aware of it), that he had been insulted
in such a way that the offense must be compensated, the
ritual statement was: "Four o'clock, at the green field."
Once the declaration had been made, provocation
ceased and all discussion ended. The two adversaries
withdrew, followed by their friends. During the classes
that followed, the news sped from bench to bench with
the names of the principals, whom their classmates
would watch out of the corner of their eyes and who
therefore affected the calm and resolution appropriate to
manliness. Inside it was another story, and even the
most courageous were distracted from their work by the
dread of seeing the moment approach when they would
have to face violence. But the members of the enemy
camp must not be given cause to snicker and to accuse
the protagonist, according to the time-honored expression, of being "scared shitless."

Jacques, having done his duty as a man by challeng-
ing Munoz, was certainly scared enough, as he was
every time he put himself in a situation where he had to

face violence and to deal it out. But he had made his decision, and in his mind there was never for an instant any question of backing out. This was the nature of things, and he knew also that the touch of nausea that would grip his heart beforehand would vanish at the moment of combat, swept away by his own violence, which in any event would hurt him tactically as much as it helped him . . . and had earned him at[1]

On the afternoon of the fight with Munoz everything took place according to ritual. The fighters were the first to arrive at the green field, followed by their supporters turned into seconds and already carrying the principals' satchels, and they in turn were followed by all those attracted to the fight, who closed a circle around the adversaries on the battlefield. The principals took off their short capes and jackets and handed them to their seconds. This time Jacques's impetuousness worked to his advantage. He attacked first, not very confidently, forcing Munoz to retreat; Munoz backed up in confusion, clumsily parrying his antagonist's fists, then landed a painful blow on Jacques's cheek that aroused a blind rage in him intensified by the shouts, the laughter, the encouragement of the crowd. He hurled himself at Munoz, rained blows on him with his fists, bewildering him, and was lucky enough to land a furious hook on the right eye of his unfortunate opponent,

---

1. The sentence ends there.

who, completely off balance, fell pitifully on his back, one eye weeping and the other immediately swelling. The black eye, a crowning blow much sought after because for several days it would visibly confirm the winner's triumph, brought a roar from the audience worthy of the Sioux. Munoz did not get to his feet immediately, and Pierre, Jacques's closest friend, quickly stepped in and authoritatively declared Jacques the winner, then helped him on with his jacket and put his cape on his shoulders, and led him away surrounded by a retinue of admirers, while Munoz got up, still crying, and dressed in his small circle of dismayed supporters. Jacques, dizzy with the rapidity of a victory he had not even hoped would be so complete, could hardly hear the congratulations around him and the already embellished accounts of the fight. He wanted to be glad, and he was glad, somewhere in the vanity of his ego, and yet, when he looked back at Munoz as he was leaving the green field, a bleak sadness suddenly seized his heart at the sight of the crestfallen face of the boy he had struck. And then he knew that war is no good, because vanquishing a man is as bitter as being vanquished.

To round out his education, he was taught without delay that the Tarpeian Rock is near the Capitol.[1] The next day, in fact, he thought he should swagger and show off in response to the backslapping admiration of his classmates. When, at the beginning of class, Munoz

---

1. In Rome, traitors were thrown to their death from the Tarpeian Rock. The meaning is: Pride goeth before a fall—*Trans.*

did not answer to his name, Jacques's neighbors commented on his absence with ironic snickers and winks to the victor, and Jacques gave in to temptation, puffed out his cheeks, and showed the others a half-closed eye; without realizing that M. Bernard was watching him, he was indulging in a grotesque mimicry that vanished in the blink of an eyelid when the master's voice resounded in the suddenly still classroom: "My poor teacher's pet," he said, deadpan, "you have as much right as the others to the 'sugar cane.' " The conqueror had to stand up, fetch the instrument of torture, and, amidst the fresh smell of cologne that surrounded M. Bernard, assume the ignominious position to be punished.

The Munoz affair was not to end on this lesson in applied philosophy. The boy's absence lasted two days, and Jacques was vaguely worried despite his swaggering air when, on the third day, an older student came in the room to inform M. Bernard that the principal was asking for the pupil Cormery. They were only summoned to the principal's office in serious cases, and the teacher, raising his bushy eyebrows, simply said: "Hurry up, kiddo. I hope you haven't done anything foolish." Jacques, his legs unsteady under him, followed the older pupil down the length of the corridor over the cement courtyard with its ornamental peppertrees that the dappled shade did not protect from the torrid heat, to the principal's office at the other end of the corridor. The first thing he saw as he entered, in front of the principal's desk, was Munoz flanked by a scowling woman and man. Although his classmate was disfigured by an eye that was swollen and completely shut, Jacques was relieved to find him still alive. But he did not have time to enjoy that relief.

"Was it you who hit your classmate?" asked the principal, a small bald man with a pink face and an energetic voice.

"Yes," Jacques said in a toneless voice.

"I told you so, Monsieur," said the woman. "André is no hooligan."

"We had a fight," said Jacques.

"I don't need to know about it," said the principal. "You know I forbid all fighting, even outside school. You injured your classmate and could have injured him even more severely. By way of a first warning, you will stand in the corner at every recess for a week. If you do it again, you will be expelled. I will inform your parents of your punishment. You may return to your class." Jacques, thunderstruck, did not move. "Go on."

"Well, Fantomâs?" said M. Bernard when Jacques returned to his class.[1] Jacques was weeping. "Go ahead, I'm listening." With a catch in his voice, the child first announced the punishment, then that Munoz's parents had complained and he had told about the fight. "Why did you fight?"

"He called me 'teacher's pet.' "

"Again?"

"No, here, during class."

---

1. Fantomâs was the masked hero of a series of pulp novels— *Trans.*

"Ah! He was the one. And you thought I hadn't suffi-ciently defended you."

Jacques gave M. Bernard a heartfelt look. "Oh no, oh no! You . . ." And he burst out in real sobs.

"Go sit down," said M. Bernard.

"It's not fair," said the child through his tears.

"Yes, it is," gently told him[1]

The next day, at recess, Jacques took his place in the corner at the end of the playground, his back turned to the yard and to the happy cries of his classmates. He shifted his weight from one leg to the other;[a] he was dying to run around with them. From time to time he glanced back and saw M. Bernard strolling in a corner of the yard with his colleagues and not looking at Jacques. But, the second day, he did not see M. Bernard come up behind him and tap him lightly on the back of his neck: "Why such a long face, shrimp? Munoz is in the corner too. Here, I give you permission to look." Munoz was indeed on the other side of the playground, alone and morose. "Your accomplices refuse to play with him for the whole week you're in the corner." M. Bernard laughed. "So you see, you're both being punished. That's the way it should be." And he leaned over the child to say to him, with an affectionate laugh that caused the heart of the convict to overflow with love: "You know, *moustique*, to look at you, you wouldn't think you could throw such a punch!"

---

1. The sentence ends there.

a. M'sieur he tripped me

This man who today was talking to his canary and who called Jacques "kiddo" though he was forty years old—Jacques had never stopped loving him, even when the years, distance, and finally the Second World War had partly, then completely cut him off from his teacher, of whom he had no news, and he was as happy as a child when in 1945 an elderly Territorial in a soldier's greatcoat rang his doorbell in Paris, and it was M. Bernard, who had enlisted again: "Not for the war," he said, "but against Hitler, and you too, kiddo, you fought— oh I knew you were made of the right stuff, you haven't forgotten your mother either I hope, that's good, your mother's the best thing in the world—and now I'm going back to Algiers, come see me," and Jacques had been going to see him for fifteen years, and each time it was the same: before leaving he would embrace the deeply moved old man who clung to his hand on the doorstep, and this man had launched Jacques in the world, taking on himself alone the responsibility for uprooting him so that he could go on to still greater discoveries.[a]

The school year was drawing to a close when M. Bernard summoned Jacques, Pierre, Fleury, a kind of prodigy who did equally well in all subjects—"he has a polytechnic brain," the teacher said—and Santiago, a handsome boy who was less gifted but succeeded by virtue of diligence: "Now," said M. Bernard when the classroom was empty. "You're my best students. I've

---

a. The scholarship

decided to nominate you for secondary-school scholarships. If you pass the examination, you'll have scholarships and you can continue your studies at the *lycée* through the baccalaureate. Elementary school is the best of schools. But it leads to nothing. The *lycée* opens all doors. And I would rather see poor boys like you go through those doors. But for that, I need your parents' authorization. Off with you!"

They left in amazement and did not even discuss it before they parted. Jacques found his grandmother at home alone picking over lentils on the oilcloth cover of the dining-room table. He hesitated, then decided to wait for his mother to arrive. She came home visibly tired, put on an apron, and came to help the grandmother sort the lentils. Jacques offered to help, and they gave him the thick white porcelain bowl where it was easier to separate the pebbles from the good lentils. Staring into his plate, he announced his news.

"What's this all about?" said the grandmother. "At what age do you do this baccalaureate?"

"In six years."

His grandmother pushed her plate away. "Did you hear that?" she asked Catherine Cormery.

She had not heard. Jacques slowly repeated the news. "Ah!" she said. "It's because you're intelligent."

"Intelligent or not, we were going to apprentice him next year. You know perfectly well we have no money. He'll bring home his pay."

"That's true," said Catherine.

Outside, the day and the heat were beginning to fade. At that time of day, with the factories all working, the neighborhood was empty and silent. Jacques gazed out at the street. He did not know what he wanted, only that he wanted to obey M. Bernard. But, at nine, he could not disobey his grandmother, nor would he know how to. Still, she was obviously hesitating. "What would you do afterwards?"

"I don't know. Maybe be a teacher, like M. Bernard."

"Yes—in six years!" She was sorting the lentils more slowly. "Ah!" she said. "No, after all, we're too poor. You tell M. Bernard we can't do it."

The next day the three others told Jacques their families had agreed. "How about you?"

"I don't know," he said, and the thought that he was even poorer than his friends left him sick at heart.

The four of them stayed after school. Pierre, Fleury, and Santiago gave their answers. "And you, *moustique?*"

"I don't know."

M. Bernard gazed at him. "All right," he said to the others. "But you'll have to work with me afternoons after school. I'll arrange it, you can go." When they had left, M. Bernard sat himself in his armchair and drew Jacques close. "Well?"

"My grandmother says we're too poor and that I have to go to work next year."

"And your mother?"

"It's my grandmother who decides."

"I know," said M. Bernard. He thought a moment, then put his arm around Jacques. "Listen: you can't blame her. Life is hard for her. The two of them alone, they've brought you up, your brother and you, and made you the good boys you are. So she's bound to be afraid. You'll need a little money besides the scholarship, and in any case you won't bring home any money for six years. Can you understand her?" Jacques nodded without looking at his teacher. "Good. But maybe we can explain it to her. Get your satchel, I'm coming with you!"

"To our place?" said Jacques.

"Yes, it will be a pleasure to see your mother again."

Minutes later M. Bernard was knocking on their door in front of a bewildered Jacques. The grandmother came to the door, wiping her hands on her apron; the strings were tied too tightly, making her old woman's paunch protrude. When she saw the teacher, she made a gesture as if to comb her hair. "So it's the grandmom," said M. Bernard, "hard at work as usual? Ah! You're a worthy woman." The grandmother invited him into the room that you had to cross to get to the dining room, seated him near the table, brought out glasses and a bottle of anisette. "Don't put yourself out, I came to have a little talk with you." He began by asking about her children, then her life on the farm, her husband; he talked about his own children. At that moment Catherine Cormery came in, panicked, called M. Bernard "Monsieur le Maître," went to her room to comb her hair and put on a clean apron, and returned to perch on the edge of a chair a little away from the table. "You," M. Bernard said to Jacques, "go out on the street and see if I'm there. You understand," he said to the grandmother, "I'm going to speak well of him and he's liable to think it's the truth." Jacques left, dashed down the stairs, and

stationed himself by the door to the building. He was
still there an hour later, and the street was already coming to life, the sky through the ficus trees was turning
green, when M. Bernard emerged from the stairs at his
back. He scratched Jacques's head. "Well!" he said.
"It's all settled. Your grandmother's a good woman. As
for your mother . . . Ah!" he said. "Don't you ever forget her."

"Monsieur," the grandmother suddenly said. She was
coming out of the hall. She was holding her apron in her
hand and wiping her eyes. "I forgot . . . you told me
you would give Jacques extra lessons."

"Of course," said M. Bernard. "And it won't be any
picnic for him, believe me."

"But we won't be able to pay you."

M. Bernard studied her carefully. He was holding
Jacques by his shoulders. "Don't worry about that," he
said, shaking Jacques. "He's already paid me."

Then he was gone, and the grandmother took
Jacques by the hand to go back to the apartment, and
for the first time she squeezed his hand, very hard, with
a kind of hopeless love. "My child," she said. "My dear
child."

For a month M. Bernard kept the four children after
school every day and made them work for two hours.
Jacques would go home both tired and exhilarated, and
then have to start on his homework. His grandmother
would look at him with mingled pride and sadness.

"He got a good head," Ernest said with conviction,
tapping his own head with his fist.

"Yes," the grandmother would say. "But what's to

become of us?" One evening she gave a start: "What about his First Communion?" Actually religion had no part in their lives.[1] No one went to Mass, no one invoked or taught the Ten Commandments, nor did anyone refer to the rewards and punishments of the hereafter. When someone's death was reported in the grandmother's presence, "Well," she would say, "he'll fart no more." If it was someone for whom she was deemed to have at least some liking, "Poor man," she would say, "he was still young," even if the deceased had long since been old enough to die. It was not a matter of ignorance on her part. For she had seen many die around her. Two of her children, her husband, her son-in-law, and all her nephews in the war. But that was just it: she was as familiar with death as she was with work or poverty, she did not think about it but in some sense lived it, and besides, the needs of the moment were even more urgent for her than they were for Algerians as a whole, who by their daily cares and their common lot were denied the funerary piety that flourishes in civilizations at their height.[a] Death for them was an ordeal to be faced, as they had faced those that preceded it, which they never spoke of, where they tried to show the courage that for them was a man's principal virtue; but meanwhile one tried to forget it or push it aside. (Hence the comic air that all interments would assume. Cousin Maurice?) If to that general inclination is added the

---

1. Three illegible lines in the margin.
a. *La Mort en Algérie.*

harsh work and struggle of daily life, not to mention, in the case of Jacques's family, the awful wear and tear of poverty, it becomes hard to find a place for religion. For Uncle Ernest, who lived by his senses, religion was what he saw; that is, the priest and the ritual. Calling on his gift for comedy, he never missed an opportunity to mimic the ceremony of the Mass, accompanying it with a [sustained] onomatopoeia to represent the Latin words, and to conclude he would play both the faithful bowing their heads at the sound of the bells and the priest seizing the opportunity offered by their bowed heads to take a surreptitious drink of the Communion wine. As for Catherine Cormery, only she with her gentleness might have suggested faith, but in fact that gentleness was her faith. She neither dissented nor agreed, laughed a little at her brother's jokes, but would call the priests she met "Monsieur Curé." She never spoke of God. In fact, that was a word Jacques never heard spoken throughout his childhood, nor did he trouble himself about it. Life, so vivid and mysterious, was enough to occupy his entire being.

With all that, if a civil burial was mentioned in the family, it was not unusual for his grandmother or even his uncle paradoxically to deplore the absence of a priest: "like a dog," they would say. This because for them, as for most Algerians, religion was part of their civic life and that alone. They were Catholic as they were French; it entailed a certain number of rituals. Actually those rituals numbered exactly four: baptism, First Communion, marriage (if they were married), and funeral rites. Between these ceremonies, which necessarily were far apart in time, they were occupied with other things, and most of all with surviving.

So it was taken for granted that Jacques would make his First Communion like Henri, who had kept a most unpleasant memory not of the ceremony itself but of its social consequences and especially the visits he was obliged to make over several days, the armband on his arm, to friends and relatives, who had to present him with a small amount of cash, which the child was embarrassed to take; the grandmother would then appropriate the entire sum, returning only a very small proportion to Henri, because Communion "cost good money." But this ceremony did not take place until around the child's twelfth year, after he had spent two years being taught the catechism. So Jacques would not have to make his First Communion until his second or third year at the *lycée*. But it was that prospect that caused the grandmother to give a start. She had a dark and somewhat frightening picture of the *lycée* as a place where you had to work ten times as much as at the neighborhood school, because these studies led to better jobs and because, to her way of thinking, no improvement in material circumstances could be gotten except by more work. She wished for Jacques to succeed with all her heart on account of the sacrifices she had just agreed to in advance, and she calculated that the time taken by catechism would be subtracted from the time for work. "No," she said, "you can't be in the *lycée* and at catechism at the same time."

"Fine. I won't make my First Communion," said Jacques, who was hoping above all to escape the ordeal

of the visits and what for him was the unbearable humil-
iation of accepting money.

The grandmother stared at him. "Why? It can be arranged. Get dressed. We're going to see the priest." She
stood up and went with a resolute air into her bedroom.
When she returned, she had taken off her camisole and
her work skirt, had put on her one going-out dress [ ][1]
buttoned to the neck, and she had knotted her black silk
scarf around her head. The strands of white hair at the
edge of her scarf, her sharp eyes and firm mouth made
her the very picture of determination.

At the sacristy of the church of Saint-Charles, a
dreadful pile of modern Gothic, she seated herself,
holding Jacques's hand while he stood beside her,
before the parish priest, a fat sixty-year-old with a
round, rather soft face, a big nose, and a good smile on
his thick lips, under a crown of silvery hair; he was
clasping his hands on his robe stretched by his parted
knees. "I want this child to make his First Communion," said the grandmother.

"Very well, Madame, we'll make a good Christian of
him. How old is he?"

"Nine."

"You're right to have him start the catechism very
early. In three years he'll be perfectly prepared for the
big day."

"No," the grandmother said curtly. "He must do it
right away."

---

1. An illegible word.

"Right away? But the Communions will be a month from now, and he can only approach the altar after at least two years of catechism."

The grandmother explained their situation. But the priest was not at all convinced that it was impossible to take religious instruction while doing secondary-school studies. With patience and kindness, he cited his own experience, gave examples . . . The grandmother stood up. "In that case he won't make his First Communion. Come, Jacques," and she pulled the child toward the exit.

But the priest hurried after them. "Wait, Madame, wait." He led her gently back to her seat, tried to reason with her.

But the grandmother shook her head like a stubborn old mule. "It's right away or he'll do without it."

At last the priest gave in. It was agreed that Jacques would make his First Communion in one month after an accelerated course of religious instruction. And the priest, shaking his head, accompanied them to the door, where he patted the child's cheek. "Listen carefully to what you're told," he said. And he looked at him with a sort of sadness.

So Jacques added the catechism classes on Thursdays and Saturday afternoons to his supplementary lessons with M. Bernard. The examination for the scholarship and the First Communion were both drawing near, and his days were overloaded, leaving no time for play, even and especially on Sundays, when, if he could put down his notebooks, his grandmother would impose domestic tasks and errands on him, citing the future sacrifices the family had agreed to for his education and the many years thereafter when he would no longer do anything for the household.

"But," said Jacques, "I might fail. The exam is hard." And in a certain sense he sometimes would wish for just that, finding that his young pride could not bear the weight of the sacrifices they were always talking to him about.

His grandmother looked at him in astonishment. She had never thought of that possibility. Then she shrugged and, not worrying about the contradiction, "Go ahead and fail," she said. "And I'll warm your ass for you." The catechism course was given by the second priest of the parish: tall, almost endlessly so in his black robe, thin, with hollow cheeks and a nose like an eagle's beak, as hard as the old priest was gentle and good. His method of teaching was recitation, and, though it was primitive, it was perhaps the only method suited to the rough, obdurate children to whom it was his mission to give their spiritual training. They had to learn the questions and responses: "Who is God?"[a] . . . These words meant absolutely nothing to the young catechumens, and Jacques, who had an excellent memory, recited them imperturbably without ever understanding them. When another child was reciting, he would let his thoughts wander, daydream, or make faces with the others. One day the tall priest caught him making one of those faces, and, believing the grimace was

a. See catechism

aimed at him, thought it right to enforce respect for the sacred character of his office; he called Jacques up before the whole assembly of children, and there, with his long bony hand, without further explanation, he hit him with all his strength. Jacques almost fell under the force of the blow. "Now go back to your place," the priest said. The child stared at him, without a tear (and for all his life it would be kindness and love that made him cry, never pain or persecution, which on the contrary only reinforced his spirit and his resolution), and returned to his bench. The left side of his face was smarting, the taste of blood was in his mouth. With the tip of his tongue, he discovered the inside of his cheek was cut by the blow and was bleeding. He swallowed his blood.

Throughout the rest of the sacramental preparation, his mind was elsewhere, and he was looking quietly at the priest, without reproach as without friendship when he spoke to him, flawlessly reciting the questions and responses about the divine nature and sacrifice of Christ; and, a hundred leagues away from the place where he was reciting, he was dreaming of that double examination that now had come to seem a single one. Immersed in his work as he was in that persisting dream, he was moved only, and in an obscure way, by the evening Masses, more and more of them in that dreadful cold church, but the organ made him listen to a music he was hearing for the first time, having until then heard nothing but stupid tunes; dreaming richer, deeper dreams featuring sacerdotal objects and vestments glistening in the semi-darkness, to meet at last the mystery,

but it was a nameless mystery where the divine person-
ages named and rigorously defined in the catechism
played no role at all, they were simply an extension of
the bare world where he lived; but the warm, inward,
and ambiguous mystery that now bathed him only
deepened the everyday mystery of his mother's silence
or her small smile when he entered the dining room at
evening and, alone in the apartment, she had not lit the
kerosene lamp, letting the night invade the room step by
step, herself a darker denser form gazing pensively out
the window, watching the brisk—but, for her, silent—
activity of the street; and the child would stop on the
doorsill, his heart heavy, full of a despairing love for his
mother, and for something in his mother that did not
belong or no longer belonged to the world and to the
triviality of the days. Then it was the First Communion,
of which Jacques remembered little except confession the day before, when he had admitted the only acts
he had been told were sinful—very few, that is—and
to "Have you had sinful thoughts?" he said, "Yes,
Father," at a guess, though he did not know how a
thought could be sinful, and till the next day he lived in
fear that he would unwittingly let out a sinful thought
or, and this was clearer to him, one of those objection-
able words that populated his schoolboy vocabulary,
and as best he could he held back the words at least until
the morning of the ceremony when, dressed in a sailor
suit with an armband, equipped with a small prayerbook
and a chaplet of little white beads, all supplied by the
least poor among their relatives (Aunt Marguerite, etc.),
holding a taper in the center aisle in a line of other chil-

dren carrying tapers under the ecstatic eyes of their families standing in the pews, and the thunder of the music
that exploded now chilled him, filled him with dread
and with an extraordinary exaltation where for the first
time he could feel his strength, his boundless ability to
prevail and to live, an exaltation that stayed with him
throughout the ceremony, taking him away from everything that was happening, including the instant of Communion, and lasting through their return home and the
meal to which their relatives had been invited, around a
[richer] than usual table, and which bit by bit excited the
guests who were accustomed to eat and drink sparingly,
so that an enormous gaiety gradually filled the room,
destroying Jacques's elation and so shaking him that
when dessert came, at the peak of the general excitement, he burst out sobbing. "What's the matter with
you?" his grandmother said.

"I don't know, I don't."

And his exasperated grandmother slapped him.
"That way you'll know why you're crying," she said.

But in truth he did know why when he looked across
the table at his mother, who was giving him her small
sad smile.

"That's well over with," said M. Bernard. "Well,
now we get to work." A few more days of hard work,
with the last lessons at M. Bernard's (describe the apartment?), and then, one morning at the trolley stop near
Jacques's home, the four pupils were grouped around
M. Bernard, each equipped with writing pad, ruler, and
pen case, and Jacques could see his mother and grand-

mother waving energetically to them from their balcony.

The *lycée* where the examination was given was all the way across town, at the other end of the arc the city makes around the bay, in a district that had once been rich and dull, but, thanks to Spanish immigrants, had become one of the most crowded and lively parts of Algiers. The *lycée* itself was a huge square building that dominated the street. You entered it by steps at either side and, in front, large monumental steps flanked on both sides by meager gardens planted with banana trees and[1] protected from student vandalism by wire fencing. The central steps led to an arcade connecting the steps at the two sides; from the arcade opened the monumental door used on major occasions, to one side of which, for everyday use, was a much smaller door that led to the glassed-in cabin of the concierge.

It was in that arcade—among the first students to arrive, who on the whole were able to hide their nervousness under a casual manner, except a few whose anxiety was betrayed by their pale countenances and their silence—that M. Bernard and his pupils were waiting in front of the closed door, in the early morning when the air was still cool and the street still damp before the sun covered it with dust. They were a good half hour early, huddled silently around their teacher, who found nothing to say to them and then left, saying he would return.

---

1. No word appears here in the manuscript.

Indeed they saw him come back in a few minutes, elegant in the felt hat and spats he had put on for the occasion, holding in each hand a package of tissue paper wrapped and twisted at the top to make a handle, and as he approached, they saw that the paper was spotted with grease. "Here are some croissants," said M. Bernard. "Eat one now and save the other for ten o'clock." They thanked him and ate, but the heavy dough once chewed was difficult to swallow. "Don't lose your head," the teacher kept saying. "Carefully read the wording of the problem and the subject of the composition. Read them over several times. You'll have time." Yes, they would read it over several times, they would obey him, with him there were no obstacles in life, it was enough to let themselves be guided by him. Now there was a hubbub by the smaller door. The students, numbering about sixty, headed in that direction. An attendant had opened the door and was reading a list. Jacques's name was one of the first to be read. He clutched his teacher's hand, he hesitated. "Go, my son," said M. Bernard. Jacques, trembling, went to the door, and, as he was going through it, he turned back to his teacher. He was there, big, solid; he was smiling calmly at Jacques and nodding reassuringly.[a]

At noon M. Bernard was waiting for them at the exit. They showed him their work papers. Santiago was the only one who had made a mistake in a problem. "Your composition is very good," he said tersely to Jacques.

---

a. check scholarship program.

At one o'clock he accompanied them back. At four o'clock he was still there, and he looked over their work. "Come on," he said, "we have to wait." Two days later the five of them were again in front of the small door at ten o'clock in the morning. The door opened and the attendant again read a list of names, this one much shorter, of the successful candidates. In the clamor Jacques did not hear his name. But he received a joyful slap on the back and heard M. Bernard say to him, "Bravo, *moustique*. You passed."

Only the nice Santiago had failed, and they gazed at him with a sort of absentminded sadness. "It doesn't matter," he said, "it doesn't matter."

And Jacques no longer knew where he was, or what was happening, they were coming back all four on the trolley; "I'll go see your parents," M. Bernard said, "I'll go to Cormery's first because he's the closest," and in the poor dining room full now of women—there were his grandmother, his mother, who had taken the day off for the occasion (?), and their neighbors the Masson women—he stayed close to his teacher's side, breathing one last time the odor of cologne, pressing against the hearty warmth of that solid body, while the grandmother beamed in front of her neighbors. "Thank you, M. Bernard, thank you," she said, and he patted the child's head.

"You don't need me anymore," he said, "you'll have teachers who know more. But you know where I am, come see me if you need me to help you." He went out, and Jacques was left alone, lost among the women; then he dashed to the window and looked out at his teacher, who waved at him one last time and who was leaving him alone henceforth, and, instead of the joy of success, a child's immense anguish wrung his heart, as if he knew in advance that this success had just uprooted him from the warm and innocent world of the poor—a world closed in on itself like an island in the society, where poverty took the place of family and community—to be hurtled into a strange world, one no longer his, where he could not believe the teachers were more learned than the one whose heart was all-knowing, and from now on he would have to learn, to understand without help, and become a man without the aid of the one man who had rescued him; would have to grow up and bring himself up alone, and it would be at the highest cost.

7 : *Mondovi: The Settlement*
and the Father

[a]Now he was grown up . . . On the road from Bône to Mondovi the car that J. Cormery was in passed slow-moving jeeps bristling with guns . . .

"M. Veillard?"

"Yes."

Framed in the doorway of his small farmhouse, the man gazing at Jacques Cormery was short but stocky, with rounded shoulders. With his left hand he held the door open, with his right he firmly gripped the jamb, so that while opening the way to his house he was at the same time barring the way. He must have been about forty, judging by the sparse graying hair that gave him a Roman look. But his tanned face with its regular features and bright eyes, his legs in khaki pants, a bit stiff but without fat or belly, his sandals and blue shirt with pockets made him seem much younger. He stood still listening to Jacques's explanation. Then: "Come in," he

---

a. Horse-drawn vehicle train ship plane.

said, and stepped aside. As Jacques went along the small whitewashed hallway, furnished with only a brown chest and a curved wooden umbrella stand, he heard the farmer laugh behind him. "So it's a pilgrimage! Well, frankly, you're just in time."

"Why?" asked Jacques.

"Come into the dining room," the farmer answered. "It's the coolest room."

The dining room was half veranda, with blinds of pliable straw, all but one of them lowered. Except for the table and buffet, both of blond wood and modern in style, the room was furnished with rattan chairs and deck chairs. When he turned around, Jacques saw that he was alone. He went to the veranda, and, through the space between the blinds, he saw a yard planted with ornamental peppertrees among which glittered two bright-red tractors. Beyond that, under a sun that at eleven was still bearable, began the rows of the vineyard. A moment later the farmer returned with a tray on which he had lined up a bottle of anisette, glasses, and a bottle of ice water.

The farmer raised his glass of milky liquid. "If you'd waited any longer, you might have found nothing here. And in any case not a single Frenchman to tell you about it."

"It's the old doctor who told me your farm is the one where I was born."

"Yes, it was part of the Saint-Apôtre property, but my parents bought it after the war." Jacques looked around. "You were certainly not born here," Veillard said. "My parents rebuilt everything."

"Did they know my father before the war?"

"I don't believe so. They had settled right by the Tunisian border, then they wanted to move closer to civilization. For them Solférino was civilization."

"They didn't hear about the former manager?"

"No. Since you're from here, you know how it is. We don't preserve anything here. We tear down and we rebuild. We think about the future and forget the rest."

"Well," said Jacques, "I took your time for nothing."

"No," the other man said, "it's a pleasure." And he smiled at him.

Jacques finished his drink. "Did your parents remain near the border?"

"No, it's the forbidden zone. Near the dam. And it's obvious you don't know my father." He too swallowed the rest of his drink, and, as if he found an extra stimulus in it, he burst out laughing: "He's a real settler. Of the old school. You know, the ones they're bad-mouthing in Paris. And it's true he's always been a hard man. Sixty years old. But long and thin like a puritan with his [horse's] head. A kind of patriarch, you see. He sweated his Arab workers, and, in all fairness, his sons also. Then, last year, when they had to evacuate, it was a real free-for-all. Life in that region had become intolerable. You had to sleep with a gun. When the Raskil farm was attacked, you remember?"

"No," said Jacques.

"Yes, the father and his two sons had their throats cut, the mother and daughter raped over and over, then killed . . . In short . . . The prefect was unfortunate

enough to tell a meeting of farmers that they would
have to reconsider [colonial] issues, how they treated
the Arabs, and that now a new day had come. Then he
had to listen to the old man tell him no one on earth was
going to lay down the law about his property. But from
that day on he didn't open his mouth. Sometimes at
night he would get up and go out. My mother would
watch him through the blinds and she'd see him walking
around his land. When the order to evacuate came, he
said nothing. His grape harvest was over, his wine was
in the vats. He opened the vats, and he went to a spring
of brackish water that he'd diverted long ago, and he
turned it back to run into his fields, and he equipped a
tractor with a trench plow. For three days, at the wheel,
bareheaded, saying not a word, he uprooted the vines
all over his property. Think of it, that skinny old man
bouncing around on his tractor, pushing the accelerator
lever when the plow wasn't getting a vine that was bigger than the others, not stopping even to eat, my mother
bringing him bread, cheese, and [*sobrasada*], which he
ate calmly, the way he had done everything, throwing
away the last chunk of bread and accelerating some
more, all this from sunrise to sunset, without even looking at the mountains on the horizon, nor at the Arabs
who'd soon found out and were watching him from a
distance—they weren't saying anything either. And
when a young captain, informed by who knows who,
arrived and demanded an explanation, he said to him,
'Young man, since what we made here is a crime, it has
to be wiped out.' When it was all finished, he headed toward the farmhouse, crossed the yard that was soaked

with wine pouring out of the vats, and began to pack his bags. The Arab workers were waiting for him in the yard. (There was also a patrol the captain had sent, no one knew just why, with a nice lieutenant who was waiting for orders.)

" 'Boss, what are we going to do?' "

" 'If I were in your shoes,' the old man said, 'I'd go join the guerrillas. They're going to win. There're no men left in France.' "

The farmer laughed: "That was blunt, eh?"

"Are they with you?"

"No, he didn't want to hear a word about Algeria. He's in Marseilles, in a modern apartment . . . *Maman* writes me that he walks around his room in circles."

"And you?"

"Oh, me, I'm staying, and to the end. Whatever happens, I'm staying. I've sent my family to Algiers, and I'll croak here. They don't understand that in Paris. Besides us, you know who're the only ones who can understand it?"

"The Arabs."

"Exactly. We were made to understand each other. Fools and brutes like us, but with the same blood of men. We'll kill each other for a little longer, cut off each other's balls and torture each other a bit. And then we'll go back to living as men together. The country wants it that way. An anisette?"

"Light," said Jacques.

A little later they went out. Jacques had asked if there was anyone left in the area who might have known his parents. No, said Veillard; besides the old doctor who had brought him into the world and who had retired right there in Solférino, there was no one. The Saint-Apôtre property had changed hands twice, many of the Arab workers had died in the two wars, many others had been born. "Everything changes here," Veillard kept saying. "It happens fast, very fast, and people forget." But maybe old Tamzal . . . He was caretaker for one of the Saint-Apôtre farms. In 1913 he must have been around twenty. In any case, Jacques would see the place where he was born.

Except to the north, the country was surrounded by distant mountains, their outlines fuzzy in the noonday heat, like enormous blocks of stone and luminous fog, with the once-swampy Seybouse plain extending between them north to the sea under a sky white with heat, its vineyards in straight lines, the leaves bluish from copper sulfate and the grapes already dark, interrupted occasionally by a row of cypresses or clumps of eucalyptus trees sheltering houses with their shade. They were following a farm path where each of their steps kicked up red dust. Ahead of them, all the way to the mountains, the air was quivering and the sunlight was throbbing. By the time they arrived at a small house behind a cluster of plane trees, they were dripping sweat. An unseen dog greeted them with angry barking.

The mulberry-wood door of the rather dilapidated house was carefully closed. Veillard knocked. The dog barked twice as hard. The sound seemed to come from a small enclosed yard on the other side of the house. But no one stirred. "See how trusting we all are," the farmer said. "They're there. But they're waiting.

"Tamzal!" he shouted. "It's Veillard.

"Six months ago they came to get his son-in-law, they wanted to know if he was supplying the guerrillas. They never heard another word about him. A month ago they told Tamzal that probably he'd been killed trying to escape."

"Ah," said Jacques. "And was he supplying the guerrillas?"

"Maybe yes, maybe not. What can you expect, it's war. But it explains why doors are slow to open in this land of hospitality."

Just then the door opened. Tamzal, small, with [ ]¹ hair, a wide-brimmed straw hat on his head, wearing patched blue overalls, smiled at Veillard, looked at Jacques.

"He's a friend. He was born here."

"Come in," said Tamzal. "You will drink tea."

Tamzal did not remember anything. Yes, perhaps. He had heard one of his uncles talk about a manager who had stayed a few months, it was after the war.

"Before," said Jacques.

Or before, that was possible, he was very young at the time, and what became of his father? He was killed in the war. *"Mektoub,"*² said Tamzal. "But war is bad."

---

1. Two illegible words.
2. In Arabic: "It was written" (in his destiny).

"There's always been war," said Veillard. "But people quickly get accustomed to peace. So they think it's normal. No, war is what's normal."[a]

"Men are crazy in wartime," said Tamzal as he went to take a platter of tea from the hands of a woman in the next room, who had turned her head away. They drank the scorching tea, thanked him, and went back along the stifling hot path through the vineyards.

"I'm going back to Solférino with my taxi," said Jacques. "The doctor invited me for lunch."

"I'm inviting myself along. Wait a moment. I'll get some food."

Later, on the plane taking him back to Algiers, Jacques was trying to sort out the information he had collected. Actually he had only gotten a little, and nothing that directly concerned his father. The night seemed strangely to rise from the earth at an almost measurable speed until at last it swallowed the plane that was pushing straight ahead, steadily, like a screw driven into the thickness of the night. But the night added to Jacques's discomfort, for he felt himself doubly confined, by the plane and by the dark, and he was breathing with difficulty. Again he saw the register of births and the names of the two witnesses, real French names like those [you] see on signs in Paris, and the old doctor, after telling him the story of his father's arrival and his own birth, had said the witnesses were local shopkeepers, the first to happen by, who agreed to do his father a

---

a. to develop

favor; they had names from the outskirts of Paris, yes, but that was no surprise, since Solférino was founded by "forty-eighters."[1]

"Oh yes," Veillard had said, "my great-grandparents were among them. That's why my old man had revolution in his genes." He went on to say that the first of his great-grandparents to come were a carpenter from Faubourg Saint-Denis and a fine-linen laundress. There was a lot of unemployment in Paris, there was unrest, and the Constituent Assembly had voted fifty million francs to send a colony of settlers.[a] They promised everyone a house and 2 to 10 hectares. "You can imagine how they applied. More than a thousand. And all of them dreaming of the Promised Land. Especially the men. The women, they were afraid of the unknown. Not the men! They hadn't made the revolution for nothing. They were the kind who believe in Santa Claus. And their Santa Claus wore a burnoose. Well, they got some kind of Santa Claus. They left in '49, and the first house was built in the summer of '54. Meanwhile . . . "

Jacques was breathing more easily now. The first darkness had finished flowing; it had ebbed like a tide, leaving behind it a cloud of stars, and now the sky was filled with stars. Now only the deafening sound of the motors was oppressing him. He tried to summon the face of the old dealer in carob and fodder who had known his father, who vaguely remembered him, and

---

1. Veterans of the Revolution of 1848—*Trans.*

a. 48 [numerals circled by the author—*Ed.*]

kept repeating: "No talker, he was no talker." But he was stupefied by the noise, it plunged him into a nasty sort of torpor where he tried in vain to evoke his father, to imagine him, but he disappeared behind this immense and hostile land, he melted into the anonymous history of the village and the plain. Details from their conversation at the doctor's came back to him on the same wave as those barges that, according to the doctor, had brought the Parisian settlers to Solférino. On the same wave, and there was no train at the time, no, no—yes, but it only went to Lyon. Then, six barges hauled by draft horses, with the "Marseillaise" and the "Chant du Départ," of course, played by the city's brass band, and the benediction by the clergy on the banks of the Seine with a flag on which was embroidered the name of the village that did not yet exist but which the passengers would create by magic. The barge was already under way, Paris was slipping away, becoming fluid, was going to disappear—may God bless your undertaking—and even the strongest of spirits, the tough ones from the barricades, they fell silent, sick at heart, their frightened wives clinging to their strength, and in the hold they had to sleep on rustling straw with the dirty water at eye level, but first the women undressed behind bedsheets that they held up in turn. Where was his father in all this? Nowhere, and yet those barges hauled a hundred years ago along the canals at the end of autumn, drifting for a month on streams and rivers covered with the last dead leaves, escorted by hazel trees and willows, bare under the gray sky, greeted in the towns by official fanfare and sent on their way with a cargo of new vagrants toward a strange country—they taught him more about the young dead man of Saint-Brieuc than the [senile] and disordered recollections that he had gone to seek. The motors now changed speed. Those dark masses, those sharp-edged dislocated chunks of the night, that was Kabylia, the wild and bloody part of the country—it had long been wild and bloody; that was where they were headed a hundred years ago, the workers of '48 piled up in a paddle-wheeler. "The *Labrador*," said the old doctor, "that was its name; can you imagine that, the *Labrador* to go to the mosquitoes and the sun?" Anyway, the *Labrador* with all its blades paddling, churning the icy water that the mistral was whipping up in a storm, its decks swept for five days and five nights by a polar wind, and the conquerors at the bottom of the hold, deathly ill, vomiting on each other and wanting to die, until they arrived at the port of Bône, with the whole population on the docks to greet the greenish adventurers with music; they had come so far, having left the capital of Europe with their wives and children and possessions to stagger ashore, after five weeks of wandering, on this land with its distant bluish background, where they encountered uneasily its strange odor compounded of fertilizer, spices, and [ ].[1]

Jacques turned in his seat; he was half asleep. He saw his father, whom he had never seen, whose very height he did not know, he saw him on the dock at Bône

---

1. An illegible word.

among the emigrants, while the pulleys hoisted off the poor possessions that had survived the voyage and disputes broke out about those that were lost. He was there, resolute, somber, teeth clenched, and, after all, was this not the same road he had taken from Bône to Solférino, almost forty years earlier, on the wagon, under the same autumn sky? But the road did not exist for the migrants: the women and children piled onto the army's gun carriages, the men on foot, cutting by guesswork across the swampy plain or the spiny brush, under the hostile eyes of occasional groups of Arabs watching them from a distance, accompanied almost constantly by a howling pack of Kabyle dogs, until at the end of the day they reached the same country his father had forty years earlier—flat, surrounded by distant heights, without a dwelling, without a single plot of cultivated land, only a handful of earth-colored military tents on it, nothing but bare empty space; to them it was the end of the world, between the deserted sky and the dangerous land,* and then the women cried into the night, from exhaustion, and fear, and disappointment.

The same arrival by night in a wretched hostile place, the same men, and then, and then . . . Oh! Jacques did not know about his father, but for the rest, that was how it was, they had to pull themselves together in front of the laughing soldiers and settle into their tents. The houses would come later, they would be built and the land would be portioned out, and work, blessed work,

---

* unknown

would save them all. "But they couldn't have it right
away, that work . . . " said Veillard. The rain, the Algerian rain, enormous, brutal, unending, had fallen for
eight days; the Seybouse had overflowed. The water
came up to the tents, and they could not go out,
brother-enemies in the filthy promiscuity of the great
tents resonating under the interminable downpour, and
to escape the stench they cut pieces of hollow reed so
they could urinate from the inside out, and as soon as
the rain stopped, they at last went to work building
flimsy huts under the orders of the carpenter.

"Ah! Those good people," said Veillard, laughing.
"They finished their little shacks in the spring, and then
they were entitled to cholera. If I can believe my old
man, that's how our ancestor the carpenter lost his
daughter and his wife—they were right to be reluctant
about the journey."

"Well yes," said the old doctor, striding up and
down, still erect and proud in his leggings; he could not
sit still. "They died ten a day. The hot season came
early, they were roasting in the huts. And as for hy-
giene . . . In short, ten of them would die a day." His
colleagues in the military were overwhelmed. Peculiar
colleagues, incidentally. They had exhausted all their
remedies. Then they had an idea. You had to dance to
stir up the blood. And every night after work the settlers
would dance between two burials to the sound of a violin. Well, it was not so badly thought out. With the heat
those good people sweated out everything they had, and
the epidemic stopped. "It's an idea to explore." Yes, it
was an idea. In the hot humid night—between the huts

where the sick were sleeping, the violinist sitting on a
crate, a lantern by him with mosquitoes and insects
buzzing around it—the conquerors in long dresses and
wearing sheets would dance, sedately sweating around a
big fire of branches, while at the four corners of the en-
campment sentinels were on watch to defend the besieged people against black-maned lions, cattle thieves,
Arab bands, and sometimes also raids by other French
settlers who were in need of distraction or supplies.
Later on, they finally gave them land, scattered plots far
from the shantytown. Later on, they built the village
with earthen walls. But two-thirds of the emigrants
were dead, there as everywhere in Algeria, without having laid hands on a spade or a plow. The others remained Parisian in the fields, plowing in top hats, gun
on the shoulder, a pipe between their teeth—and only
pipes with covers were allowed, never cigarettes, because of fires—and quinine in their pockets, quinine
sold in the cafés in Bône and in the canteen in Mondovi
as an ordinary drink, to your health, accompanied by
their wives in silk dresses. But always the gun and the
soldiers around, and even to do the laundry in the Seybouse an escort was needed for those who in the old
days would hold a peaceful salon while working at the
washhouse in the rue des Archives; and the village itself
was often attacked at night, as in '51 during one of the
uprisings when hundreds of cavalrymen in burnooses
circling the walls fled seeing the stovepipes the besieged
people aimed at them to simulate cannons, building and
working in an enemy land that refused to be occupied
and took its revenge on whatever it found, and why was

Jacques thinking about his mother while the plane rose and now was coming down? Picturing that wagon bogged down on the road from Bône, where the settlers had left a pregnant woman to go for help and found her with her belly slit and her breasts cut off.

"It was war," said Veillard.

"Let's be fair," added the old doctor. "We shut them up in caves with their whole brood, yes indeed, yes indeed, and they cut the balls off the first Berbers, who themselves . . . and so on all the way back to the first criminal—you know, his name was Cain—and since then it's been war; men are abominable, especially under a ferocious sun."

And after lunch they had walked through the village, similar to hundreds of other villages all over the country, a few hundred small houses in the simple style of the end of the nineteenth century, laid out on several streets that met at right angles where the larger buildings were—the cooperative, the farm bank, the recreation hall—and everything led to the metal-framed bandstand, looking like a carousel or a large Métro entrance, where for years the village men's choir or the military band had given concerts on holidays, while couples in their Sunday best strolled around it, in the heat and the dust, shelling peanuts. Today was also a Sunday, but the army's psychological warfare branch had installed loudspeakers in the bandstand, the crowd was mostly Arab, and they were not strolling around the square; they were standing still and listening to the Arab music that alternated with speeches, and the French people lost in the crowd all had the same look, somber and turned to the future, like those who long ago had come here on the *Labrador*, or those who landed other places in the same circumstances, with the same suffering, fleeing poverty or persecution, finding sorrow and stone. Such were the Spaniards of Mahon, ancestors of Jacques's mother, or those Alsatians who in '71 had rejected German rule and chosen France, and they were given the land of the Arab rebels of '71, who were dead or imprisoned—dissidents taking the places kept warm by insurgents, persecuted-persecutors from whom his father descended, who, forty years later, arrived in this place, with the same somber and determined manner, his thoughts only on the future, like those who have no love for their past and renounce it; an emigrant himself like those who lived and had lived on this land without leaving a trace except on the worn and greened-over slabs in the small settler cemeteries such as the one Jacques had visited with the old doctor at the end of the day after Veillard had left. On one side, hideous new construction in the latest funerary fashion, embellished by the cheap religious art on which contemporary piety is expended. On the other, under the old cypresses, between paths covered with pine needles and cypress cones, or else by damp walls with the oxalis and its yellow flowers growing at their feet, old tombstones, hardly distinguishable from the earth, that had become illegible.

Whole mobs had been coming here for more than a century, had plowed, dug furrows, deeper and deeper in some places, shakier and shakier in others, until the dusty earth covered them over and the place went back to its wild vegetation; and they had procreated, then disappeared. And so it was with their sons. And the sons and grandsons of these found themselves on this land as he himself had, with no past, without ethics, without guidance, without religion, but glad to be so and to be in the light, fearful in the face of night and death. All those generations, all those men come from so many nations, under this magnificent sky where the first portent of twilight was already rising, had disappeared without a trace, locked within themselves. An enormous oblivion spread over them, and actually that was what this land gave out, what fell from the sky with the night over the three men returning to the village, their hearts made anxious by the approach of night, filled with that dread* that seizes all men in Africa when the sudden evening descends on the sea, on the rough mountains and the high plateaus, the same holy dread that has the same effect on the slopes of Delphi's mountain, where it makes temples and altars emerge. But on the land of Africa the temples have been destroyed, and all that is left is this soft unbearable burden on the heart. Yes, how they died! How they were still dying! In silence and away from everything, as his father had died in an incomprehensible tragedy far from his native land, after a life without a single free choice—from the orphanage to the hospital, the inevitable marriage along the way, a life that grew around him, in spite of him; until the war killed and buried him; from then and forever unknown

---

* anxiety

to his people and his son, he too was returned to that immense oblivion that was the ultimate homeland of the men of his people, the final destination of a life that began without roots—and so many reports in the libraries of the time about the use of foundlings for this country's settlement, yes, all these found and lost children who built transient towns in order to die forever in themselves and in others. As if the history of men, that history that kept on plodding across one of its oldest territories while leaving so few traces on it, was evaporating under the constant sun with the memory of those who made it, reduced to paroxysms of violence and murder, to blazes of hatred, to torrents of blood, quickly swollen and quickly dried up, like the seasonal streams of the country. Now the night was rising from the land itself and began to engulf everything, the dead and the living, under the marvelous and ever-present sky. No, he would never know his father, who would continue to sleep over there, his face forever lost in the ashes. There was a mystery about that man, a mystery he had wanted to penetrate. But after all there was only the mystery of poverty that creates beings without names and without a past, that sends them into the vast throng of the nameless dead who made the world while they themselves were destroyed forever. For it was just that that his father had in common with the men of the *Labrador*. The Mahon people of the Sahel, the Alsatians on the high plateaus, with this immense island between sand and sea, which the enormous silence was now beginning to envelop: the silence of anonymity; it enveloped blood and courage and work and instinct, it was at once cruel and compassionate. And he who had wanted to escape from the country without name, from the crowd and from a family without name, but in whom something had gone on craving darkness and anonymity—he too was a member of the tribe, marching blindly into the night near the old doctor who was panting at his right, listening to the gusts of music coming from the square, seeing once more the hard inscrutable faces of the Arabs around the bandstands, Veillard's laughter and his stubborn face—also seeing with a sweetness and a sorrow that wrung his heart the deathly look on his mother's face at the time of the bombing—wandering through the night of the years in the land of oblivion where each one is the first man, where he had to bring himself up, without a father, having never known those moments when a father would call his son, after waiting for him to reach the age of listening, to tell him the family's secret, or a sorrow of long ago, or the experience of his life, those moments when even the ridiculous and hateful Polonius all of a sudden becomes great when he is speaking to Laertes; and he was sixteen, then he was twenty, and no one had spoken to him, and he had to learn by himself, to grow alone, in fortitude, in strength, find his own morality and truth, at last to be born as a man and then to be born in a harder childbirth, which consists of being born in relation to others, to women, like all the men born in this country who, one by one, try to learn to live without roots and without faith, and today all of them are threatened with eternal anonymity and the loss of the only consecrated traces of their passage on this earth, the illegible slabs in the cemetery that the night has now covered over; they had to learn how to live in relation to others, to the immense host of the conquerors, now dispossessed, who had preceded them on this land and in whom they now had to recognize the brotherhood of race and destiny.

Now the plane was descending to Algiers. Jacques was thinking about the little cemetery of Saint-Brieuc where the soldiers' graves were better kept than those in Mondovi.* The Mediterranean separates two worlds in me, one where memories and names are preserved in measured spaces, the other where the wind and sand erases all trace of men on the open ranges. He had tried to escape from anonymity, from a life that was poor, ignorant, and mulish; he could not live that life of blind patience, without words, with no thought beyond the present. He had traveled far and wide, had built, had created, had loved people and abandoned them, his days had been full to overflowing. And yet now he knew from the bottom of his heart that Saint-Brieuc and what it represented had never been anything to him, and he thought of the worn and green-encrusted gravestones he had just left, acknowledging with a strange sort of pleasure that death would return him to his true homeland and, with its immense oblivion, would obliterate the memory of that alien and ordinary man who had

* Algiers

grown up, had built in poverty, without help or deliverance, on a fortunate shore and in the light of the first mornings of the world, and then alone, without memories and without faith, he had entered the world of the men of his time and its dreadful and exalted history.

PART TWO

The Son or The First Man

1 : *Lycée*

^aWhen, on October 1st of that year, Jacques Cor-
mery^b—unsteady on his thick new shoes, bundled up in
a new shirt that still had its stiffening in it, weighed
down with a satchel that smelled of varnish and
leather—saw the motorman, next to whom Pierre and
he were standing at the front of the motorcar, pull his
crank back to first gear and the heavy vehicle leave the
Belcourt stop, he turned back to try to catch a glimpse
of, a few meters away, his mother and grandmother still
leaning out the window to keep him company for a bit
longer on this first journey to the mysterious *lycée*, but
he could not see them because the man next to him was
reading the inside pages of *La Dépêche Algérienne*. So he
turned to the front and gazed at the steel rails that the

---

a. Begin either by going to school and the rest in order, or else
by introducing the adult alien and then return to the period from
going to school to the illness.

b. physical description of the child.

motorcar was steadily swallowing and above them the trolley wires vibrating in the cool of the morning, turning his back, his heart somewhat heavy, on his home, on the old neighborhood that he had never really left except for a few expeditions (they said "go to Algiers" when they went downtown), traveling faster and faster now and, despite Pierre's brotherly shoulder practically glued to his, with a sense of solitude, uneasy about a strange world where he did not know how he would have to behave.

Actually no one could have given them advice. Pierre and he realized very soon that they were on their own. M. Bernard himself, whom they in any case would not dare disturb, could tell them nothing about this *lycée* he did not know. At home ignorance was still more complete. For Jacques's family, Latin, for example, was a word that had absolutely no meaning. That there had been (besides primitive times, which they on the other hand could imagine) times when no one spoke French, that civilizations (and the word itself meant nothing to them) had succeeded each other with such different customs and languages—these truths had not reached them. Neither the images, nor things written, nor word of mouth, nor the veneer of culture acquired in everyday conversation had reached them. In this home where there were no newspapers, nor, until Jacques brought them in, any books, no radio either, where there were only objects of immediate utility, where no one but relatives visited, a home they rarely left and then only to meet other members of the same ignorant family—what Jacques brought home from the *lycée* could not be assimilated, and the silence grew between him and his family. At the *lycée* itself, he could not speak of his family; he sensed their peculiarity without being able to articulate it, even if he could have overcome the insuperable reticence that sealed his lips on the subject.

It was not even differences of class that set them apart. In this country of immigration, of quick fortunes and spectacular collapses, the boundaries between classes were less clear-cut than between races. If the children had been Arab, their feeling would have been more painful and bitter. Besides, though they had Arab classmates in school, there were few in the *lycée*, and they were always sons of wealthy notables. No, what set them apart, and Jacques even more than Pierre, because their peculiarity was more pronounced in his home than in Pierre's family, was that it was impossible for him to connect his family to traditional values and stereotypes. To the questions asked at the beginning of the year, he could of course answer that his father was killed in the war, that after all was a position in society, and that he was a "pupil of the nation,"[1] which everyone understood. But after that the difficulties began. In the printed forms they were given, he did not know what to put under "parents' occupation." At first he put "homemaker" while Pierre put "post office employee." Pierre explained to him that homemaker was not an occupation but was said of a woman who kept her own home and did her own housework.

---

1. Children of men killed in the war, who were entitled to a small stipend for school supplies—*Trans.*

"No," said Jacques, "she takes care of other people's houses, especially the shopkeeper across the street."

"Well," Pierre said hesitantly, "I think you have to put down 'domestic.' "

That idea had never occurred to Jacques, for the simple reason that this all-too-rare word was never spoken in his home—and this for the reason that no one there had the feeling that she was working for others; she was working first of all for her children. Jacques started to write the word, stopped, and all at once he knew shame and all at once[1] the shame of having been ashamed.

A child is nothing by himself; it is his parents who represent him. It is through them that he defines himself, that he is defined in the eyes of the world. He feels it is through them that he is truly judged—judged, that is, without right of appeal, and this judgment by the world was what he had just discovered, and, with it, his own judgment on the hard heart that was his. He could not know that once become a man, one is less deserving for not recognizing these evil feelings. For one is judged, for better or for worse, by what one is and much less on one's family, since it even happens that the family is judged in its turn by the child become a man. But it would have taken a heart of rare and heroic pureness for Jacques not to suffer from the discovery he had just made, just as it would have taken an impossible humility for him not to react with anger and shame to what his suffering had revealed to him about his own nature. He

---

1. *sic*

had none of those qualities; instead there was a hard and nasty arrogance that helped him at least on this occasion, making him write the word "domestic" on the form with a firm hand and take it, his face expressionless, to the monitor, who did not even notice it. Along with all that, Jacques had not the slightest desire to have a different family or station in life, and his mother as she was remained what he loved most in the world, even if that love was hopeless. Besides, how can it be made clear that a poor child can sometimes be ashamed without ever being envious?

On another occasion, when he was asked his religion, he answered: "Catholic." Asked if he should be enrolled in the course in religious instruction, and remembering his grandmother's fears, he said no. "In short," the monitor said deadpan, "you are a non-practicing Catholic." Jacques could explain nothing of what went on in his home, nor could he say the bizarre way his people dealt with religion. So he firmly answered, "Yes," which made people laugh and won him a reputation for stubbornness at the very moment he felt himself most at sea.

Another day, the literature teacher, having handed out to the students a form concerning some internal matter, asked them to bring it back signed by their parents. The form, which enumerated the things students were forbidden to bring to school, from weapons to magazines and including playing cards, was written in such choice language that Jacques had to summarize it in simple terms for his mother and grandmother. His mother was the only one able to put a crude signature at the bottom of the form.[a] Because, after her husband's death, she received* her war widow's pension every quarter, and because the government, in this case the Treasury—but Catherine Cormery just said she was going to the treasure, for to her it was just a name, void of any meaning; to the children, on the other hand, it suggested a mythic place with limitless resources where their mother was admitted from time to time to draw small amounts of money—asked for her signature each time, after the first time when she had problems, a neighbor (?) had taught her to copy a sample of the signature "Widow Camus,"[1] and she managed to do this more or less well, but anyway it was always accepted. However, the next morning Jacques discovered that his mother, who left long before him to clean a store that opened early, had forgotten to sign the form. His grandmother did not know how to sign. She managed to keep her accounts with a system of circles that, according to whether they were crossed once or twice, represented ones, tens, and hundreds. Jacques had to return the form unsigned, saying that his mother had forgotten, was asked if no one in his home could sign, answered no, and discovered from the teacher's surprised look that this circumstance was more unusual than he had believed.

He was even more disconcerted by the French boys

---

a. the reminder.

* collect

1. *sic*

brought to Algiers by the vagaries of their father's ca-
reers. The one who gave him the most to think about
was Georges Didier;[a] their common liking for French
classes and reading drew them into a very close friendship, of which Pierre moreover was jealous. Didier was
the son of a very devout Catholic. His mother "made
music," his sister (whom Jacques never saw, but he
dreamed delightfully about her) did embroidery, and
Didier, according to what he said, intended to enter the
priesthood. Extremely intelligent, he was uncompro-
mising on questions of faith and of morals, where his
convictions were dogmatic. He was never heard to utter
a dirty word, nor to refer, as other children did with
endless self-satisfaction, to the body's natural functions
or to those of reproduction, which in any case were not
as clear in their minds as they liked to say. The first
thing he sought from Jacques, once their friendship was
established, was that he give up dirty words. Jacques
had no difficulty giving them up with him. But with
others those words would easily slip back into his conversation. (Already taking shape in him was the many-
faceted nature that would make so many things easy for
him, would make him adept at talking anyone's language, at getting along in any surroundings, at playing
any role, except . . .) With Didier, Jacques understood
what it was to be a middle-class French family. His
friend had a family home in France where he went on
vacations; he was forever talking or writing to Jacques

---

a. come back to him at his death.

about it, that house with an attic full of old trunks, where they saved the family's letters, souvenirs, photos. He knew the history of his grandparents and his great-grandparents, also an ancestor who was a sailor at Trafalgar, and this long history, vivid in his imagination, also provided him with examples and precepts for everyday behavior. "My grandfather would say . . . Papa thinks that . . . " and in that way he would justify his sternness, his imperious purity. When he spoke of France, he would say "our country" and he accepted in advance the sacrifices that country might demand ("your father died for our country," he would say to Jacques . . .), whereas this notion of country had no meaning to Jacques, who knew he was French, and that this entailed a certain number of duties, but for whom France was an abstraction that people called upon and that sometimes laid claim to you, a bit like that God he had heard about outside his home, who evidently was the sovereign dispenser of good things and bad, who could not be influenced, but who on the other hand could do anything with the people's destiny. And this impression of his was even stronger among the women who lived with him. "*Maman*, what is our country?"[a] he asked one day.

She looked frightened as she did each time she did not understand. "I don't know," she said. "No."

"It's France."

"Oh, yes." And she seemed relieved.

---

a. discovery of the Fatherland in 1940.

Whereas Didier did know what it was; the family through its generations was a potent presence to him, and the country where he was born through its history—he called Joan of Arc by her first name—and so were good and evil defined for him as was his present and future destiny. Jacques, and Pierre also, though to a lesser degree, felt themselves to be of another species, with no past, no family home, no attic full of letters and photos, citizens in theory of a nebulous nation where snow covered the roofs while they themselves grew up under an eternal and savage sun, equipped with a most elementary morality that, for example, forbade them to steal, enjoined them to protect their mothers and women, but was silent on a great number of questions concerning women, and relations with their superiors . . . (etc.)—children, in short, unknown to and ignorant of God, unable to imagine a future life when this life seemed so inexhaustible each day under the protection of the indifferent deities of sun, of sea, or of poverty. And in truth, if Jacques was so devoted to Didier, no doubt it was because of the boy's heart that was so smitten with the absolute, so utterly loyal to his passions (the first time Jacques heard the word "loyalty," which he had read a hundred times, was from Didier) and capable of a charming tenderness, but it was also because he was so different, in Jacques's eyes, his charm being truly exotic, and attracting him all the more, just as Jacques later on, when he was grown, would feel himself irresistibly drawn to foreign women. The child of the family, of tradition, and of religion had the allure for Jacques of some tanned adventurers who return from the tropics guarding a strange and incomprehensible secret.

But the Kabyle shepherd who, on his mountain that the sun has scaled and eroded, watches the storks go by while dreaming of the North from which they came after a long voyage—he may dream all day long, in the evening he still goes back to the dish of mastic leaves, to the family in long robes, to the wretched hut where he has his roots. In the same way, while Jacques might be intoxicated with the foreign potions of bourgeois (?) tradition, he remained devoted to the one who was most like him, and that was Pierre. Every morning at quarter after six (except Sunday and Thursday), Jacques would go down the stairs of his building four at a time, running in the mugginess of the hot season or the violent rain of winter that made his short cape swell up like a sponge; then at the fountain he would turn in to Pierre's street, and, still on the run, climb the two stories to knock softly at the door. Pierre's mother, a handsome woman with an ample build, would open the door that led directly to the sparsely furnished dining room. At the other end of the dining room a door on either side led to a bedroom. One was Pierre's, which he shared with his mother, the other was his two uncles', rough railroad men who smiled a lot and said little. As you entered the dining room, to the right was a room without air or light that served as both kitchen and bathroom. Pierre was chronically late. He would be sitting at the table with its oilcloth cover, the kerosene lamp lit if it was winter, holding a big brown bowl of glazed clay in both hands, and trying to swallow the scorching coffee

his mother had just poured him without burning himself. "Blow on it," she would say. He blew on it, he
sucked it in and smacked his lips, and Jacques shifted his
weight from foot to foot while he watched him.[a] When
Pierre had finished, he still had to go to the candlelit
kitchen, where, at the zinc sink, a glass of water awaited
him and, lying across it, a toothbrush spread with a
thick ribbon of a special kind of toothpaste, for he suffered from pyorrhea. He slipped on his short cape, his
cap, and his satchel, and, all rigged out, gave his teeth a
long and vigorous brushing, then spat loudly in the
sink. The pharmaceutical odor of the toothpaste mingled with the smell of the coffee. Jacques, a bit disgusted
and at the same time impatient, would let that be
known, and it was not unusual for this to result in one of
those sulks that are the cement of a friendship. Then
they would go down the stairs to the street in silence
and walk unsmiling to the trolley stop. But other times
they would chase each other, laughing, or while running they would pass one of the satchels back and forth
like a rugby ball. At the stop they waited, watching for
the red trolley to see with which of two or three motormen they were going to ride.

For they always scorned the two trailer cars and
climbed up into the motorcar to work their way to the
front, with difficulty, since the trolley was packed with
workers going downtown and their satchels hindered
their progress. At the front, they took advantage of each

---

a. schoolboy's cap.

departing passenger to press closer to the motorman's iron and glass cab and the high narrow controller, on the flat top of which a gearshift handle moved around a circle with a big steel notch to mark neutral, three other marks for the forward gears, and a fifth for reverse. Only the motormen had the right to work the gearshift, and they enjoyed the prestige of demigods in the eyes of the children, who were forbidden by a sign overhead to speak to them. They wore an almost military uniform, with a cap with molded leather visor, except the Arab drivers, who wore a tarboosh. The children told them apart by their appearance. There was the "nice little young one," who looked like a leading man and had thin shoulders; the "brown bear," a big sturdy Arab with thick features who always stared straight ahead; the "friend of the animals," an old Italian with clear eyes in a drab face, all bent over his gearshift, who owed his nickname to the fact that he once almost stopped his trolley to avoid hitting an absentminded dog and another time to avoid a dog that was nonchalantly relieving himself between the rails; and "Zorro," a tall fellow with the face and small moustache of Douglas Fairbanks.[a] The friend of the animals was dear to the children's hearts. But they ardently admired the brown bear; imperturbable, solidly fixed on his legs, he would drive his noisy vehicle at top speed, holding the wooden handle firmly in his enormous left hand and pushing it into third gear as soon as traffic permitted, his right hand

---

a. The cord and the bell.

vigilant on the big brake wheel to the right of the gear-box, ready to give the wheel a few vigorous turns while he moved his gearshift to neutral, and then the motorcar would skid heavily on the rails. It was with the brown bear that, on curves or switches, the trolley pole attached with a spiral spring to the roof of the motorcar was most likely to leave the electric wire overhead, which it was fitted to by a small wheel with a hollow rim, and then stand straight up with a great racket of vibrating wires and flying sparks. The conductor would jump down from the motorcar, seize the long trolley-catcher wire, attached to the end of the pole that was automatically unrolled from a cast-iron box at the back of the vehicle, and, pulling with all his strength to overcome the resistance of the steel spring, would bring the trolley pole back and, letting it up slowly, try to insert the wire once more into the hollow rim of the wheel, all in the midst of flaring sparks. Leaning out of the motor-car, or, if it was winter, with their noses pressed against the windows, the children followed the action, and when it was crowned with success, they would announce it in a stage whisper to inform the motorman without committing the infraction of speaking directly to him. But the brown bear was unmoved: he waited, according to regulation, until the conductor gave him the departure signal by pulling on the cord that hung at the back of the motorcar and activated a bell at the front. He would then set the trolley in motion again, without further precaution. Clustered together in front, the children would watch the metallic tracks race past under and over them, on a rainy or sparkling morning, rejoicing when the trolley, going full speed, would pass a horse-drawn cart or for a time would keep pace with a wheezing automobile. At each stop the trolley would unload part of its cargo of Arab and French workmen, take on a clientele that got better dressed the closer they were to downtown, then start off again at the clang of the bell and so would travel from one end to the other of the arc along which the city lay, until the moment when they suddenly emerged at the port before the immense space of the bay that stretched out to the big blue mountains at the end of the horizon. Three stops more and it was the end of the line, the place du Gouvernement, where the children got off. This square, bordered on three sides by trees and buildings with arcades, opened out to the white mosque and, beyond it, the expanse of the port. In its center stood the statue of the Duke of Orléans on a prancing horse, all verdigris under the dazzling sky; but in bad weather the bronze turned black and dripped rainwater (and they told the inevitable story that the sculptor committed suicide, having forgotten to put a curb chain on the harness), while from the horse's tail water trickled endlessly into the little garden protected by the railing that framed the monument. The rest of the square was surfaced with small shiny paving stones, which the children, jumping off the trolley, would fling themselves across, in long skids, toward the rue Bab-Azoun that brought them to the *lycée* in five minutes.

Bab-Azoun was a narrow street made still more narrow by the arcades on both sides that stood on enormous square pillars, leaving just enough room for the trolley tracks, used by another company, that connected this area to the higher districts of the city. On hot days the thick blue sky lay over the street like a steaming lid, and the shade was cool under the arcades. On rainy days the whole street was nothing but a deep trench of wet shiny stone. Under the arcades were rows of shops: wholesale textile dealers, their façades painted in dark colors, piles of light-colored cloth glowing softly in the shade; groceries that smelled of clove and coffee; small shops where Arab tradesmen sold pastries dripping with oil and honey; dark deep-set cafés where the coffeemakers were percolating at that time of day (whereas in the evening, lit up by glaring lamps, they were full of noise and voices, a crowd of men trampling the sawdust on the floor, pushing up to the bar where there were glasses of opalescent liquid and little saucersful of lupines, anchovies, cut-up celery, olives, fries, and peanuts); and, finally, bazaars for tourists where they sold hideous Eastern glass trinkets, displayed in windows framed by postcards in rotating racks, and Moorish scarves in garish colors.

One of these bazaars, in the middle of the arcades, was run by a fat man who was always sitting behind his windows, in the shade or under an electric light; he was huge and pale, with bulging eyes, like those creatures you find by lifting stones or in old tree trunks, and, above all, he was absolutely bald. Because of this feature the *lycée* students nicknamed him "the flies' skating rink" and "the mosquitoes' bicycle racetrack," and they would claim that when the insects traveled across the bare surface of that skull, they would miss the turn and be unable to keep their balance. Often in the evening the children would dash by his shop like a flight of starlings, shouting the unfortunate man's nicknames and imitating the flies' supposed skids with a sound of "zzzzz." The fat shopkeeper cursed them; once or twice he was presumptuous enough to try to chase them, but had to give it up. Then all at once he remained silent before the volley of shouts and scoffing, and for several evenings he let the children grow bolder, until they came right up and yelled in his face. And suddenly, one evening, some young Arabs, paid by the shopkeeper, emerged from behind the pillars where they had been hiding and set out in pursuit of the children. That evening Jacques and Pierre escaped punishment only because of their exceptional speed. Jacques took a single blow on the back of his head, then, once recovered from his surprise, was able to outrun his adversary. But two or three of their schoolmates took a severe beating. The students plotted to sack the shop and physically destroy its owner, but the fact is they never acted on their dark plans; they stopped persecuting their victim, and they adopted the habit of passing by angelically on the other side of the street.

"We chickened out," Jacques said bitterly.

"After all," Pierre answered, "we were in the wrong."

"We were in the wrong and we were afraid of being beaten up."

Later on, he would remember that incident when he came (truly) to understand that men pretend to abide

by what is right and never yield except to force.[a] Halfway up the rue Bab-Azoun the street widened and on
one side the arcade gave way to the church of Sainte-
Victoire. This little church occupied the site of a vanished mosque. A kind of offertory (?), always full of
flowers, had been carved in its whitewashed façade.
Flower sellers had set up on the open sidewalk and were
already displaying their wares by the time the children
passed by; they offered enormous bunches of iris, carna-
tions, roses, or anemones, according to the season, set in
tall tin cans, the rims always rusted by the water that
was always being sprinkled on the flowers. On the same
side of the street there was also a little shop selling Arab
fritters; it was really a nook that would hardly hold
three men. A fireplace had been dug out at one side of
this nook. Its sides were lined with blue-and-white
earthenware, and a huge basin of boiling oil was bub-
bling on its surface. A strange person sat cross-legged in
front of the fireplace. He wore Arab pantaloons, his
chest was half naked during the summer and in the heat
of the day; on other days he wore a European jacket
closed at the top of the lapel with a safety pin; and with
his shaved head, thin face, and toothless mouth he
looked like a Gandhi without glasses. With a red
enamel skimmer in his hand, he watched over the cooking of the fritters browning in the oil. When a fritter
was ready—that is, when the outside was golden while

a. himself like the rest.

the very fine dough inside had become both translucent and crisp (like a transparent fried potato)—he would carefully reach under the fritter with his ladle and lift it deftly out of the oil, drain it over the basin by shaking the ladle three or four times, then put it in front of him in a glassed-in stand with several perforated shelves on which already prepared fritters were lined up, on one side the long honey fritters, on the other, flat and round, the plain fritters.[a] Pierre and Jacques were mad about these pastries, and on those rare occasions when one or the other had a bit of money, they took a moment to stop and get a plain fritter on a piece of paper immediately made transparent by the oil, or the long fritter that the seller before giving it to them had dipped in a nearby jar, alongside the stove, full of dark honey speckled with fritter crumbs. The children would take these splendid things and bite into them as they ran to the *lycée,* head and shoulders bent over to avoid dirtying their clothes.

The departure of the swallows took place each year, soon after the opening of school, in front of the church of Sainte-Victoire. Electrical wires and even high-power lines, used at one time to drive the trolleys, now abandoned but never taken down, stretched over the street where it had been widened. The swallows[b] usually flew over the waterfront boulevards, on the square in front of the *lycée,* or in the sky over the poor neigh-

---

a. Zlabias, Makroud.
b. See the sparrows of Algeria mentioned by Grenier.

borhoods, sometimes picking with piercing cries at a ficus fruit, some floating garbage, or fresh manure; but at the first cold weather—only relatively cold since there was never a frost; still you could feel it after the enormous weight of the hot months—the swallows would appear one by one in the corridor of rue Bab-Azoun, flying low toward a trolley, then abruptly veering up to disappear in the sky over the houses. Suddenly one morning they appeared by the thousands on all the lines over the little square at Sainte-Victoire, on top of the houses, squeezed in next to each other, nodding their heads over their little black-and-white necks, shaking their tails and moving their feet a bit to make room for a newcomer, covering the sidewalk with their tiny ashlike droppings, all together making what was a single constant chirp, punctuated with brief cackles, a continuing confidential dialogue that had been going on above the street all morning, and would get gradually louder and become almost deafening by evening, when the children were running to the homeward-bound trolleys; then the chirp would stop suddenly, on an invisible command, and thousands of sleeping birds would bow their little heads and their black-and-white tails. For two or three days, coming from every corner of the Sahel, and sometimes even farther, they would arrive in feathery little bands, trying to find room between the first arrivals, and, little by little, they would settle on all the cornices along the street on both sides of the main place of assembly, the sound of their wings beating and their chirping over the passersby growing louder and louder until it became deafening. And then one morning, just as abruptly, the street was empty. In the night, just before dawn, the birds had left all together for the South. For the children that was when winter began, well before its date, since they had never known a summer without the shriek of the swallows in the still warm sky of evening.

The rue Bab-Azoun ended at a big square where the *lycée*, on the left, faced the barracks on the right. The steep damp streets of the Arab city began their uphill climb behind the *lycée*. The barracks faced away from the sea. Beyond the *lycée* was the Marengo gardens; beyond the barracks, the poor, half-Spanish Bab-el-Oued district. A few minutes past quarter after seven, Pierre and Jacques, having climbed the stairs at full speed, would enter with a flood of children through the concierge's small entrance next to the monumental door. They started up the main stairs, with the honor rolls posted on either side, still running at top speed, and arrived at the main floor, where the stairs to the upper floors began on the left; it was separated from the main courtyard by a glassed-in arcade. There, behind one of the main floor columns, they spotted the Rhinoceros watching for latecomers. (The Rhinoceros was a chief supervisor, a small nervous Corsican who owed his nickname to his curled moustache.) Another life began.

Pierre and Jacques had received scholarships that included half-board because of their "family situation." So they spent all day at the *lycée* and had their lunch in the dining hall. Classes began at eight or nine o'clock, according to the day, but breakfast for the boarding students was served at 7:15, and the half-boarders were entitled to it. The families of the two children could not imagine that anyone would give up anything to which he was entitled, they who were entitled to so little; thus Jacques and Pierre were among the few half-boarders to arrive at 7:15 in the big white circular dining hall, where sleepy boarding students were already seating themselves at long zinc-covered tables, before big bowls and huge baskets with thick slices of dry bread, while the waiters swaddled in long aprons made of crude canvas, most of whom were Arab, went along the rows carrying big coffeepots with curved spouts that had once been shiny, and poured into the bowls a boiling liquid that contained more chicory than coffee. Having used their prerogative, the children could go a quarter of an hour later to the study hall, where, presided over by a monitor who was himself a boarding student, they could review their homework before classes began.

The great difference here from the neighborhood school was the number of teachers. M. Bernard knew everything and taught everything he knew in the same way. At the *lycée,* the teacher changed with the subject, and the method changed with the man.[a] Now you could compare; you had to choose, that is, between those you liked and those you did not. From this point of view a teacher in the school is more like a father: he takes over his role almost entirely; he is as inevitable and he is part of what is necessary in your life. So the question of lov-

---

a. M. Bernard was loved and admired. At best the *lycée* teacher could only be admired and you did not dare love him.

ing or not loving him does not really arise. Usually you love him because you are absolutely dependent on him. But if it happens that the child likes him little or not at all, dependence and necessity remain, and that is not far from resembling love. At the *lycée,* on the other hand, the teachers were like those uncles you are entitled to choose among. That is, you could dislike them, and so there was a certain physics teacher, who was very elegant in his attire, authoritarian and crude in his speech, whom neither Jacques nor Pierre could stomach, though they had him two or three times over the years. The literature teacher, whom the children saw more often than the others, was the one they would have been most likely to love, and in fact Jacques and Pierre clung to him in almost all those classes[a] without however being able to depend on him, since he knew nothing about them and since, once class was over, he went off to a different life and so did they, leaving for that distant neighborhood where there was no possibility a *lycée* teacher would settle, so different that they never met anyone, neither teachers nor students, on their trolley line—only red cars served the lower districts (the C.F.R.A.), while the upper sections, reputed to be more elegant, were served by a line with green cars, the T.A. Furthermore, the T.A. went right to the *lycée,* whereas the C.F.R.A. line ended at the place du Gouvernement, you [ ][1] the *lycée* from below. So it was that when their

---

a. say which? and develop?

1. An illegible word.

day was over, the children felt their separateness at the very door to the *lycée*, or only a bit farther, at the place du Gouvernement, when, leaving the merry group of their schoolmates, they headed toward the red trolleys that went to the poorest neighborhoods. And it was just their separateness they felt, not inferiority. They were from somewhere else, that was all.

During the school day, on the other hand, there was no such difference. Their smocks might be more or less elegant, they all looked alike. The only rivalries were those of intelligence in class and physical agility in sports. In these two sorts of competitions, the two children were far from being the last. The solid instruction they had received in the neighborhood school had given them an advantage that, from the first year, put them in the top group of the class. Their sure spelling, their reliable arithmetic, their trained memory, and most of all the respect[ ][1] inculcated in them for all kinds of knowledge were major assets, at least at the beginning of their studies. If Jacques had not been so rambunctious, which repeatedly kept him off the honor roll, and if Pierre had taken more to Latin, their success would have been complete. At any rate, they were encouraged by their teachers and they were respected. As for sports, it was above all soccer, and from the first recesses Jacques found what would be his love for so many years. Their matches were played during the recess after lunch at the dining hall and the one-hour recess that, for boarders

---

1. An illegible word.

and half-boarders and day students in detention, came before the last class at four o'clock. An hour recess at that time gave the children the opportunity to eat their snack and relax before the two-hour study hall, when they could do their homework for the following day.[a] For Jacques a snack was out of the question. Obsessed with soccer, he would dash out to the cement courtyard, which was surrounded on its four sides by arcades supported by thick pillars (under which the studious and well-behaved boys strolled and chatted), with four or five green benches at its sides, and big ficus trees protected by an iron railing. Two teams took their sides of the yard, the goalies assumed their positions between the pillars at each end, and a big foam-rubber ball was placed at the center. No referee, and at the first kick the shouting and sprinting began. It was on this field that Jacques, who already could meet the best students in the class on equal terms, made himself respected and liked also by the worst, some of whom fate had endowed, for want of a strong mind, with sturdy legs and inexhaustible lungs. This was where for the first time he parted company with Pierre, who did not play, though he was naturally well coordinated; he had become more frail, growing faster than Jacques, and becoming more blond, as if being transplanted had not worked as well with him.[b] Jacques's growth was delayed, which earned him the delightful nicknames "shrimp" and "short-ass," but

a. the yard less crowded because the day students were gone.
b. to develop.

he paid no attention, and running madly, dribbling the ball between his feet, dodging first a tree and then an opponent, he felt himself king of the field and king of the world. When the drum sounded the end of recess and the beginning of study hall, he really fell from the sky, stopped short on the cement, panting and sweating, furious that the hours were so short; then bit by bit he returned to the present, hurried to line up with the others, mopped the sweat off his face with both his sleeves—and suddenly took fright at the thought of the wear on the studs in the soles of his shoes, which he anxiously examined at the beginning of study hall, trying to evaluate the difference in their shininess from the previous day, and was reassured by the very difficulty he had in discerning how worn they were. Except when some irreparable damage—a detached sole, or torn upper, or twisted heel—left no doubt as to how he would be received when he went home, and then he would swallow his saliva, his stomach queasy, during the two hours of the study hall, trying to redeem his sin by devoting himself more strenuously to his work, from which however, and despite his best efforts, he was inevitably distracted by the fear of being beaten. This last study hall was also the one that seemed the longest. To begin with, it lasted two hours. And besides it took place at night or when night was falling. The high windows looked out on the Marengo gardens. The students around Jacques and Pierre, sitting side by side, were quieter than usual, tired from work and play, absorbed in their last assignments. Especially at the end of the year, night would fall on the big trees, the flower beds, and the clusters of banana trees in the park. The sky became greener and greener; it seemed to swell as the sounds of the city grew fainter and more distant. When it was very hot and one of the windows was half open, they heard the cries of the last swallows over the little garden, and the scent of seringas and of the big magnolias came in to drown the more acid and bitter smells of ink and ruler. Jacques would daydream, his heart strangely heavy, until he was called to order by the young monitor, who was himself doing his assignments for the University. They had to wait for the last drum.

[a]At seven o'clock came the rush out of the *lycée;* they ran in noisy groups the length of the rue Bab-Azoun, where all the stores were lit up and the sidewalk under the arcades was so crowded that sometimes they had to run in the street itself, between the rails, until a trolley came in sight and they had to dash back under the arcades; then at last the place du Gouvernement opened up before them, its periphery illuminated by the stalls and stands of the Arab peddlers lit by acetylene lamps giving off a smell the children inhaled with delight. The red trolleys were waiting, already jammed—whereas in the morning there were fewer passengers—and sometimes they had to stand on the running board of a trailer car, which was both forbidden and tolerated, until some passengers got off at a stop, and then the two boys would press into the human mass, separated, unable in any case to talk to each other, and

---

a. the homosexual's assault.

could only work their way slowly with elbows and bodies to get to one of the railings where they could see the dark port with its big steamers outlined by lights that seemed, in the night of the sea and the sky, like skeletons of burned-out buildings where the fire had left its embers. The big brightly lit trolleys rode with a great racket over the water, then forged a bit inland and passed between poorer and poorer houses to the Belcourt district, where the children had to part company and Jacques climbed the never lighted stairs toward the circle of the kerosene lamp that lit the oilcloth table cover and the chairs around the table, leaving in the shadow the rest of the room, where Catherine Cormery was occupied at the buffet preparing to set the table, while his grandmother was in the kitchen reheating the stew from lunch and his older brother was at the corner of the table reading an adventure novel. Sometimes he had to go to the Mzabite grocer for the salt or quarter-pound of butter needed at the last minute, or go get Uncle Ernest, who was holding forth at Gaby's café. Dinner was at eight, in silence unless Uncle Ernest recounted an incomprehensible adventure that sent him into gales of laughter, but in any event there was no mention of the *lycée*, except if his grandmother would ask if he had gotten good grades, and he said yes and no one said any more about it, and his mother asked him nothing, shaking her head and gazing at him with her gentle eyes when he confessed to good grades, but always silent and a bit distracted; "Sit still," she would say to her mother, "I'll get the cheese," then nothing till the meal was over, when she stood up to clear the table.

"Help your mother," his grandmother would say, because he had picked up *Pardaillan* and was avidly reading it. He helped out and came back to the lamp, putting the big volume that told of duels and courage on the slick bare surface of the oilcloth, while his mother, pulling a chair away from the lamplight, would seat herself by the window in winter, or in summer on the balcony, and watch the traffic of trolleys, cars, and passersby as it gradually diminished.[a] It was, again, his grandmother who told Jacques he had to go to bed because he would get up at five-thirty the next morning, and he kissed her first, then his uncle, and last his mother, who gave him a tender, absentminded kiss, then assumed once more her motionless position, in the shadowy half-light, her gaze lost in the street and the current of life that flowed endlessly below the riverbank where she sat, endlessly, while her son, endlessly, watched her in the shadows with a lump in his throat, staring at her thin bent back, filled with an obscure anxiety in the presence of adversity he could not understand.

---

a. Lucien—14 EPS—16 Insurance.

The Chicken Coop and
Cutting the Hen's Throat

That dread of death and the unknown, which he always felt when coming home from the *lycée,* was already taking hold of him at the end of the day, as fast as the darkness that rapidly devoured the light and the earth, and would not cease until his grandmother lit the suspension lamp, setting the glass chimney down on the oilcloth, her [stance] up a bit on the balls of her feet, her thighs pressed against the edge of the table, her body leaning forward, her head twisted so she could better see the burner of the lamp under the shade, one hand holding the copper key that regulated the wick under the lamp, the other scraping the wick with a lit match until it stopped smoldering and gave a beautiful clear light; and then the grandmother would replace the chimney, which would squeak a little against the chiseled tabs of the copper gallery into which she pressed it, and, again standing erect at the table, one arm raised, she adjusted the wick until the hot yellow light was cast evenly on the table in a large and perfect circle, and, as if reflected by the oilcloth, it lit with a gentler glow the faces of the woman and the child who was watching the ritual from the other side of the table—and his heart gradually grew easy as the light grew brighter.

It was the same dread he tried sometimes to overcome out of pride or vanity when his grandmother would on certain occasions order him to go get a hen from the yard. It was always in the evening, before a major holiday—Easter or Christmas—or else before a visit from better-off relatives whom they wished as much to honor as to deceive, for the sake of propriety, about the family's actual circumstances. In one of his first years at the *lycée*, the grandmother had asked Uncle Josephin to bring her some Arab hens from his Sunday trading expeditions, and had drafted Uncle Ernest to build her a crude chicken coop on the sticky damp earth at the far end of the yard, where she kept five or six fowls that gave her their eggs and at times their lives. The family was at dinner the first time the grandmother decided to conduct an execution, and she asked the older of the boys to go get her the victim. But Louis[1] said he couldn't; he said point-blank that he was afraid. The grandmother sneered, and railed against these children of the rich, not like those in her time— out in the depths of the bush, they were afraid of nothing. "Jacques is braver than that, I'm sure of it. Go ahead, you." To tell the truth, Jacques did not feel at all braver. But once it had been said, he could not back down, and so he went to it on that first evening. He had

---

1. Jacques's brother is sometimes called Henri, sometimes Louis.

to feel his way in the dark down the stairs, turn left in the hall that was always dark, and find the door to the yard and open it. The night outside was less dark than the hall. You could make out the four slippery greenish steps down to the yard. To the right, a weak light trickled through the blinds of the small building occupied by the barber and the Arab family. Across the yard he could see the whitish[a] splotches of the animals asleep on the ground or on their manure-splattered perches. Once he had reached the coop, as soon as he touched the unsteady coop, squatting with his fingers above his head in the big mesh of the cage, a soft cackling began to rise with the warm nauseating smell of the droppings. He opened the little lattice door at ground level, bent over to reach his hand and arm in, was disgusted at the touch of the earth or of a dirty stick, and hastily withdrew his hand, gripped with fear as the coop exploded in a turmoil of wings and feet, the birds fluttering and running all over the place. Yet he had to make up his mind to it, since he had been designated as the more courageous one. But he was horrified by this commotion among the animals in the dark, in this dim and filthy place—it turned his stomach. He waited, gazing up at the immaculate night above him, the sky full of calm clean stars; then he threw himself forward, grabbed the first claw within reach, dragged the crying terrified animal to the little door, took hold of the second foot with his other hand and roughly yanked the hen out of the coop, al-

a. distorted.

ready tearing off some of its feathers against the door-jamb, while the whole coop burst into piercing panic-stricken cackling, and the old Arab, vigilant, appeared framed in a sudden rectangle of light. "It's me, M. Tahar," the child said in a toneless voice. "I'm getting a hen for my grandmother."

"Oh, it's you. All right, I thought it was robbers," and he went back inside, leaving the yard dark again. Now Jacques ran, while the hen struggled desperately and he bumped it against the wall of the hallway or the rungs of the stairs, sick with fear and disgust at the feel of its cold, thick, scaly claws in his hand, ran still faster on the landing and in the hall of the building, and victoriously entered the dining room. The victor stood framed in the doorway, hair mussed, knees green from the moss in the yard, holding the hen as far as possible from his body, his face white with fear. "You see," the grandmother said to the older boy. "He's younger than you are, but he puts you to shame." Jacques waited to preen with justified pride until the grandmother had taken a firm grip on the feet of the hen, which suddenly grew quiet as if understanding that from now on it was in the hands of the inexorable. His brother ate his dessert without looking at him, except to make a scornful face that made Jacques even more satisfied with himself. However, that satisfaction was brief. Glad to have found she had a manly grandson, his grandmother invited him to the kitchen to take part in cutting the hen's throat. She was already wearing a big blue apron and, still holding the hen's feet in one hand, she put a deep earthenware dish on the floor, with the long kitchen knife that Uncle Ernest sharpened periodically on a long black stone, so that the blade, worn till it was very thin and narrow, was no more than a shining edge. "You go over there." Jacques went to the designated place, across the kitchen, while the grandmother placed herself in the doorway, blocking the exit to the hen as well as to the child. His back to the sink, his [left] shoulder against the wall, he watched in horror the sure movements of the sacrificer. The grandmother pushed the plate just into the light shed by the little kerosene lamp set on a wooden table, to the left of the doorway. She laid the animal on the floor, and, putting her knee to the ground, trapped the hen's feet, pressed it flat with her hands to keep it from struggling, then seized the head with her left hand and pulled it back over the plate. With the razor-sharp knife she slowly cut its throat at the place where a man has his Adam's apple, opening the wound by twisting the head while the knife cut with a dreadful sound more deeply into the cartilage, holding still the animal that was shaking all over with terrible twitches while the blood ran bright red into the white dish; and Jacques watched, his legs trembling, as if it were his own blood he felt draining away. "Take the dish," the grandmother said after an interminable time. The animal was no longer bleeding. Jacques carefully placed the dish on the table, with the blood already turning dark. The grandmother tossed the hen down next to the dish; its plumage was already dim, and the round creased lid was closing over its glassy eye. Jacques stared at the motionless body, the toes of its feet drawn together and hanging limp, the crest faded and flaccid—death, in short—then he went out to the dining room.[a]

"Me, I can't watch that," his brother said with suppressed anger that first night. "It's disgusting."

"No, it's not," Jacques said uncertainly. Louis was looking at him with an expression that was both hostile and inquisitorial. And Jacques straightened up. He subdued his fear, the panic that took hold of him in the face of night and that appalling death, and he found in pride, only in pride, a will to courage that finally served as courage itself. "You're scared, that's all," he said at last.

"Yes," said the grandmother, coming back in the room. "It's Jacques who'll go to the chicken coop in the future."

"Good, good," said Uncle Ernest, beaming, "he got courage."

Jacques, rooted to the spot, looked at his mother, who was sitting a bit apart from the others, darning socks stretched over a wooden egg. His mother gazed at him. "Yes," she said, "that's good, you're brave." And she turned back to the street, and Jacques, seeing nothing but her, felt unhappiness swelling once more in his heavy heart.

"Go to bed," said the grandmother. Jacques, without lighting the small kerosene lamp, undressed in the bedroom by the light from the dining room. He lay down on the side of the double bed, to avoid having to touch

---

a. The next day, the smell of raw chicken on the fire.

his brother, or disturb him. He went right to sleep, worn out with fatigue and emotion, awakened at times by his brother, who climbed over him to sleep by the wall because he got up later than Jacques, or by his mother, who sometimes bumped into the wardrobe while undressing in the dark, and who climbed softly into her bed and slept so lightly you could think she was lying awake, and Jacques did sometimes think so; he felt like calling her but he told himself she would not hear him anyway, then forced himself to stay awake as long as she did, just as quietly, motionless, and making no sound, until sleep overcame him as it had already overcome his mother after a hard day of laundry or housework.

Thursdays and Vacations

Only on Thursdays and Sundays could Jacques and Pierre get back to their own world. (Except on some Thursdays when Jacques was in detention—as stated in a note from the chief monitor's office, which Jacques would ask his mother to sign after summarizing its contents with the word "punishment"—and had to spend two hours, from eight to ten o'clock, sometimes four in serious cases, at the *lycée*, in a special room with other offenders, under the supervision of a monitor who usually was furious at being drafted on that day, doing some particularly unrewarding task.)[a] Pierre, in eight years of *lycée*, never suffered detention. But Jacques was too rambunctious, and also too vain, and he played the fool for the sake of showing off, and so he collected detentions. Try as he might to explain to the grandmother that these punishments were for conduct, she could not see the difference between stupidity and bad

---

a. At the *lycée* it was called a *castagne* not a *donnade*.

behavior. To her, a good student would of necessity be virtuous and well behaved; accordingly, virtue led straight to knowledge. So Thursday's punishment was made worse, at least in the first years, by Wednesday's beating.

On Thursdays when there was no punishment, and on Sundays, mornings were devoted to errands and work around the home. And in the afternoon Pierre and Jean[1] could go out together. During the summer there was the Sablettes beach, and the parade grounds, a big vacant lot that included a roughly laid out soccer field and several areas for *boules* players. Usually they played soccer with a ball made of rags, and teams of Arab and French boys that were put together on the spot. But during the rest of the year the two children went to the Home for Disabled Veterans at Kouba,[a] where Pierre's mother, who had left the post office, was chief laundress. Kouba was the name of a hill to the east of Algiers, at the end of a trolley line.[b] In fact, the city ended there, and the gentle countryside of the Sahel began, with its symmetrical knolls, its relatively abundant waters, meadows that seemed practically opulent, and fields of savory red soil, separated here and there by hedges of tall cypress or reeds. Grapevines, fruit trees, corn grew in abundance and without too much effort. Also, for those who came from the city and its damp and

---

1. The reference is to Jacques.
a. Is that its name?
b. the fire.

hot lower districts, the air was bracing and believed to be good for the health. For those people from Algiers who, once they had some wealth or income, would flee the Algiers summer for a more temperate France, it was enough if the air they breathed someplace was just slightly cool, for them to dub it "French air." So in Kouba they breathed the air of France. The old soldiers' home, started for crippled veterans soon after the war, was five minutes from the end of the trolley line. It was a former convent, vast, complex in its architecture, and spread out over several wings, with very thick white-washed walls, covered arcades, and big cool halls with arched ceilings where the dining rooms and the various services had been set up. The laundry, headed by Mme. Marlon, Pierre's mother, was in one of these big halls. That was where she first greeted the children, amidst the smell of hot irons and damp linen, with the two employees, one Arab the other French, who were under her orders. She would give them each a piece of bread and chocolate; then, rolling up the sleeves on her lovely arms, so strong and youthful: "Put that in your pocket for four o'clock and go out in the garden, I have work to do."

First the children would wander through the arcades and the inside courtyards, and most often they ate their snack right away to be rid of the cumbersome bread and the chocolate that melted between their fingers. They would encounter the disabled veterans, some missing an arm or a leg, others installed in little carts with bicycle wheels. There were no disfigured or blind men, only cripples; they were neatly dressed, often wearing a medal, the sleeve of the shirt or jacket, or the pantsleg, carefully taken up and fastened with a safety pin around the invisible stump, and it was not gruesome, there were so many of them. Once past the surprise of the first day, the children looked on them as they did on everything new they discovered and immediately incorporated into their view of the world. Mme. Marlon had explained to them that these men had lost an arm or a leg in the war, and as it happened that the war was part of their universe and they heard about it all the time, it had influenced so many things around them that they had no difficulty understanding that you could lose an arm or a leg to it, and even that it could be defined as a time of life when legs and arms were lost. That was why this world of cripples was in no way sad for the children. Some of the men were closemouthed and somber, it is true, but most were young, smiling, and even joked about their disability. "I only have one leg," one of them would say—he was blond, with a strong square face, and radiantly healthy; they often saw him prowling around the laundry—"but I can still give you a kick in the ass," he would tell the children. And, leaning on the cane in his right hand with his left hand on the parapet of the arcade, he would pull himself erect and swing his one foot in their direction. The children laughed with him, then fled as fast as they could. It seemed normal to them that they were the only ones who could run or use both arms. On just one occasion the thought occurred to Jacques, who had sprained his ankle playing soccer and was limping for a few days, that the Thursday cripples would for all their lives be unable, as he was now, to run and catch a moving trolley, or kick a ball. Suddenly he was struck by the miraculous nature of the body's mechanics, along with an unreasoning fear at the idea that he too might be mutilated, and then he forgot about it.

They* would wander alongside the dining halls with their shutters half closed, the big tables entirely surfaced with zinc glowing faintly in the shade, then the kitchens with their huge containers, caldrons, and casseroles, from which a persistent smell of meat scraps drifted. In the last wing they saw bedrooms with two or three beds covered with gray blankets, and blond-wood closets. Then they went down an outside stairs to the garden.

The soldiers' home was surrounded by a big park that was almost entirely neglected. A few residents had taken on the task of caring for some clumps of rose-bushes and flower beds around the building, not to mention a small vegetable garden enclosed by big hedges of dry reeds. But beyond that the park, which had once been superb, had gone back to nature. Huge eucalyptuses, royal palms, coconut palms, rubber trees[a] with great trunks and low branches that took root farther off, thus making a labyrinth of vegetation full of shade and secrets, thick solid cypresses, vigorous orange trees, clumps of extraordinarily tall pink and white laurels— all these overshadowed the secluded paths where clay had swallowed the gravel; nibbling at the paths' edges

---

* the children
a. the other big trees.

were odorous tangles of syringas, jasmines, clematis, passionflowers, bushes of honeysuckles, and they in turn were invaded at ground level by an energetic carpet of clover, oxalis, and wild grasses. To wander in this fragrant jungle, to crawl in it, to snuggle your face in the grass, to cut a passage through grown-over paths with a knife and come out with mud streaked legs and water all over your face—this was rapture.

But the manufacture of frightful poisons also took up a large part of the afternoon. Under an old stone bench that backed on a section of wall, the children had piled up a whole assortment of tin aspirin tubes, medicine jars, old inkwells, fragments of dishes, and chipped cups that constituted their laboratory. There, hidden in the densest part of the park, away from all eyes, they would prepare their mysterious potions. Their base was oleander, simply because they had often heard it said around them that its shadow was deadly and that anyone so imprudent as to go to sleep at the foot of an oleander would never awaken. So they ground up oleander leaves, and flowers in season, between two stones, to make an evil (unhealthy) pulp, the mere sight of which promised a terrible death. This pulp was left in the open air, where it immediately took on colors of particularly frightening iridescence. During this time, one of the children would run to fill an old bottle with water. Now it was the turn of the cypress cones to be ground up. The children were sure of their malevolence for the unsure reason that the cypress is the cemetery tree. But the fruits were collected from the tree, not on the ground where drying out and hardening gave them a distressingly healthy appearance.[a] Next, the two mashes were mixed in an old bowl and diluted with water, then filtered through a dirty handkerchief. The children handled the liquid thus obtained, of an alarming green, with all the care one would exercise with a virulent poison. They carefully decanted the liquid into aspirin tubes or pharmaceutical jars, which they restoppered while prudently avoiding touching the contents. They mixed what was left with various mashes of all the berries they could gather, so as to make a series of more and more intense poisons, carefully numbered and put away under the stone bench until the next week, so that fermentation would make them definitively deadly. When this sinister work was finished, J. and P. would gaze enraptured at their collection of terrifying flasks and sniff delightedly the sharp acid smell that rose from the stone stained with green mash. These poisons were not actually intended for anyone. The chemists calculated the number of people they could kill, sometimes optimistically stretching it to the point of supposing they had manufactured a quantity sufficient to depopulate the whole city. Yet they had never thought that these magical drugs might rid them of a classmate or teacher they detested. But to tell the truth, there was no one they hated, which would greatly hinder them when they were adults, in the world where they then had to live.

But the grandest days were those of the wind. A side of the building that faced the park ended in what had

---

a. put back in chronological order.

once been a terrace, with its stone railing now lying in the grass in front of the huge red-tiled cement footing. From the terrace, open on three sides, you looked out over the park and, beyond it, a ravine that separated the Kouba hill from one of the high plains of the Sahel. The terrace was so oriented that on days when the east wind rose, always violent in Algiers, it would whip straight across it. On those days the children would dash to the closest palms, where long dried palm branches were always lying around. They scraped the ends to remove the thorns and so they could hold on with both hands. Then, dragging the branches behind them, they ran to the terrace; the wind blew furiously, whistling through the big eucalyptuses that were wildly waving their top branches, disheveling the palms, making a sound of paper crumpling as it shook the big shiny leaves of the rubber trees. The idea was to climb up on the terrace, lift the palm branches and turn their backs to the wind. The children would get a good grip on the dry rustling branches, partly shielding them with their bodies, then would abruptly turn around. The branch would immediately be plastered against them, they would breathe its smell of dust and straw. The game was to advance into the wind while lifting the branch higher and higher. The winner was the one who first reached the end of the terrace without letting the wind tear the branch from his hands, then he would stand erect holding the palm branch at arm's length, one leg extended with all his weight on it, struggling victoriously for as long as possible against the raging force of the wind. There, standing erect over the park and the plain seething with trees, under the sky crossed by huge clouds traveling at full speed, Jacques could feel the wind from the farthest ends of the country coursing down the length of the branch and down his arms to fill him with such a power and an exultation that he cried out endlessly, until his arms and shoulders gave way under the strain and he let go of the branch, which the storm instantly carried off along with his cries. And that night lying in bed, worn out, in the silence of the room where his mother was lightly sleeping, he could still hear the howling and the tumult of the wind that he would love for all his life.

Thursday[a] was also the day Jacques and Pierre would go to the public library. Jacques had always devoured any books that came to hand, and he consumed them with the same appetite he felt for living, playing, or dreaming. But reading enabled him to escape into a world of innocence where wealth and poverty were equally interesting because both were utterly unreal. *L'Intrépide*, that series of thick collections of illustrated stories that he and his friends passed around until the board binding was gray and rough and the pages dog-eared and torn, was the first to transport him to a world of comedy or heroism where his two basic appetites for joy and for courage were satisfied. The taste for heroism and panache was certainly strong in the two boys, judging by their incredible consumption of cloak-and-dagger novels, and by how easily they added the

---

a. separate them from their environment.

characters of *Pardaillan* to their everyday lives. Indeed, their favorite writer was Michel Zevaco,[1] and the Renaissance, especially in Italy, with its atmosphere of stilettos and poisons, in settings of Roman or Florentine palaces and royal or papal pomp, was the favorite kingdom of these two aristocrats, who could sometimes be seen in the yellow dusty street where Pierre lived, hurling challenges at each other as they unsheathed their long varnished [ ][2] rulers fighting impetuous duels among the garbage cans that would leave long-lasting marks on their fingers.[a] At the time, they could hardly find any other sort of books, for the reason that few people read in that neighborhood and all they could buy for themselves—and only rarely at that—were the cheap volumes lying around in the bookstores.

But about the same time they started at the *lycée*, a public library was opened in the area, halfway between the street where Jacques lived and the heights where the more refined districts began, with their villas surrounded by little gardens full of scented plants that thrived on the hot humid slopes of Algiers. These villas circled the grounds of Sainte-Odile, a religious board-

---

1. Author of the *Pardaillan* stories—*Trans*.

2. An illegible word.

a. Actually they were fighting over who would be D'Artagnan or Passepoil. No one wanted to be Aramis or Athos, Porthos if necessary. [All characters in Alexandre Dumas's *The Three Musketeers*, except Passepoil, who is from *Le Bossu* by Paul Feval—*Trans*.]

ing school that took only girls. It was in this neighborhood, so near and yet so far from their own, that
Jacques and Pierre experienced their deepest emotions
(that it is not yet time to discuss, that will be discussed,
etc.). The frontier between these two worlds (one dusty
and treeless, where all the space was devoted to its residents and the stone that sheltered them, the other
where flowers and trees supplied this world's true lux-
ury) was described by a rather wide boulevard with superb plane trees planted along its two sidewalks. Villas
stretched along one bank of this frontier and low-cost
buildings along the other. The public library was built
on that border.

It was open three times a week, including Thursday,
in the evening after work, and all morning Thursday. A
quite unattractive-looking young teacher, who volun-
teered several hours a week at this library, would be sitting behind a rather large blond-wood table and was in
charge of books for loan. The room was square, the
walls entirely filled with blond wood bookcases and
black clothbound books. There was also a small table
with a few chairs around it for those who wanted
quickly to refer to a dictionary, for it was only a lending
library, and an alphabetical card catalogue that neither
Jacques nor Pierre ever looked into, their method con-
sisting of wandering along the shelves, choosing a book
by its title or, less often, by its author, then making note
of its number and writing it on the blue slip that you
used to request permission to borrow the work. To be
entitled to borrow books, you just had to show a rent
receipt and pay a minimal fee. Then you received a

folding card where borrowed books were noted, as well as in the book kept by the young teacher.

Most of the books in the library were novels, but many were set aside and forbidden to those under fifteen. And the children's strictly intuitive method made no real selection among the books that remained. But chance is not the worst method in matters of culture, and, devouring everything indiscriminately, the two gluttons swallowed the best at the same time as the worst, not caring in any event whether they remembered anything, and in fact retaining just about nothing, except a strange and powerful emotion that, over the weeks, the months, and the years, would give birth to and nurture a whole universe of images and memories that never yielded to the reality of their daily lives, and that surely was no less immediate to these eager children who lived their dreams as intensely as they did their lives.[a] [b]

Actually the contents of these books mattered little. What did matter was what they first felt when they went into the library, where they would see not the walls of black books but multiplying horizons and expanses that, as soon as they crossed the doorstep, would take them away from the cramped life of the neighborhood. Then came the moment when—each of them provided with the two books they were allowed, holding them close against their sides with their elbows—they slipped out

---

a. Pages of Quillet's dictionary, smell of the plates.

b. *Mademoiselle*, Jack London, is that good?

onto the boulevard, dark by this time; they squashed underfoot the fruits of the big plane trees while calculating the delights they were going to extract from their books, comparing them already with those of the previous week, until, having arrived on the main street, they would first open them by the uncertain light of the first streetlight, to pick out some phrase (for ex.: "his was a most uncommon strength") that would heighten their joyous and avid hopes. They would part quickly and dash to the dining room to open the book on the oilcloth by the light of the kerosene lamp. A strong smell of glue rose from the crude binding that also was rough to the touch.

The way the book was printed would give the reader advance notice of the pleasure he would derive from it. P. and J. did not like books set in large type with wide margins, such as pleased readers of more refined tastes, but rather pages set in small type stretching all the way across tightly justified lines, filled to the brim with words and sentences, like those enormous rustic dishes you can eat at long and heartily without ever emptying them, and are all that can satisfy some gigantic appetites. They had no use for subtleties; they knew nothing and wanted to know everything. It mattered little if the book was poorly written and crudely printed, as long as the writing was clear and it was full of violent activity; those books, and those alone, would feed their dreams, and on that they could go into a heavy sleep.

Moreover, each book had its own smell according to the paper on which it was printed, always delicate and discreet, but so distinct that with his eyes closed J.

could have told a book in the Nelson series[1] from one of the contemporary editions Fasquelle was then publishing. And each of those odors, even before he had begun reading, would transport Jacques to another world full of promises already [kept], that was beginning even now to obscure the room where he was, to blot out the neighborhood itself and its noises, the city, and the whole world, which would completely vanish as soon as he began reading with a wild exalted intensity that would transport the child into an ecstasy so total that even repeated commands could not extract him:[a] "Jacques, for the third time, set the table." Finally he would set the table, his expression empty and without color, a bit staring, as if drunk on his reading, and he would return to his book as if he had never put it down. "Jacques, eat," and finally he would eat food that, heavy as it was, seemed less real and less solid than what he found in the books; then he cleared the table and went back to his book. Sometimes his mother came to him before seating herself in her usual place. "It's the library," she would say. She mispronounced this word she had heard spoken by her son that had no meaning to her, but she recognized the jackets of books.[b] "Yes," Jacques said without looking up. Catherine Cormery leaned over his shoulder. She looked at the double rectangle under the light, the regular rows

---

1. A series of classics—*Trans.*
a. to develop.
b. They made him (Uncle Ernest) a small desk of blond wood.

of the lines; she would inhale the odor, and sometimes she would run her swollen fingers, wrinkled by the water from doing laundry, across the page, as if she were trying better to understand what a book was, to come a little closer to these mysterious signs, incomprehensible to her, but where her son so often and for hours on end found a life unknown to her and from which he would return with such an expression, looking at her as if she were a stranger. Her gnarled hand gently caressed the boy's head; he did not react; she sighed, then went and sat down, far from him. "Jacques, go to bed." The grandmother repeated the command. "You'll be late tomorrow." Jacques got to his feet, prepared his satchel for the next day's classes, not letting go of his book, which he held in his armpit, and then, like a drunkard, he fell into a heavy sleep, after slipping the book under his bolster.

So, for years, Jacques's existence was divided unequally into two lives between which he was unable to make any connection. For twelve hours, to the sound of the drum, in a society of children and teachers, amidst games and study. For two or three hours of daily life, in the home in the old neighborhood, close to his mother, whom he did not really join except in the sleep of the poor. Although the earliest part of his life was this neighborhood, his present and even more his future were at the *lycée*. So that in a sense the neighborhood eventually blended in with night, with sleep and with dreams. Moreover, did this neighborhood even exist, and was it not the desert it became for the child one evening when he was unconscious? He had fallen on cement . . . At the *lycée*, in any case, there was no one he could talk to about his mother and his family. In his family no one he could talk to about the *lycée*. No friend, no teacher ever came to his home during all the years before he received his baccalaureate. And as for his mother and grandmother, they never came to the *lycée*, except once a year, when awards were given, at the beginning of July. On that day, it is true, they would enter by the monumental door, in a crowd of dressed-up parents and students. The grandmother put on the black dress and scarf she wore for major outings; Catherine Cormery wore a hat adorned with brown net and black waxen grapes, a brown summer dress, and the only pair of shoes with heels that she owned. Jacques wore a short-sleeved white shirt with an open-necked collar, pants that were first short then long, but always carefully ironed by his mother on the previous evening; and, walking between the two women, he himself led them to the red trolley, at about one o'clock in the afternoon, settled them on a seat in the motorcar while he remained standing at the front, looking back through the glass partition at his mother, who smiled at him from time to time and throughout the journey checked the angle of her hat or whether her stockings were falling, or the position of the small golden medal of the Virgin she wore at the end of a thin chain. At the place du Gouvernement began the daily journey along the length of the rue Bab-Azoun, which he made just once in the year with the two women. Jacques sniffed the [lampero] lotion on his mother, which she had liberally applied for the occasion, the grandmother walking erect and proud, scold-

ing her daughter when she complained about her feet
("That'll teach you to wear shoes too small for you
at your age"), while Jacques persisted in showing
them the stores and shopkeepers that had come to
have such an important place in his life. At the *lycée*,
the monumental door was open, potted plants adorned
the monumental stairs from top to bottom, stairs that the
first parents and students were beginning to climb, the
Cormerys naturally being far ahead of time, as the poor
always are, for they have few social obligations and
pleasures, and are afraid of not being punctual for those
few.[a] Then they arrived at the older students' courtyard,
full of rows of chairs rented from a firm that staged
dances and concerts, while at the far end, under the
great clock, the whole width of the courtyard was occupied by a platform filled with chairs and armchairs; it
too was decorated, and profusely, with green plants.
Little by little the yard was filled up with light-colored
outfits, women being in the majority. The first arrivals
chose places sheltered from the sun, under the trees.
The others fanned themselves with Arab fans made of
fine plaited straw decorated with red woolen tassels on
their rims. Above the audience the blue of the sky congealed and became harder and harder as it baked in the
heat.

At two o'clock a military orchestra, out of sight in

---

a. and those whom fate has poorly endowed cannot help thinking somewhere inside that they are responsible and they feel they
must not add to this general culpability by any small failings . . .

the upper arcade, launched into the "Marseillaise," all the spectators rose to their feet, and the teachers entered in their square caps and long gowns trimmed in colors that differed according to their discipline, led by the headmaster and the official personage (usually a high-ranking bureaucrat in the colonial administration) drafted this year for the occasion. Another military march covered for the seating of the teachers, and right after that the official personage took the podium and gave his opinions on France in general and education in particular. Catherine Cormery listened without hearing, but with no sign of impatience or weariness. The grandmother could hear, but did not understand very much. "He speaks well," she said to her daughter, who assented with conviction. This encouraged the grandmother to turn and smile at her neighbor to the left, confirming with a nod of her head the opinion she had just expressed. The first year, Jacques noticed that his grandmother was the only person wearing the old Spanish woman's black mantilla, and he was embarrassed by it. To tell the truth, this false sense of shame had never left him; he just decided he could do nothing about it after he timidly ventured to mention a hat to his grandmother and she answered that she had no money to waste and besides the mantilla kept her ears warm. But when his grandmother spoke to her neighbors during the awards ceremony, he felt himself meanly blushing. After the official personage, the youngest teacher rose to speak; he was usually newly arrived that year from France and was traditionally entrusted with delivering the formal address. The speech could last from half an hour to an hour, and the young academician never failed to stuff it with cultural allusions and humanist subtleties that made it utterly unintelligible to this Algerian audience. With the help of the heat, attention flagged, and the fans waved faster. Even the grandmother showed her lassitude by glancing around. Only Catherine Cormery, attentive, received without blinking the rain of erudition and wisdom that was falling on* her without interruption. As to Jacques, he was squirming; he looked around for Pierre and his other friends, signaled discreetly to them, and began a long conversation that consisted of making faces. At last, vigorous applause thanked the orator for being kind enough to conclude, and the announcement of the awards began. First came the upper classes, and, in the early years, the two women spent the entire afternoon sitting and waiting for them to come to Jacques's class. The awards for excellence were the only ones to be saluted with a fanfare of invisible music. The winners, who became younger and younger, rose, walked the side of the courtyard, went up on the platform, received a handshake sprinkled with fine words from the official personage, then from the headmaster, who presented each with his bundle of books (after getting it from an attendant, who preceded the award-winner to the platform, at the foot of which rolling carts full of books

----

* bouncing off

had been stationed). Then, in the midst of music and applause, the award-winner came back down, his books under his arm, radiant and looking around for his happy relatives, who were wiping away their tears. The sky became a little less blue, losing some of its heat through an invisible cleft somewhere over the sea. The prizewinners went up and returned, one fanfare followed another, the courtyard gradually emptying out, while the sky began now to turn a greenish hue, and they came to Jacques's class. As soon as his class was announced, he stopped fooling around and became serious. At the sound of his name, he rose, his head buzzing. Behind he could barely hear his mother, who had not heard, saying: "Did he say Cormery?"

"Yes," said the grandmother, her face flushed with excitement. The cement path he walked along, the platform, the official's vest with his watch chain, the headmaster's good smile, sometimes a friendly look from one of his teachers in the crowd on the platform; then returning accompanied by the music to the two women who were already standing in the aisle, his mother gazing at him with a sort of astonished joy, and he gave her the thick list of awards to keep, his grandmother with a look calling her neighbors to witness—it all happened too fast after the interminable afternoon, and Jacques was in a hurry to go home and look at the books he had been given.[a]

---

a. *Les Travailleurs de la mer*. [By Victor Hugo—*Trans.*]

They usually went home with Pierre and his mother,[a] the grandmother silently comparing the height of the two stacks of books. At home, Jacques took the award list, and, at his grandmother's request, turned down the corners of the pages where his name appeared, so she could show them to the neighbors and family. Then he made an inventory of his treasures. He had not finished when he saw his mother come back—already having removed her dress—in slippers, buttoning her linen blouse, and drawing her chair toward the window. She smiled at him. "You did good work," she said, and she shook her head as she gazed at him. He returned her gaze; he was waiting, for what he did not know, and she turned to the street, in the posture that was familiar to him, far away now from the *lycée* she would not see for another year, while shadows invaded the room and the first lights came on above the street,* where no one was passing by but faceless pedestrians.

But if his mother was leaving forever that *lycée* she had hardly glimpsed, Jacques found himself suddenly back for good in the midst of his family and his neighborhood.

Vacations also returned Jacques to his family, at least in the first years. No one in his home had a vacation; the men worked the year round without respite. Only an

---

a. She had never seen the *lycée* nor anything of its daily life. She had attended a program arranged for the relatives. That was not the *lycée*, it was . . .

* the sidewalks.

accident at work, when they were employed by firms that had insured them against such risks, could give them any time off, and their vacation came by way of the hospital or the doctor. For example, Uncle Ernest, one time when he felt worn out, had "put himself on insurance," as he said, by deliberately shaving a thick slice of meat off his palm with a plane. As for the wives, and Catherine Cormery, they worked without a break for the good reason that a rest meant poorer meals for all of them. Unemployment, for which there was no insurance at all, was the calamity they most dreaded. That explained why these workers, in Pierre's home as in Jacques's, who in their daily lives were the most tolerant of men, were always xenophobes on labor issues, accusing in turn the Italians, the Spaniards, the Jews, the Arabs, and finally the whole world of stealing their work—an attitude that is certainly disconcerting to those intellectuals who theorize about the proletariat, and yet very human and surely excusable. It was not for mastery of the earth or the privileges of wealth and leisure that these unexpected nationalists were contending against other nationalities; it was for the privilege of servitude. Work in this neighborhood was not a virtue but a necessity that, in order to survive, led to death.

In any case, and no matter how hard the Algerian summer was, while overloaded boats took bureaucrats and well-off people to recuperate in the good "French air" (and those who returned brought back fabulous and unbelievable descriptions of lush fields where the water was flowing right in the middle of August), nothing at all changed in the lives of the poor neighborhoods, and, far from being half emptied, as were the downtown districts, their population seemed to increase because of the great numbers of children pouring out into the streets.[a]

For Pierre and Jacques, wandering in the dry streets, wearing espadrilles with holes, cheap pants, and skimpy undershirts with round necks, vacation meant above all the hot season. The last rains fell in April, or May at the latest. Over the weeks and the months, the sun, more and more intense, hotter and hotter, had dried, then dried out, then roasted the walls, had ground plaster, stone, and tile into a fine dust that, blown at random by the wind, would cover the streets, the store windows, and the leaves of all the trees. In July the entire neighborhood became a sort of gray-and-yellow[b] labyrinth, deserted during the day, all the shutters of all the houses carefully closed, ruled by the ferocious sun, felling dogs and cats on the doorsteps of buildings, forcing living beings to hug the walls to stay out of its reach. In August the sun disappeared behind the thick oakum of a sky that was gray with heat, heavy and humid, shedding a diffuse, whitish light, tiring to the eyes, which erased the last traces of color from the streets. In the coopers' workshops, the sound of the hammers slackened, and the workers stopped occasionally to put their sweaty heads and chests under the cool stream of water from the pump.[c] In the apartments, the bottles of water and,

---

a. above toys carousel useful presents.

b. wild

c. Sablettes? and other summer activities.

less often, wine were swaddled in damp cloth. Jacques's grandmother moved around the shady rooms bare-footed, wearing a plain shift, mechanically shaking her straw fan, working in the morning, dragging Jacques to bed for the siesta, then waiting for the first cool of the evening to go back to work. Thus for weeks the sum-mer and those subject to it would crawl along under the heavy, sweaty, and roasting sky, until even the memory of winter's cool and its waters* was lost, as if the earth had never known the wind, nor the snow, nor light wa-ters, and from the Creation to this day in September nothing had existed but this enormous desiccated min-eral structure tunneled with overheated corridors where sweating and dust-covered beings, a bit haggard, eyes staring, were slowly moving about. And then, all at once, the sky contracted until it broke open under the stress. The first rain of September, violent and abun-dant, flooded the city. All the streets of the neighbor-hood began to gleam, along with the shiny leaves of the ficus trees, the overhead wires, and the trolley rails. Over the hills that looked down on the city came the scent of damp earth from more distant fields, bringing a message of open space and freedom to the prisoners of the summer. Then the children dashed into the streets, running through the rain in their scanty clothes and wallowing happily in the big frothing streams in the street, making a circle in the big puddles while holding each other's shoulders, faces full of shouts and laughter

* rains.

turned up into the incessant rain, trampling out this new vintage in unison so that it gave forth a gush of dirty water more intoxicating than wine.

Oh yes, the hot season was terrible, and often it drove almost everyone crazy, nerves more on edge day by day and without the strength or energy to react, to shout, to insult or strike out, and exasperation accumulated, like the heat itself, until, here and there in the sad and untamed neighborhood, it exploded—like that day when, in the rue de Lyon, almost at the border of the Arab district known as the Marabout, by the cemetery cut into the red clay of the hillside, Jacques saw an Arab, dressed in blue with his head shaved, come out of a dusty Moorish barbershop; he took a few steps on the sidewalk in front of the child, in a strange posture, his body leaning forward, his head thrown back farther than seemed possible, and in fact it was not possible. The barber had gone mad while shaving him, and with a single blow of his long razor had cut the exposed throat; all the Arab felt from the smooth slicing was the blood choking him, and he went out, running like a duck with its throat poorly cut, while the barber, immediately subdued by other customers, was howling horribly—like the heat itself during these interminable days.

Then the water from the cataracts of the sky would roughly scrub the summer's dust off the trees, the roofs, the walls, and the streets. The muddy water quickly filled the gutters, gurgled fiercely in the drains, would in most years burst the sewer lines themselves and flood the streets, spraying out before cars and trolleys like two very streamlined yellow fins. The sea itself would turn muddy on the beach and in the port. The first sun after that would make steam rise from the buildings and the streets, from the whole city. The heat might return, but it no longer ruled; the sky was more open, it was easier to breathe, and, through the depth of the sun, a vibration in the air, a promise of water heralded autumn and the start of the school year.[a] "Summer's too long," said the grandmother; she welcomed with the same sigh of relief the autumn rain and the departure of Jacques, whose bored stamping around the shuttered rooms during the torrid days only added to her exasperation.

Besides, she did not understand why a part of the year should be specially set aside for doing nothing. "As for me, I never had any vacation," she would say, and it was true, she had never known either school or leisure time; she had worked as a child, and worked without respite. She could accept that her grandson would not bring home any money for a few years in return for a greater gain. But from the first day, she had been brooding over those three lost months, and when Jacques was going into his fourth year, she judged that it was time to put his vacation to use. "You're going to work this summer," she told him at the end of the school year, "and bring home some money. You can't just stay here doing nothing."[b] Actually, Jacques thought he had a lot

---

a. in the *lycée*—subscription card—*renew monthly*—the exhilaration of answering: "Subscriber" and the triumphant verification.

b. the mother speaks up—He'll be tired.

to do, what with going swimming, the expeditions to Kouba, sports, roaming the streets of Belcourt, reading illustrated stories, popular novels, the Vermot almanac, and the Saint-Étienne company's inexhaustible catalogue.[a] Not including errands for the household and small tasks imposed on him by his grandmother. But, to her, all that amounted to doing nothing at all, since the child was not bringing home any money nor was he working as he did during the school year, and in her eyes this free ride was as glaring as the fires of hell. The simplest thing to do was to find him a job.

In truth it was not so simple. Of course you could find help-wanted listings for junior clerks or errand boys in the classified ads in the newspapers. And Mme. Bertaut, the dairywoman whose shop alongside the barbershop smelled of butter (unusual to these noses and palates accustomed to oil), would read the ads to the grandmother. But the employers always required applicants to be at least fifteen years old, and it would take audacity to lie about Jacques's age, for he was not very big for thirteen. Furthermore, the employers always hoped for employees who would make their career with them. The first ones to whom the grandmother (rigged out as she was for major outings, including the infamous mantilla) offered Jacques found him too young or else flatly refused to hire an employee for two months.

"You'll just have to say you'll stay," the grandmother said.

---

a. His reading earlier? the upper neighborhoods?

"But that's not true."

"It doesn't matter. They'll believe you."

That was not what Jacques meant, and actually he did not worry about whether he would be believed. But it seemed to him that this sort of lie would stick in his throat. Of course he had often lied at home, to avoid punishment, to keep a two-franc coin, and far more often for the pleasure of talking or bragging. But if to lie to his family seemed a venial sin, with strangers it seemed mortal. In an obscure way he felt that you do not lie on essentials to those you love, because then you could no longer live with them or love them. All the employers could learn of him was what he told them, and so they would not know him, the lie would be absolute. "Let's go," said the grandmother, knotting her mantilla, one day when Mme. Bertaut told her a big hardware store in the Agha district wanted a young filing clerk. The hardware store was on one of the slopes that led up to the central districts; the mid-July sun was roasting the street and intensifying the smells of urine and asphalt that rose from its surface. There was a narrow but very deep store at street level, divided the long way by a counter displaying samples of iron parts and latches; the walls were largely occupied by drawers bearing mysterious labels. To the right of the entrance, a wrought-iron grille had been installed above the counter with a window for the cashier. The soft, day-dreaming lady behind the grille asked the grandmother to go up to the office, on the second floor. A wooden stairway, at the end of the store, did in fact lead to a big office laid out and oriented in similar fashion to the store, where five or six employees, men and women, were seated at a big table in the middle. A door on one side led to the manager's office.

The manager, in his sweltering office, was in shirt-sleeves with his collar loosened.[a] A small window at his back opened on to a yard where the sun did not reach, though it was two o'clock in the afternoon. He was short and fat, he hitched his thumbs in his wide sky-blue suspenders, and he was short of breath. You could not clearly see the face, from which came a low breathless voice inviting the grandmother to be seated. Jacques inhaled the odor of iron that permeated the whole building. It seemed to Jacques that the manager's motionless stance meant he was suspicious, and he felt his legs tremble at the thought of the lies they would tell this powerful, fearsome man. As for the grandmother, she did not tremble. Jacques was going to be fifteen, he had to find a position and start without delay. According to the manager, he didn't look fifteen, but if he was intelligent . . . and by the way, did he have his *certificat d'études?* No, he had a scholarship. What scholarship? For the *lycée*. So he was going to the *lycée?* What class? Fourth year? And he was leaving the *lycée?* The manager was even more still, his face could be seen better now, and his round milky eyes shifted from the grandmother to the child. Jacques quaked under that gaze.

"Yes," said the grandmother. "We're too poor."

The manager relaxed imperceptibly. "That's too

---

a. collar button, detachable collar.

bad," he said, "because he was gifted. But there are good positions to be achieved in business also." The good position started modestly, it is true. Jacques would earn 150 francs a month for being present eight hours a day. He could start the next day.

"You see," said the grandmother. "He believed us."

"But how will I explain it to him when I leave?"

"Leave that to me."

"All right," the child said submissively. He looked up at the summer sky over their heads and thought of the smell of iron, the office full of shadows, that he would have to get up early tomorrow, and that his vacation was over when it had barely begun.

For two years Jacques worked during the summer. First in the hardware store, then for a ship broker. Each time he feared the approach of September 15th, the date he had to give notice.[1]

It was really over, even though the summer was the same as before, with its heat, its boredom. But summer had lost what used to transfigure it, its sky, its open spaces, its clamor. Jacques no longer spent his days in the untamed poverty of his neighborhood, but downtown where the cement of the rich replaced the rough casting of the poor, giving the houses a more distinguished and sadder tone of gray. At eight o'clock, when Jacques entered the store that smelled of iron and shade, a light in him went out, the sky had vanished. He greeted the cashier and climbed up to the big poorly lit

---

1. Passage circled by the author.

office on the second floor. There was no room for him at
the main table. The old bookkeeper, his moustache
stained yellow by the hand-rolled cigarettes he sucked
on all day long; the assistant bookkeeper, a half-bald
man of about thirty with a bull-like face and chest; two
younger clerks, one of whom, thin, brown-haired, muscular, with a handsome straight profile, always arrived
with his shirt wet and sticking to his body, and gave off
a good smell of the sea because he went swimming from
the pier every morning before burying himself in the
office for the day, and the other, fat and laughing, who
could not restrain his jovial vitality; and lastly Mme.
Raslin, the manager's secretary, a bit horsey but quite
pleasant to look at in her linen or duckcloth dresses, always pink, but who gazed on the world with a stern
eye—these were enough to fill up the table with their
files, their account books, and their machine. So Jacques
was stationed on a chair to the right of the manager's door, waiting to be given some work to do,
which usually consisted of filing invoices or business
correspondence in the card-index file on either side of
the window—where at first he liked to pull out the sliding drawers, handle the cards, and sniff them, until the
smell of paper and glue, at first exquisite, finally became
the very odor of boredom for him; or else he was asked
to go over a lengthy addition once more, and he did it in
his lap, sitting on his chair; or else the assistant bookkeeper would ask Jacques to "collate" a series of numbers with him and, always standing, he would carefully
check the numbers that the assistant read off, in a dole-
ful low voice so as not to disturb his colleagues. From

the window you could see the street and the buildings across it, but never the sky. Sometimes, but not often, Jacques was sent on an errand, to get office supplies from the nearby stationery store or to the post office to send an urgent money order. The central post office was located two hundred meters away, on a broad boulevard that led from the port up to the summits of the hills on which the city was built. Jacques would rediscover space and light on this boulevard. The post office itself, in an immense rotunda, was lit by three large doors and light trickling through a huge cupola.[a] But more often, unfortunately, Jacques was made to post the mail at the end of the day, after leaving the office, and then it was just more drudgery, for he had to run, at the time when the day was beginning to fade, to a post office besieged by a crowd of customers, get in line at the windows, and the wait made his workday still longer. The long summer was practically used up for Jacques in dark days without sparkle and in trivial occupations. "You can't go on without doing anything," his grandmother said. But it was precisely in the office that Jacques felt he wasn't doing anything. He was not unwilling to work, though for him nothing could take the place of the sea or the games of Kouba. But to him real work consisted of what was done at the cooperage, for example—a lengthy physical effort, a series of skillful, precise actions by hard, quick-moving hands—and you saw the result of your labor take shape: a new barrel, well fin-

_____

a. postal transactions?

ished, without a crack, something the worker could contemplate.

But this office work came from nowhere and led nowhere. Selling and buying, everything turned on these ordinary, petty actions. Although he had lived till then in poverty, it was in this office that Jacques discovered the mundane, and he wept for the light he had lost. His co-workers were not the cause of the feeling that he was being smothered. They were nice to him, they never rudely ordered him around, and even the stern Mme. Raslin sometimes smiled at him. Among themselves they spoke little, with that mix of jovial heartiness and indifference characteristic of Algerians. When the manager arrived, a quarter-hour after them, or when he emerged from his office to give an order or check an invoice (for serious matters, he would summon the old bookkeeper or the employee involved to his office), they would better reveal their characters, as if these men and this woman could not express themselves except in their relations with authority—the old bookkeeper discourteous and independent, Mme. Raslin lost in some austere daydream, and the assistant bookkeeper, by contrast, utterly servile. But, for the rest of the day, they would retreat into their shells, and Jacques sat on his chair waiting for the order that would cause him to do some absurd hurrying about—what his grandmother called "work."[a]

------

a. Summer lessons after the baccalaureate—the stupefied head in front of him.

When he could stand it no longer, when he was literally boiling over on his chair, he would go down to the yard behind the store and hide between the cement walls of the poorly lit Turkish toilet, with its sour pervading odor of urine. In this dark place he would close his eyes, and, breathing the familiar smell, he would dream. Something obscure was stirring in him, something irrational, something in his blood and in his nature. At times he would recall the sight of Mme. Raslin's legs that day when, having knocked over a box of pins in front of her, he knelt to pick them up and, raising his head, saw her parted knees under her skirt and her thighs in lace underwear. Till then he had never seen what a woman wore under her skirts, and this sudden vision made his mouth dry and caused him to tremble almost uncontrollably. A mystery was being revealed to him that, despite his many experiences, he would never resolve.

Twice a day, at noon and at six o'clock, Jacques would dash outside, run down the sloping street, and jump onto a packed trolley, lined with clusters of passengers on every running board, which was taking workers [back] to their neighborhoods. Squeezed against each other in the heavy heat, they were silent, the adults and the child, looking toward the home that was expecting them—quiet, perspiring, resigned to this existence divided among a soulless job, long trips coming and going in an uncomfortable trolley, and at the end an abrupt sleep. On some evenings it would sadden Jacques to look at them. Until then he had only known the riches and the joys of poverty. But now heat and boredom and fatigue were showing him their curse, the curse of work so stupid you could weep and so interminably monotonous that it made the days too long and, at the same time, life too short.

At the ship broker's, summer was more pleasant because the office looked out on boulevard Front-de-Mer and especially because some of his work was at the port. Jacques actually had to go on board the ships of all nationalities that put in at Algiers and that the broker, a handsome pink-cheeked old man with curly hair, represented to the various government offices. Jacques brought the ship's papers to the office, where they were translated, and, after a week, he himself was assigned to translating lists of supplies and certain bills of lading when they were written in English and addressed to the customs authorities or the big import companies that took delivery of merchandise. So Jacques had regularly to go to the Agha commercial port to get those papers. The heat ravaged the streets leading down to the port. The heavy cast-iron ramps alongside them were so burning hot that you could not touch them with your hand. The sun created a void on the huge piers, except around the ships that had just moored, side against the pier, where the longshoremen were busying themselves—men dressed in blue pants rolled to mid-calf, with bare bronzed torsos, and on their heads a cloth that covered their shoulders and back to the waist, on which they loaded sacks of cement or coal or sharp-edged packages. They came and went on the gangplank that sloped down from the deck to the pier, or else they entered straight into the belly of the freighter by the wide open door of the hold, walking rapidly across a beam laid between the hold and the pier. Beyond the smell of sun and dust rising from the piers and that of the overheated decks where the tar was melting and all the fixtures were roasting, Jacques could recognize the particular odor of each freighter. Those from Norway smelled of wood, those from Dakar or the Brazilian ships brought with them the scent of coffee and spices, the Germans smelled of oil, the English of iron. Jacques would climb up the gangplank, show the broker's card to a sailor, who did not understand it. Then he was led through passageways where even the shade was hot to the cabin of an officer or sometimes the captain.[a] Along the way he would cast covetous glances at those narrow bare cabins where the essence of masculine life was concentrated, and that he was coming to prefer that to the most luxurious of quarters. They greeted him kindly because he himself smiled pleasantly, and he liked these men's rough faces, the appearance that a certain kind of solitary life gave them all, and he let them see his liking for them. Sometimes one of them spoke a little French and would question him. Then, in good spirits, he went back to the flaming pier, the burning ramps, and work in the office. It was just that running these errands in the heat exhausted him; he slept heavily, and September found him thinner and fidgety.

He was relieved at the approach of the days when he would spend twelve hours at the *lycée*, at the same time

---

a. The longshoreman's accident? See diary.

that he was increasingly embarrassed at having to inform the office that he was leaving. The hardware store was the hardest. He would cravenly have preferred that he not go to the office and that his grandmother go and give whatever explanation. But the grandmother thought it was easy enough to skip the formalities: all he had to do was collect his pay and never go back, with no further explanation. Jacques, who would have found it quite natural to send his grandmother to endure the manager's thunder—and in a sense it is true she was responsible for the situation and the lie it entailed—was nonetheless indignant at the idea of this evasion, without being able to explain why; in addition, he found the clinching argument: "But the boss will send someone here."

"That's true," the grandmother said. "Well then, you'll just have to tell him you're going to work at your uncle's." Jacques was already leaving with damnation in his heart when his grandmother told him: "And above all collect your pay first. Then talk to him."

That evening the manager called each employee to his lair to give him his pay. "Here, kid," he said to Jacques, offering him his envelope. Jacques was reaching out a hesitant hand when the manager smiled at him. "You're doing very well, you know. You can tell your parents that." Jacques was already speaking, saying he would not be coming back. The manager looked at him, amazed, his hand still outstretched to him. "Why?" He had to lie, and the lie would not come out. Jacques remained silent, and with so woeful an air that the manager understood. "You're going back to the *lycée?*"

"Yes," said Jacques, and in the midst of his fear and
distress a sudden feeling of relief brought tears to his
eyes. Furious, the manager got to his feet. "And you
knew it when you came here. And your grandmother
knew it too." Jacques could only say yes with a nod.
Vocal thunderclaps filled the room: they were dishonest,
and he, the manager, hated dishonesty. Did he know
that he had the right not to pay him, and he'd be pretty
foolish, no he wouldn't pay him, let his grandmother
come, she'd get a warm reception all right, if they'd told
him the truth, he might have hired him anyway, but oh!
that lie—"he can't stay at the *lycée*, we're too poor"—
and he'd let himself be had.

"It was because of that," the bewildered Jacques suddenly said.

"Why because of that?"

"Because we're poor"; then he was silent, and it was
the manager who went on after looking at him: ". . . that
you did that, that you made up that story?" Jacques,
teeth clenched, stared at his feet. The silence was interminable. Then the manager took the envelope from the
table and held it out: "Take your money. Get out," he
said harshly.

"No," said Jacques.

The manager stuffed the envelope into Jacques's
pocket: "Get out." In the street Jacques was running,
and now he was crying and gripping his collar with both
hands to avoid touching the money that was burning in
his pocket.

To lie for the right to have no vacation, to work far
from the summer sky and the sea he so loved, and to lie

again for the right to return to his work at the *lycée*—
this injustice made him desperately unhappy. For the
worst of it was not the lies that after all he was unable to
utter, ready as he always was to lie for pleasure but incapable of doing so out of necessity, the worst of it was
the delights he had lost, the season's light and the time
off that had been taken away from him, and now the
year consisted of nothing but a series of hasty awaken-
ings and hurried dismal days. He had to lose what was
royal in his life of poverty, the irreplaceable riches that
he so greatly and gluttonously enjoyed, to earn a little
bit of money that would not buy one-millionth of those
treasures. And yet he understood that he had to do it,
and there was even something in him that, at the very
time he was most rebellious, was proud of having done
it. For he had found the sole compensation for those
summers sacrificed to the misery of the lie on his first
payday when—entering the dining room where his
grandmother was peeling potatoes that she then tossed
in a basin of water; Uncle Ernest, seated, was picking
fleas off the patient Brillant whom he held between his
legs; and his mother, who had just arrived, was at the
buffet opening a small bundle of dirty laundry she had
been given to wash—Jacques had stepped forward and,
without a word, placed on the table the 100-franc bill
and the large coins he had been clutching in his hand all
the way home. Without a word, the grandmother
pushed a 20-franc piece back toward him and picked up
the rest. With her hand she touched Catherine Cormery
on the side to get her attention and showed her the
money: "That's your son."

"Yes," his mother said, and her sorrowful eyes briefly caressed the child.

The uncle nodded while holding on to Brillant, who had thought his ordeal was over. "Good, good," he said. "You a man."

Yes, he was a man, he had paid a bit of what he owed, and the idea of having diminished the poverty of this household by a little filled him with that almost wicked pride that comes to men when they begin to feel themselves free and subject to nothing. And in fact, when he entered the fifth-year courtyard at the start of the next school year, he was no longer the disoriented child who four years earlier had left Belcourt in the early morning—unsteady on his studded shoes, anxious at the thought of the strange world awaiting him—and his expression as he looked at his classmates had lost some of its innocence. Besides, by that time many things were beginning to pull him away from the child he had been. And if one day he who till then had patiently accepted being beaten by his grandmother as if it were one of the inevitable obligations of childhood, if he tore the leather whip out of her hands, suddenly crazed, in a furious rage, so determined to strike that white head whose bright cold eyes were driving him out of his mind that the grandmother understood him—she recoiled and went to close herself in her room, sobbing certainly over the misfortune of having raised unnatural children but already knowing she would never beat Jacques again, and in fact never again did she beat him—it was because the child had indeed died in this thin muscular adolescent, with his brush-cut hair and his fiery expression, this youth who had worked all summer to bring home wages, who had just been named first-string goalie on the *lycée* team, and who, three days earlier, had had his first faltering taste of a girl's lips.

2 : *A Mystery to Himself*

Oh yes, that was how it was, the life of this child was like that: that was how life was in the neighborhood's island of poverty, bound together by stark necessity, in an ignorant and handicapped family, with his youthful blood boiling, a ravenous appetite for life, an untamed and hungry intellect, and all the while an ecstasy of joy punctuated by the sudden counterpunches inflicted by a world unknown to him, leaving him abashed at the time, but he would quickly recover, trying to understand, to learn, to assimilate this world he did not know, and he did assimilate it, because he seized upon it so avidly, not trying to worm his way in; he was willing to go along but would not abase himself, and finally he was never without a sure confidence, yes a certainty, since he was guaranteed that he would achieve everything he desired and nothing would ever be impossible for him, nothing that is of this world and only of this world; he was preparing himself (and was prepared also by the bareness of his childhood) to find his place anywhere, because there was no position he wanted, but only joy, and free spirits, and energy, and all that life has that is good, that is mysterious, that is not and never will be for sale. Preparing himself even by dint of poverty to be able one day to receive money without ever seeking it or submitting to it, to be as he was now—he, Jacques, at age forty, holding sway over so much and yet so certain that he was less than the least of people, and nothing in any case next to his mother. Yes, that was how he lived, in those games by the sea, in the wind, in the street, under the weight of summer and the heavy rains of the brief winter, with no father, with no heritage handed down, but finding a father for a year, just when he needed him, and learning through the people and the things of [ ],[1] through the knowledge that revealed itself to him to fashion something that resembled a style of behavior (sufficient at the time for his circumstances, insufficient later on when confronting the cancer of the world) and to create his own heritage.

But was that all there was: that style, those games, that daring, that ardor, the family, the kerosene lamp and the dark stairs, the palms in the wind, birth and baptism in the sea, and finally those gloomy laborious summers? There was that, oh yes, that is how it was, but there was also the secret part of his being, something in him that through all those years had been blindly stirring like those measureless waters under the earth which from the depths of rocky labyrinths have never seen the light of day and yet dimly reflect a light, come from

---

1. An illegible word.

who knows where, drawn perhaps from the glowing center of the earth through stone capillaries to the black air of those buried caverns in which glutinous and [com-pacted] plants find food enough to live where any life seems impossible. And this blind stirring in him, which had never ceased, which he still felt now, a dark fire buried in him like one of those peat fires, gone out at the surface but still burning inside, making the outer fis-sures of the peat move in rough eddies of vegetation, so that the muddy surface moves in the same rhythm as the peat of the bog, and these dense imperceptible waves would cause, day after day, the most violent and the most terrible of his desires, as well as his most barren anxieties, his most fruitful nostalgia, his sudden need for bareness and sobriety, his yearning also to be nobody—yes this mysterious stirring through all those years was well matched to this immense country around him; as a small child he had felt its weight and that of the im-mense sea before him, and behind him the endless ex-panse of mountains, plains, and desert called the interior, and between the two the constant danger no one spoke of because it seemed natural; but Jacques sensed it in Birmandreis, in the little farmhouse with arched ceilings and whitewashed walls, when his aunt went around the bedrooms at bedtime to make sure the huge bolts on the thick, solid wooden shutters had been properly closed, this was the very country into which he felt he had been tossed, as if he were the first inhabitant, or the first conqueror, landing where the law of the jun-gle still prevailed, where justice was intended to punish without mercy what custom had failed to prevent—

around him these people, alluring yet disturbing, near and separate, you were around them all day long, and sometimes friendship was born, or camaraderie, and at evening they still withdrew to their closed houses, where you never entered, barricaded also with their women you never saw, or if you saw them on the street you did not know who they were, with faces half veiled and their beautiful eyes sensual and soft above the white cloth, and they were so numerous in the neighborhoods where they were concentrated, so many of them that by their sheer numbers, even though exhausted and submissive, they caused an invisible menace that you could feel in the air some evenings on the streets when a fight would break out between a Frenchman and an Arab, just as it might have broken out between two Frenchmen or two Arabs, but it was not viewed the same way; and the Arabs of the neighborhood, wearing their faded blue overalls or their wretched cloaks, would slowly approach, coming from all directions in a continuous movement, until this steadily agglutinating mass by the mere action of its coalescing would without violence eject the few Frenchmen attracted by witnesses to the fight, and the Frenchman who was fighting would in backing up find himself suddenly confronting both his antagonist and a crowd of somber impenetrable faces, which would have deprived him of what courage he possessed had he not been raised in this country and therefore knew that only with courage could you live here; and so he would face up to the threatening crowd that nonetheless was making no threat except by its presence and by the movement it could not help mak-

ing, and most often it was they who took hold of the
Arab fighting in a transport of rage to make him leave
before the arrival of the police, who were quickly informed and quick to come, and who without debate
would take away the fighters, manhandling them as they
passed by Jacques's windows on the way to the police
station. "Poor fellows," his mother would say, seeing
the two men firmly held and shoved along by their
shoulders, and after they were gone, violence, fear, and
menace prowled the street in the child's mind, and a
nameless dread made his mouth go dry. This night inside him, yes these tangled hidden roots that bound him
to this magnificent and frightening land, as much to its
scorching days as to its heartbreakingly rapid twilights,
and that was like a second life, truer perhaps than the
everyday surface of his outward life; its history would
be told as a series of obscure yearnings and powerful in-
describable sensations, the odor of the schools, of the
neighborhood stables, of laundry on his mother's hands,
of jasmine and honeysuckle in the upper neighborhoods, of the pages of the dictionary and the books he
devoured, and the sour smell of the toilets at home and
at the hardware store, the smell of the big cold class-
rooms where he would sometimes go alone before or
after class, the warmth of his favorite classmates, the
odor of warm wool and feces that Didier carried around
with him, of the cologne big Marconi's mother doused
him with so profusely that Jacques, sitting on the bench
in class, wanted to move still closer to his friend; the
scent of the lipstick Pierre swiped from one of his aunts
and that several of them sniffed together, excited and

uneasy, like dogs that enter a house where there has been a female in heat, imagining that this was what a woman was, this sweet-smelling chunk of bergamot and cosmetic cream that, in their rough world of shouting, sweating, and dust, revealed to them a world refined[a] and delicate and inexpressibly seductive, from which even the foul language they were mouthing all together over the lipstick could not succeed in protecting them; and, since earliest childhood, his love of bodies, of their beauty, which made him laugh with bliss on the beaches, of their warmth that never stopped attracting him, with nothing particular in mind, like an animal—it was not to possess them, which he did not know how to do, but just to enter into their radiance, to lean his shoulder against his friend's with a great sensation of confidence and letting go, and almost to faint when a woman's hand lingered a moment on his in the crowd of the trolley—the longing, yes, to live, to live still more, to immerse himself in the greatest warmth this earth could give him, which was what he without knowing it hoped for from his mother; he did not get it and perhaps did not dare to get it, but he found it with the dog Brillant when he stretched out alongside him and breathed his strong smell of fur, or in the strongest and most animal-like odors where the marvelous heat of life was somehow preserved for him who could not do without it.

From the darkness within him sprang that famished

---

a. add to the list

ardor, that mad passion for living which had always been part of him and even today was still unchanged, making still more bitter—in the midst of the family he had rediscovered and facing the images of his childhood—the sudden terrible feeling that the time of his youth was slipping away, like the woman he had loved, oh yes, he had loved her with a great love, with all his heart and his body too, yes, with her it was a fervent desire, and when he withdrew from her with a great silent cry at the moment of orgasm he was in passionate harmony with his world, and he had loved her for her beauty and for the openhearted and despairing passion for life that was hers, and that made her deny, deny that time could pass, though she knew it was passing at that very moment, not wanting people to be able one day to say she was still young, but rather to stay young, always young; she burst into sobs one day when, laughing, he told her youth was passing and the days were waning: "Oh no, oh no," she said through her tears, "I'm so in love with love," and, intelligent and outstanding in so many ways, perhaps just because she truly was intelligent and outstanding, she rejected the world as it was. As it had been those days when, returning after a brief stay in the foreign country where she was born—those funereal visits, those aunts about whom she was told: "It's the last time you'll see them," and actually see their faces, their bodies, their ruins, and she wanted to go out screaming; or else those family dinners on a tablecloth embroidered by a great-grandmother who was long since dead and whom no one thought about, except she who was thinking about her great-grandmother when she was young, about her pleasures, about her appetite for living, like herself, marvelously beautiful in the bloom of her youth, and everyone at the table was paying her compliments, and on the wall around the table were hanging portraits of beautiful young women who were the ones who were complimenting her now and who were all decrepit and worn out. Then, her blood on fire, she wanted to flee, flee to a country where no one would grow old or die, where beauty was imperishable, where life would always be wild and radiant, and that did not exist; she wept in his arms when she returned, and he loved her desperately.

And he too, perhaps more than she, since he had been born in a land without forefathers and without memory, where the annihilation of those who preceded him was still more final and where old age finds none of the solace in melancholy that it does in civilized lands [ ],[1] he, like a solitary and ever-shining blade of a sword, was destined to be shattered with a single blow and forever, an unalloyed passion for life confronting utter death; today he felt life, youth, people slipping away from him, without being able to hold on to any of them, left with the blind hope that this obscure force that for so many years had raised him above the daily routine, nourished him unstintingly, and been equal to the most difficult circumstances—that, as it had with endless generosity given him reason to live, it would also give him reason to grow old and die without rebellion.

---

1. An illegible word.

Interleaves

(4) On the ship. Siesta with child + war of 14.

(5) At his mother's—the bombing.

(6) Journey to Mondovi—siesta—the settlement.

(7) At his mother's. Childhood continued—he recaptures childhood and not his father. He learns he is the first man. Madame Leca.

"When, having kissed him two or three times with all her strength, holding him tight against her, and after letting him go, she looked at him and took him in her arms again to kiss him once more, as if, having measured her affection to its fullness (which she had just done), she had decided that one measure was still missing and.[1] And then, right afterwards, turned away, she seemed no longer to be thinking of him nor

---

1. The sentence ends there.

for that matter of anything, and even sometimes looked at him with a strange expression as if now he were in the way, disturbing the empty, closed, confined universe where she circled."

SHEET II

A settler wrote to a lawyer in 1869:

"For Algeria to survive her doctors' treatments she has to be hard to kill."

Villages surrounded by moats or walls (and turrets at the 4 corners).

Of 600 settlers sent in 1831, 150 died in the tents. Hence the great number of orphanages in Algeria.

In Boufarik, they plow with a gun on their shoulder and quinine in their pocket. "He looks like Boufarik." 19% died in 1839. Quinine is sold as a drink in the cafés.

Bugeaud marries off his soldier settlers in Toulon after having written the mayor of Toulon to select 20 energetic fiancées. These were "shotgun weddings." But, once confronted with it, they exchange mates as best they can. It's the birth of Fouka.

Communal work at the beginning. These are military collective farms.

Settling "by region." Chéragas was settled by 66 families of horticulturists from Grasse.

In most cases the town halls of Algeria *have no archives*.

. . .

The people from Mahon landed in small bands with a trunk and their children. Their word is their bond. Never hire a Spaniard. They created the wealth of the Algeria seaboard.

Birmandreis and the house of Bernarda.

The story of [Dr. Tonnac], the first settler in Mitidja.

Cf. de Bandicorn, *Histoire de la colonisation de l'Algérie*, p. 21.

Pirette's history, *idem*, pp. 50 and 51.

SHEET III

10—Saint-Brieuc[1]

14—Malan

20—Childhood games
30—Algiers. The father and his death (+ the bombing)
42—The family
69—M. Germain and the School
91—Mondovi—the settlement and the father

II

101—*Lycée*

140—Unknown to himself
145—The adolescent[2]

---

1. The numbers correspond to the pages of the manuscript.
2. The manuscript stops at page 144.

SHEET IV

Also important is the theme of performing for others. What rescues us from our worst sorrows is the feeling of being abandoned and alone, yet not so alone that "others" do not "take notice" of us in our unhappiness. It is in this sense that our moments of happiness are sometimes those when the feeling that we are abandoned inflates us and lifts us into an endless sadness. In the sense also that happiness often is no more than self-pity for our unhappiness.

Striking among the poor—God put resignation alongside despair like the cure alongside the disease.[a]

When I was young, I asked more of people than they could give: everlasting friendship, endless feeling.

Now I know to ask less of them than they can give: a straightforward companionship. And their feelings, their friendship, their generous actions seem in my eyes to be wholly miraculous: a consequence of grace alone.

Marie Viton: airplane

SHEET V

He was the prince of the world, with a crown of shining talent, of passions, of strength, of joy, and it was from all that that he was coming to beg her forgiveness, she who had been a submissive slave to life and the passing days, who knew

---

a. death of the grandmother.

nothing, desired nothing, and did not dare to desire, and who nonetheless had preserved intact a truth he had lost and that was all that justified our existence.

Thursdays in Kouba
    Practice, sports
    Uncle
    Baccalaureate
    Illness
    O mother, O love, dear child, greater than my times, greater than the history that subjected you to itself, more true than all I have loved in this world, O mother, forgive your son for having fled the night of your truth.

The grandmother, a tyrant, but she serves standing up at the table.

The son who makes his mother respected and strikes at his uncle.

The First Man (Notes and Sketches)

Or else

Conversation about terrorism:

Objectively she is responsible (answerable)

Change the adverb or I'll hit you

What?

Don't take what's most asinine from the West. Don't say objectively or I'll hit you.

Why?

Did your mother lie down in front of the Algiers-Oran train? (the trolleybus)

I don't understand.

The train blew up, four children died. Your mother didn't move. If objectively she is nonetheless responsible,* then you approve of shooting hostages.

---

* answerable

She didn't know.

Neither did *she*. Never say objectively again.

Concede that there are innocent people or I'll kill you too.

You know I could do it.

Yes, I've seen you.

[a]Jean is the first man.

Then use Pierre as a reference point and give him a past, a country, a family, a morality (?)—Pierre—Didier?

Adolescent loves on the beach—and night falling on the sea—and nights of stars.

Meeting the Arab in Saint-Étienne. And this befriending by the two exiles in France.

Mobilization. When my father was called to the colors, he had never seen France. He saw it and was killed.

(What a modest family like mine has given to France.)

Last conversation with Saddok when J. is already against terrorism. But he receives Saddok, the right of asylum being sacred. At his mother's. Their conversation takes place in his mother's presence. At the end, "Look," said J., indicating his mother. Saddok got up, went to his mother, hand on his heart, to kiss his mother while bowing in the Arab manner. "She is my mother," he said. "Mine is dead. I love and respect her as if she were my mother."

(She fell because of a terrorist attack. She isn't well.)

. . .

---

a. Cf. *Histoire de la colonisation*.

Or else:

Yes I hate you. For me honor in the world is found among the oppressed, not those who hold power. And it is from that alone that dishonor arises. When just once in history an oppressed person understands . . . then . . .

Goodbye, said Saddok.

Stay, they'll catch you.

That's better. Them I can hate, and I join them in hatred. You're my brother and we're separated . . .

J. is on the balcony at night . . . In the distance they hear two shots and speeding . . .

What is it? said the mother.

It's nothing.

Ah! I was afraid for you.

He falls against her . . .

Then he is arrested for harboring.

They would send to be baked   the two francs in

The grandmother, her authority,   the hole

her energy

He stole the change.

The sense of honor among Algerians.

Learning justice and morality means to decide whether an emotion is good or bad according to its consequences. J. can give in to women—but if they take all his time . . .

"I've lived too long, and acted and felt, to say this one is right and that one wrong. I've had enough of living according to the image others show me of myself. I'm resolved on autonomy, I demand independence in interdependence."

Would Pierre be the actor?

...

Jean's father a teamster?

After Marie's illness, Pierre has an outburst like Clamence (I don't love anything . . .), then it's J. (or Grenier) who responds to the fall.[1]

Contrast the mother and the universe (the airplane, the most distant countries brought together).

Pierre a lawyer. And lawyer for Yveton.[2]

"Men like us are good and proud and strong . . . if we had a faith, a God, nothing could undermine us. But we had nothing, we had to learn everything, and living for honor alone has its weaknesses . . ."

At the same time it should be the history of the end of a world . . . with regret for those years of light running through it . . .

Philippe Coulombel and the big farm in Tipasa. Friendship with Jean. His death in a plane over the farm. They found him with the stick in his side, his face crushed against the instrument panel. A bloody pulp sprinkled with glass splinters.

Title: The Nomads. Begin with a move and end with evacuation from Algerian soil.

...

---

1. Clamence is the protagonist of Camus's *The Fall—Trans.*

2. Communist activist who put explosives in a factory. Guillotined during the Algerian war.

Two exaltations: the poor woman and the world of paganism (intelligence and happiness).

Everyone likes Pierre. J.'s success and his conceit make him enemies.

Lynching scene: 4 Arabs thrown off the Kassour.

His mother *is* Christ.

Have others speak about J., bring him on, show him, through the contradictory picture that together they paint of him.

Cultivated, athletic, debauched, a loner and the best of friends, spiteful, unfailingly dependable, etc., etc.

"He doesn't like anyone," "No one could be more noble in spirit," "cold and distant," "warm and passionate," everyone thinks he's an energizer except he himself, always lying down.

Thus *expand* the personality.

When he speaks: "I began to believe in my innocence. I was Tsar. I reigned over everything and everyone, at my disposal (etc.). Then I found out I didn't have enough heart truly to love and I thought I would die of contempt for myself. Then I recognized that others don't truly love either and that I just had to accept being like just about everyone.

"Then I decided no, I would blame myself alone for not being great enough and be comfortable in my hopelessness until I was given the opportunity to become great.

"In other words, I'm waiting for the time when I'll be Tsar and won't enjoy it."

. . .

Or else:

One cannot live with truth—"knowingly"—, he who does so sets himself apart from other men, he can no longer in any way share their illusion. He is an alien—and that is what I am.

Maxime Rasteil: the ordeal of the 1848 settlers. Mondovi—
   Insert history of Mondovi?
   Ex: 1) the grave the return and the [ ][1] at Mondovi
      1A) Mondovi in 1848 → 1913.

His Spanish side   sobriety and sensuality
                                    energy and *nada*

J.: "No one can imagine the pain I've suffered . . . They honor men who do great things. But they should honor even more those who, in spite of what they are, have been able to restrain themselves from committing the worst crimes. Yes, honor me."

Conversation with the paratroop lieutenant:
   "You talk too well. We're going to give you the third degree and see if you're still so smart."
   "All right, but first I want to warn you because no doubt you've never encountered any real men. Listen carefully. I am holding you responsible for what's going to happen in that third degree, as you call it. If I don't crack, it doesn't matter. I'll just spit in your face in public on the day it becomes possible for me to do so. But if I crack and if I get out

_____

1. Word illegible.

alive, and whether it takes a year or twenty years, I personally will kill you."

"Take good care of him," said the lieutenant, "he's a wise guy."[a]

J.'s friend kills himself "to make Europe possible." To *make* Europe requires a willing victim.

J. has four women at the same time and thus is leading an *empty* life.

C.S.: when the soul suffers too much, it develops a taste for misfortune . . .

Cf. History of the *Combat* movement.[1]

Darling who dies in the hospital while her neighbor's radio is blaring nonsense.

—Heart disease. Living on borrowed time. "If I commit suicide, at least it will be my choice."

"You alone will know why I killed myself. You know my principles. I hate those who commit suicide. Because of what they do *to others*. If you have to do it, you must disguise it. Out of kindness. Why am I telling you this? Because you love misfortune. It's a present I'm giving you. *Bon appétit!*"

---

a. (he meets him again unarmed [and provokes] a duel).

1. *Combat* was a Resistance newspaper of which Camus was editor—*Trans*.

. . .

J.: A life that is surging, reborn, a multitude of people and experiences, the capacity for renewal and [propulsion] (Lope)—

The end. She lifts her knotted hands to him and strokes his face. "You, you're the greatest one." There was so much love and adoration in her somber eyes (under the somewhat worn brow) that something in him—the one who knew—rebelled . . . A moment later he took her in his arms. Since she, who saw more clearly, loved him, he had to accept it, and to admit that to love he had to love himself a little . . .

A Musil theme: the search for salvation of the soul in the modern world—D: [meeting] and parting in *The Possessed*.

Torture. Executioner by proxy. I could never get close to another man—now we are side by side.

The Christian condition: pure feeling.

The book *must be* unfinished. Ex.: "And on the ship bringing him back to France . . ."

Jealous, he pretends not to be and plays the man of the world. And then he is no longer jealous.

At age 40, he realizes he needs someone to show him the way and to give him censure or praise: a father. Authority and not power.

X sees a terrorist fire at . . . He hears someone running after him in a dark street, stands still, turns suddenly, trips him so he falls, the revolver drops. He takes the weapon and trains it on the man, then realizes he cannot turn him in, takes him to a remote street, makes him run ahead of him and fires.

The young actress in the camp: the blade of grass, the first grass amidst the slag and that acute feeling of happiness. Miserable and joyful. Later on she loves Jean—because he is *pure*. I? Those who arouse love, even if it is disappointed, are princes who make the world worthwhile.

28 *Nov. 1885*: birth of Lucien C. in Ouled-Fayet: son of Baptiste C. (age 43) and Marie Cormery (age 33). Married 1909 (*13 Nov.*) to Mlle. Catherine Sintès (born 5 *Nov.* 1882). Died in Saint-Brieuc 11 Oct. 1914.

When he is 45, he discovers by comparing the dates that his brother was born two months after the wedding? But the uncle who has just described the ceremony speaks of a long slender dress . . .

It is a doctor who delivers the second son in the new home where the furniture is piled up.

She leaves in *July 14* with the child swollen with mosquito bites from the Seybouse. August, mobilization. The husband goes directly to his [unit] in Algiers. He gets out one night to kiss his two children. They will not see him again till word of his death.

A settler who, expelled, destroys the vines, lets in brackish water . . . "If what we did here is a crime, it must be wiped out . . ."

. . .

Maman (about N.): the day you "graduated"—"when they gave you the bonus."

Criklinski and ascetic love.

He expresses surprise that Marcelle, who has just become his mistress, takes no interest in her country's misfortune. "Come," she says. She opens a door: her nine-year-old child—delivered with forceps motor nerves smashed—paralyzed, speechless, left side of the face *higher* than the right, must be fed, washed, etc. He closes the door.

He knows he has cancer, but does not say he knows. Others think they are fooling him.

1st part: Algiers, Mondovi. And he meets an Arab who speaks to him of his father. His relations with Arab workers.

J. Douai: L'Écluse.

Beral's death in the war.

How F. cries out in tears when she learns of his affair with Y.: "Me too, I'm beautiful also." And Y.'s cry: "Ah! Let someone come and carry me off."

Later, long after the tragedy, F. and M. meet.

Christ did not set foot in Algeria.

The first letter he received from her and his feeling on seeing his own name in her handwriting.

. . .

Ideally, if the book were written to the mother, from beginning to end—and if one learned only at the end that she cannot read—yes, that would be it.

And what he wanted most in the world, which was for his mother to read everything that was his life and his being, that was impossible. His love, his only love, would be forever speechless.

Rescue this poor family from the fate of the poor, which is to disappear from history without a trace. The Speechless Ones.
They were and they are greater than I.

Begin with the night of the birth. Chap. I, then chap. II: 35 years later, a man would get off the train at Saint-Brieuc.

Gr,[1] whom I acknowledge as father, was born where my real father died and was buried.

Pierre with Marie. At the beginning he could not take her: *that is why* he came to love her. On the contrary, J. with Jessica, immediate bliss. That is why it takes him time to really love her—her body conceals her.

The hearse on the high plains [Figari].

The story of the German officer and the child: nothing makes it worth dying for him.

. . .

---

1. Grenier.

The pages of the Quillet dictionary: their smell, the plates.

The odors of the cooperage: the chip that smells more [ ][1] than sawdust.

Jean, eternally unsatisfied.

He leaves home as an *adolescent* in order to *sleep alone*.

Discovery of religion in Italy: through art.

End of chap. I: during this time, Europe was tuning its cannons. They went off six months later. The mother arrives in Algiers, holding a four-year-old by the hand, another child in her arms, this one swollen with bites from the Seybouse mosquitoes. They arrive at the grandmother's, three rooms in a poor neighborhood. "Mother, thank you for taking us in." The grandmother erect, looking at her with hard clear eyes: "Daughter, you'll have to go to work."

Maman: like an ignorant Myshkin. She does not know Christ's life, except on the cross. Yet who is closer to it?

One morning, in the courtyard of a provincial hotel, waiting for M. That feeling of happiness he could never experience except in what was temporary, illicit—which by the fact that it was illicit guaranteed the happiness could never last—infected him most of the time, except the few times, like now, when it appeared in its pure state, in the gentle light of morning, among dahlias still shiny with dew . . .

. . .

———

1. An illegible word.

Story of XX.

She arrives, pushes her way in, "I'm free," etc., plays the emancipated woman. Then she gets in bed naked, does everything for . . . a bad [ ]¹ Unfortunate.

She leaves her husband—in despair, etc. The husband writes to the other man: "You're responsible. Go on seeing her or she'll kill herself." Actually, sure failure: infatuated with the absolute, and in that case trying to woo the impossible—so she killed herself. The husband came. "You know what brings me here." "Yes." "All right, it's your choice, I kill you or you kill me." "No, it's you who has to bear the burden of the choice." "Go ahead and kill." Actually, the kind of predicament that the victim is really not accountable for. But [no doubt] she was responsible for something else she never paid for. Foolishness.

XX. She has in her a disposition toward destruction and death. She is [dedicated] to God.

A naturist: in an eternal state of suspicion about food, air, etc.

In occupied Germany:
    Good evening, *herr offizer*.
    Good evening, says J., closing the door. He is surprised at the tone of his voice. And he understands that many conquerors use that tone only because they are embarrassed to be conquering and occupying.

J. wants not to be. What he does, loses his reputation, etc.

. . .

---

1. An illegible word.

Character: Nicole Ladmiral.

The father's "African sadness."

End. Takes his son to Saint-Brieuc. On the little square, standing facing each other. How do you live? says the son. What? Yes, who are you, etc. (Happy) he feels the shadow of death thickening around him.

V.V. We men and women of that time, of this city, in this country, we embraced each other, rejected and took each other back, and finally parted. But through all that time we never stopped helping each other to live, with that marvelous complicity of those who have to fight and suffer together. Ah! that is what love is—love for all.

At the age of 40, having ordered meat very rare in restaurants all his life, he realized he actually liked it medium and not at all rare.

Free oneself from any concern with art and form. Regain direct contact, without intermediary, thus innocence. To give up art here is to *give up one's self*. Renouncing the self, not through virtuousness. On the contrary, accept one's hell. One who wants to be better prefers his self, one who wants to enjoy prefers his self. The only one who renounces his self, his I, is one who accepts *whatever happens* with its consequences. Then this one is in direct contact.

Regain the greatness of the Greeks or the great Russians through this distanced innocence. Do not fear. Fear nothing. But who will help me!

That afternoon, on the road from Grasse to Cannes, where in a moment of incredible rapture he discovers, suddenly, after an affair lasting years, that he loves Jessica, that at last he loves her, and that the rest of the world becomes like a shadow beside her.

I was not in any of what I said or wrote. It was not I who married, not I who was a father, who . . . etc . . .

Many documents about sending *foundlings* to settle in Algeria. Yes. All of us here.

The morning trolley, from Belcourt to the place du Gouvernement. In front, the motorman with his levers.

I am going to tell the story of an alien.
  The story I am going to tell . . .

Maman and history: She is told about sputnik: "Oh, I wouldn't like it up there!"

Chapter *going backwards*. Hostages Kabyle village. Emasculated soldier—roundup, etc., step by step to the first shot fired in the settlement. But why stop there? Cain killed Abel. Problem in technique: a single chapter or in countermelody?

Rasteil: a settler with a thick moustache, graying sideburns.
  His father: a carpenter from Faubourg Saint-Denis; his mother: a fine-linen laundress.
  All the settlers were Parisian anyway (and many were forty-eighters). Many unemployed in Paris. The Constituent had voted fifty million to send a "colony":
  For each settler:
  a dwelling
  2 to 10 hectares

seeds, cultures, etc.

food rations

No railroad (it only went as far as Lyon). From there canals—*on barges* hauled by draft horses. "Marseillaise," "Chant du Départ," benediction by the clergy, flag to take to Mondovi.

Six barges 100 to 150 meters each. Cooped up, on straw mattresses. The women, to change underwear, undress behind bedsheets they hold up one after the other.

Almost a month journey.

In Marseilles, at the big Lazaret[1] (1,500 people), for a week. Then loaded on an old paddlewheeler: the *Labrador*. Leave in a mistral. Five days and five nights—everyone sick.

Bône—with the whole population on the dock to greet the settlers.

Things piled up in the hold that disappear.

From Bône to Mondovi (on the army's gun carriages, to leave room and air for the women and children) *no road*. By guesswork in the swampy plain or in the brush, under the hostile eyes of the Arabs, accompanied by the howling pack of Kabyle dogs—12/8/48.[2] Mondovi did not exist, some military tents. During the night the women were weeping—8 days of Algerian rain on the tents, and the wadis were overflowing. The children relieved themselves in the tents. The carpenter put up light shelters draped with sheets to protect the furniture. Hollow reeds cut on the banks of the Seybouse so the children could urinate from the inside out.

Four months in the tents, then temporary wooden huts; each double hut had to lodge *six families*.

---

1. hospital—*Trans.*
2. Circled by the author.

Spring 49: untimely hot season. They are roasting in the huts. Malaria then cholera. 8 to 10 deaths a day. The carpenter's daughter, Augustine, dies, then his wife. His brother-in-law also. (They bury them in a layer of tuff.)

The doctors' prescription: *dance* to heat the blood.

And they dance every night to a fiddler between two burials.

The land grants would not be distributed until 1851. The father dies. Rasine and Eugéne are left alone.

To go wash their laundry in a tributary of the Seybouse they needed an escort of soldiers.

Walls built + ditches by the army. Cabins and gardens, they build with their hands.

Five or six lions roar around the village. (Numidian lion with black mane.) Jackals. Boars. Hyena. Panther.

Attacks on the villages. Theft of livestock. Between Bône and Mondovi, a wagon bogs down. The travelers leave to get reinforcements, except a pregnant young woman. They find her with her belly slit and breasts cut off.

The first church: four clay walls, no chairs, a few benches.

The first school: a shack made of poles and branches. Three sisters.

The lands: scattered plots, they plow with a gun on their shoulder. At night you go back to the village.

A column of 3,000 French soldiers passing by raids the village during the night.

June 51: uprising. Hundreds of cavalrymen in burnooses around the village. Simulating cannons with stovepipes on the little ramparts.

In actual fact, the Parisians in the fields; many went to the fields wearing top hats and their wives with silk dresses.

Smoking cigarettes forbidden. Only the covered pipe was permitted. (Because of fires.)

. . .

The houses built in *54*.

In the department of Constantine, 2/3 of the settlers died almost without having laid a hand on a spade or plow.

Old settler cemetery, immense oblivion.[1]

Maman. The truth is that, in spite of all my love, I had not been able to live that life of blind patience, without words, without plans. I could not live her life of ignorance. And I had traveled far and wide, had built, had created, had loved people and abandoned them. My days had been full to overflowing—but nothing had filled my heart like . . .

He knew he was going to leave again, make a mistake again, forget what he knew. But actually what he knew was that the truth of his life was there in that room . . . No doubt he would flee that truth. Who can live with his own truth? But it is enough to know it is there, it is enough to know it at last and that it feeds a secret and silent [fervor] in the self, in the face of death.

Maman's Christianity at the end of her life. The poor, unfortunate, ignorant woman [ ][2] show her sputnik? May the cross sustain her!

In 72, when the paternal branch settled, it was following:

—the Commune,

—the Arab uprising of 71 (the first one killed in Mitidja was a teacher).

The Alsatians occupied the land of the *insurgents*.

---

1. "immense oblivion" circled by the author.
2. An illegible word.

...

The measure of the era

The mother's ignorance in countermelody to all the [ ][1] of history and the world.

Bir Hakeim: "it's far" or "over there."

Her religion is visual. She knows what she has seen without being able to interpret it. Jesus is suffering, he dies, etc.

Woman warrior.

Write one's [ ][2] in order to find the truth.

1ST PART: THE NOMADS

(1) Birth during the move. 6 months after the war.[a] The child. Algiers, the father in Zouave uniform wearing a straw hat going over the top.

(2) 40 years later. The son facing the father in the Saint-Brieuc cemetery. He returns to Algeria.

(3) Arrival in Algeria in time for the "events." Look up. Trip to Mondovi. He finds childhood and not the father. He learns he is the first man.[b]

---

1. An illegible word.
2. Two illegible words.
a. Mondovi in 48.
b. The settlers from Mahon in 1850—the Alsatians in 72-73—
14.

2ND PART: THE FIRST MAN

Adolescence: The punch
Sports and morality
The Man: (Political activity [Algeria], the Resistance)

3RD PART: THE MOTHER

Loves
The kingdom: the old playmate, the old friend, Pierre, the old teacher, and the story of his two enlistments
The mother[1]
In the last part, Jacques explains to his mother the Arab question, Creole civilization, the fate of the West. "Yes," she says, "yes." Then full confession and the end.

There was a mystery about this man, and a mystery he wanted to clear up.

But at the end there was nothing but the mystery of poverty that creates people without a name and without a past.

Youth at the beaches. After days full of shouting, of sunlight, of strenuous activity, of dull or intense desire. Night falls on the sea. A swift cries high in the sky. And anguish seizes his heart.

Finally he takes Empedocles as his model. The [ ][2] philosopher who lives alone.

---

1. The author drew a box around this whole passage.
2. An illegible word.

. . .

I want to write the story of a pair joined by the same blood and every kind of difference. She similar to the best this world has, and he quietly abominable. He thrown into all the follies of our time; she passing through the same history as if it were that of any time. She silent most of the time, with only a few words at her disposal to express herself; he constantly talking and unable to find in thousands of words what she could say with a single one of her silences . . . Mother and son.

Freedom to use any style.

Jacques, who until then had felt himself at one with all victims, now recognizes that he is at one with the executioners. His sorrow. Definition.

You would have to live as an onlooker to your own life. To add to it the dream that would complete it. But we live, and others dream your life.

He looked at her. Everything had come to a standstill, and time passed with a sputter. As at the movies when, the picture having vanished through some malfunction, you hear nothing in the darkness of the hall except the sound of the machinery going on . . . with an empty screen.

The jasmine necklaces sold by the Arabs. The scented string of yellow and white flowers [ ].[1] The necklaces quickly fade

---

1. Six illegible words.

[ ]¹ the flowers turn yellow [ ]² but the odor lingers, in the poor room.

Paris days in May when the white pods of the chestnut flowers are floating everywhere in the air.

He had loved his mother and his child, everything that it was not up to him to choose. And after all he, who had challenged everything, questioned everything, he had never loved anything except what was inevitable. The people fate had imposed on him, the world as it appeared to him, everything in his life he had not been able to avoid, his illness, his vocation, fame or poverty—in a word, his star. For the rest, for everything he had to choose, he had made himself love, which is not the same thing. No doubt he had known the feeling of wonderment, passion, and even moments of tenderness. But each moment had sent him on to other moments, each person to others, and he had loved nothing he had chosen, except what was little by little imposed on him by circumstance, had lasted as much by accident as by intention, and finally became necessary: Jessica. The heart, the heart above all is not free. It is inevitability and the recognition of the inevitable. And he, in truth, had never wholeheartedly loved other than the inevitable. All that was left for him was to love his own death.

ᵃTomorrow, six million yellow people, billions of yellow, black, and dark-skinned people will pour onto the shore of

---

1. Two illegible words.
2. Two illegible words.
a. he dreams it during his siesta:

Europe . . . and at best would [convert her]. Then everything that had been taught, to him and to those like him, also everything he had learned, on that day the men of his race, all the values he lived for, would die of uselessness. Then what will still be worthwhile? His mother's silence. *He laid down his arms before her.*

M. at 19. He was 30 then, and they did not know each other. He realizes we cannot set the clock back, prevent the loved one from having been, and done, and experienced, we possess nothing of what we choose. For we would have to choose with the first cry at birth, and we are born apart—except from the mother. We possess only what is inevitable, and we must return to it and (see preceding note) submit to it. And yet, what nostalgia and what regrets!

One must relinquish. No, learn to love what is imperfect.

To conclude, he asks his mother's forgiveness—Why you've been a good son— But it is because of all the rest she cannot know or even imagine [ ]¹ that she is the only one who can forgive (?)

Since I've inverted it, show Jessica old *before* showing her young.

He marries M. because she has never known a man and he is fascinated by that. In short, he marries for what is wanting in himself. Then he will learn to love women who have been used—that is—to love the awful necessity of life.

A chapter on the war of 14. Incubator of our era. As seen by the mother? Who knows neither France, nor Europe, nor

---

1. An illegible word.

the world. Who thinks shells explode of their own volition, etc.

Alternate chapters would give the mother's voice. Commenting on the same events but with her vocabulary of 400 words.

In short, I wanted to speak of those I loved. And of that only. Intense joy.

[a]Saddok:

(1) "But why get married that way, Saddok?"

"Should I marry the French way?"

"The French or any other way! Why subject yourself to a tradition you believe is foolish and cruel?"[b]

"Because my people are identified with this tradition, they have nothing else, they stopped there, and to part with that tradition is to part with them. That is why I will go into that room tomorrow, and I will strip a stranger of her clothes, and I will rape her to the sound of gunshots."

"All right. In the meantime, let's go swimming."

(2) "So what?"

"They say that for the time being the anti-Fascist front must be consolidated, that France and Russia must join in self-defense."

"Can't they defend themselves and at the same time establish justice at home?"

––––––––

a. All this in a [not-true-to-life] style that is lyrical and not exactly realistic.

b. The French are right, but their rightness is oppressive to us. And that is why I choose Arab madness, the madness of the oppressed.

"They say that will come later, that we have to wait for that."

"Justice can't be delayed here, and you well know it."

"They say if you don't wait, objectively you'll be aiding Fascism."

"And that's why prison is the right place for your former comrades."

"They say it's too bad, but they can't do otherwise."

"They say, they say. And you say nothing."

"I say nothing."

He looked at him. It was beginning to get hot.

"So, you're betraying me?"

He had not said: "you're betraying us" because betrayal concerns the flesh, the single individual, etc . . .

"No. I'm leaving the Party today . . ."

(3) "Remember 1936."

"I'm not a terrorist for the Communists. I'm one against the French."

"I'm French. She is too."

"I know. Too bad for you."

"So you are betraying me."

Saddok's eyes shone with a kind of fever.

If I finally choose chronological order, Madame Jacques or the doctor will be descendants of the first settlers in Mondovi.

Let's not feel sorry for ourselves, said the doctor, just imagine our first ancestors here, etc . . .

(4)—And Jacques's father killed at the Marne. What remains of that obscure life? Nothing, an impalpable memory—the light ash of a butterfly wing incinerated in a forest fire.

. . .

The *two* Algerian nationalisms. Algeria 39 and 54 (rebellion). What becomes of French values in an Algerian sensibility, that of the first man. The account of the two generations explains the present tragedy.

The holiday camp at Miliana, the barracks' trumpets morning and evening.

Loves: he would have wanted them all virgin, with no past and no men. And the only one he ever met who actually was, he vowed his life to her but could not himself be faithful. So he wanted women to be what he himself was not. And what he was sent him back to women who were like him and whom he loved and possessed with anger and passion.

Adolescence. His drive to live, his faith in life. But he is spitting blood. So that is what life will be, a hospital, death, solitude, this absurdity. Hence the parting. And in his very depths: no, no, life is something else.

Inspiration on the road from Cannes to Grasse . . .
    And he knew that even if he had to go back to that barren cold where he had always lived, he would dedicate his life, his heart, the gratitude of his entire being, which had enabled him once, perhaps only once, but once, to yield . . .

Begin the last part with this scene:
    The blind donkey who for years patiently turns his wheel in a circle, enduring beatings, the ferocity of nature, the sun, the flies, still enduring, and from that slow circular motion, seemingly fruitless, monotonous, painful, water endlessly flows . . .

. . .

1905. L.C.'s[1] war in Morocco. But, at the other end of Europe, Kaliayev.

The life of L.C. Entirely involuntary, except his will to be and to keep on. Orphanage. Farm laborer obliged to marry his wife. Thus his life evolves despite him—and then the war kills him.

He goes to see Grenier: "Men like me, I've conceded it, have to obey. They need a guiding rule, etc. Religion, love, etc.: impossible for me. So I have decided to vow obedience to you." What follows (news).

After all, he does not know who his father is. But who is he himself? 2nd Part.

The silent movie, reading the subtitles to the grandmother.

No, I am not a good son: a good son is one who stays put. I've traveled far and wide, I've betrayed her with trivialities, fame, a hundred women.
    "But, you loved no one but her?"
    "Ah! I've loved no one but her?"

When, by his father's grave, he felt the time go out of joint—this new course of time is that of the book.

He is a man of excess: women, etc.
    So the [hyper] in him is punished. Then he knows.

. . .

---

1. Probably Lucien Camus, his father.

The dread in Africa when the sudden twilight falls on the sea or on the high plateaus or on the rough mountains. It is the dread of the sacred, fear of eternity. The same as at Delphi, where nightfall produces the same effect, it makes the temples come forth. But on the soil of Africa the temples have been destroyed, all that remains is this immense weight on the heart. Then how they die! In silence, away from everything.

What they did not like in him was the Algerian.

His dealings with money. Owing in part to poverty (he never bought anything for himself), and on the other hand to his arrogance: he never bargained.

Confession to his mother to conclude.

"You do not understand me, and yet you are the only one who can forgive me. Plenty of people offer to do it. Many also shout in all sorts of ways that I am guilty, and I am not guilty when they tell me I am. Others have the right to say it to me, and I know they are right and that I should seek their forgiveness. But one asks forgiveness of those one knows can forgive. Just that, to forgive, and not to ask you to deserve forgiveness, to wait. [But] just to talk to them, to tell them everything and receive their forgiveness. The men and women of whom I could ask it, I know that somewhere in their hearts, despite their good intentions, they neither can nor do they know how to forgive. One person alone could have forgiven me, but I was never guilty toward him and I gave him my heart entire, and yet I could have gone to him, I often did so in silence, but he is dead and I am alone. You alone can do it, but you do not understand me and cannot read me. And I am speaking to you, I am writing, to you, to you alone, and when it is finished, I will ask forgiveness without further explanation and you will smile on me . . ."

Jacques, at the time of the escape from the clandestine editorial office, kills a pursuer (he grimaced, staggered, a bit bent forward. Then Jacques felt a terrible fury rising in him: he hit him once more from below in the [throat], and a huge hole burst open immediately at the base of the neck; then, crazed with disgust and anger, he hit him again [ ]¹ right in the eyes without looking where he was striking . . .) . . . then he goes to Wanda's.

The poor and ignorant Berber peasant. The settler. The soldier. The White with no land. (He loves them, those people, not those half-breeds with pointed yellow shoes and scarves who have only adopted the worst from the West.)

The end.
   Return the land, the land that belongs to no one. Return the land that is neither to be sold nor to be bought (yes and Christ never set foot in Algeria, since even the monks owned property and land grants there).
   And he cried out, looking at his mother, then the others:
   "Return the land. Give all the land to the poor, to those who have nothing and who are so poor that they never wanted to have and to possess, to those in the country who are like her, the immense herd of the wretched, mostly Arab and a few French, and who live and survive here through stubbornness and endurance, with the only pride that is worth anything in the world, that of the poor, give them the

---

1. Four illegible words.

land as one gives what is sacred to those who are sacred, and then I, poor once more and forever, cast into the worst of exiles at the end of the earth, I will smile and I will die happy, knowing that those I revered, she whom I revered, are at last joined to the land I so loved under the sun where I was born."

(Then shall the great anonymity become fruitful and envelop me also—I shall return to this land.)

Revolt. Cf. *Demain* in Algeria, p. 48, Servier.

Young political commissars in the F.L.N. who took Tarzan as their pseudonym.

Yes, I command, I kill, I live in the mountains, under the sun and the rain. What do you offer me that's better: laborer in Béthune.

And Saddok's mother, cf. p. 115.

Confronting . . . in the oldest story in the world we are the first men—not men on the wane as they shout in the [ ]¹ newspaper but men of a different and undefined dawn.

Children without God or father, the masters they offered us horrified us. We lived without legitimacy— Pride.

What they call the skepticism of the new generations—a lie.

Since when is an honest man who refuses to believe the liar a skeptic?

The nobility of the writer's occupation lies in resisting oppression, thus in accepting isolation.

. . .

---

1. An illegible word.

What has helped me bear an adverse fate will perhaps help me accept an overly favorable outcome—and what has most sustained me was the great vision, the very great vision I have of art.

Except in [antiquity]
    Writers started out in slavery.
    They won their freedom—no question [ ]¹

K.H.: Everything exaggerated is trivial. But Monsieur K.H. was trivial before becoming exaggerated. He wanted to be both.

---

1. Four illegible words.

Two Letters

19 November 1957

Dear Monsieur Germain,

I let the commotion around me these days subside a bit before speaking to you from the bottom of my heart. I have just been given far too great an honor, one I neither sought nor solicited. But when I heard the news, my first thought, after my mother, was of you. Without you, without the affectionate hand you extended to the small poor child that I was, without your teaching, and your example, none of all this would have happened. I don't make too much of this sort of honor. But at least it gives me an opportunity to tell you what you have been and still are for me, and to assure you that your efforts, your work, and the generous heart you put into it still live in one of your little schoolboys who, despite the years, has never stopped being your grateful pupil. I embrace you with all my heart.

Albert Camus

My dear child,

I have received, addressed in your handwriting, the book *Camus* that its author Monsieur J.-Cl. Brisville was kind enough to inscribe to me.

I do not know how to express the delight you gave me with your gracious act nor how to thank you for it. If it were possible, I would give a great hug to the big boy you have become who for me will always be "my little Camus."

I have not yet read this work, other than the first few pages. Who is Camus? I have the impression that those who try to penetrate your nature do not quite succeed. You have always shown an instinctive reticence about revealing your nature, your feelings. You succeed all the more for being unaffected, direct. And good on top of that! I got these impressions of you in class. The pedagogue who does his job conscientiously overlooks no opportunity to know his pupils, his children, and these occur all the time. An answer, a gesture, a stance are amply revealing. So I think I well know the nice little fellow you were, and very often the child contains the seed of the man he will become. Your pleasure at being in school burst out all over. Your face showed optimism. And I never suspected the actual situation of your family from studying you. I only had a glimpse when your mother came to see me about your being listed among the candidates for the scholarship. Anyway, that happened when you were about to leave me. But until then you seemed to me to be in the same position as your classmates. You always had what you needed. Like your brother, you were nicely dressed. I don't think I can find a greater compliment to your mother.

To return to Monsieur Brisville's book, it is amply illustrated. It was very moving to know, from his photograph, your poor *papa* whom I have always considered "my comrade." Monsieur Brisville was kind enough to quote me: I will thank him for it.

I saw the ever-lengthening list of works that are about you or speak of you. And it gives me very great satisfaction to see that your fame (this is the exact truth) has not gone to your head. You have remained Camus: bravo.

I have followed with interest the many vicissitudes of the play you adapted and also staged: *The Possessed*. I love you too much not to wish you the greatest success: it is what you deserve. What's more, Malraux wants to provide you with a theatre. But . . . can you manage all these various activities? I fear that you misuse your talents. And, permit your old friend to point out, you have a nice wife and two children who need their husband and *papa*. On this subject, I am going to tell you what the head of our normal school used to tell us now and then. He was very hard on us, which kept us from seeing, from feeling, that he *really* loved us. "Nature keeps a great book in which she scrupulously records every one of the excesses we commit." I must say that this wise advice has often restrained me when I was about to disregard it.

So listen, try to leave a blank on the page reserved for you in nature's Great Book.

Andrée reminds me that we saw and heard you on a literary program on television, a program about *The Possessed*. It was moving to see you answer the questions that were asked. And I could not keep myself from making the malicious observation that you well knew I would, after all, see and hear you. That makes up a bit for your absence from Algiers. We haven't seen you for quite a while . . .

Before closing, I want to tell you how troubled I am, as a secular teacher, by the menacing plots aimed at our schools. I believe that throughout my career I have respected what is most sacred in a child: the right to seek out his own truth. I loved you all and I believe I did my best not to show my opinions and thus to influence your young minds. When it was a matter of God (it was in the curriculum), I said some believed, others did not. And in the fullness of his rights, each did as he pleased. Similarly, on the subject of religion, I limited myself to listing the ones that existed, to which those who so desired belonged. To be accurate, I added that there were people who practiced no religion. I am well aware this does not please those who would like to make teachers fellow travelers for religion and, more precisely, for the *Catholic* religion. At the normal school of Algiers (it was then at the parc de Galland) my father, like his classmates, was *required* to go to Mass and take Communion every Sunday. One day, exasperated by this requirement, he put the "consecrated" host in a prayerbook and closed it! The head of the school was informed of this and did not hesitate to expel my father. That is what the promoters of the "Free school"[1] (free . . . to

---

1. "Free" meaning private, usually Catholic, as opposed to the secular state school—*Trans.*

think as they do) want. With the current membership of the Chamber of Deputies, I fear this plot may succeed. *Le Canard Enchâiné*[1] reported that in one department a hundred secular schools function with a crucifix hanging on the wall. I see in that an abominable attack on the children's minds. What may it come to in time? These thoughts make me very sad.

My dear child, I am coming to the end of my 4th page: I'm taking advantage of your time and I beg you to forgive me. All goes well here. Christian, my son-in-law, starts his 27th month in service tomorrow!

Know that, even when I do not write, I often think of all of you.

Madame Germain and I warmly embrace all four of you. Affectionately.

Louis Germain

I remember the time you came to visit our class with your fellow communicants. You were obviously proud of the suit you were wearing and the feast day you were observing. Honestly, I was happy for your pleasure, believing that if you were making your Communion it was because you wanted to. So . . .

---

1. The satirical weekly—*Trans.*